DATA ARCHITECTURE: THE INFORMATION PARADIGM

Books and Training Products From QED

DATABASE

Data Analysis: The Key to Data Base Design
Diagnostic Techniques for IMS Data Bases
The Data Dictionary: Concepts and Uses
DB2: The Complete Guide to Implementation
and Use
Logical Data Base Design
DB2 Design Review Guidelines
DB2: Maximizing Performance of Online
Production Systems

SYSTEMS DEVELOPMENT

Effective Methods of EDP Quality Assurance
Handbook of Screen Format Design
The Complete Guide to Software Testing
A User's Guide for Defining Software
Requirements
A Structured Approach to Systems Testing
Practical Applications of Expert Systems
Expert Systems Development: Building
PC-Based Applications
Storyboard Prototyping for Systems Design
Designing and Implementing Ethernet
Networks
The Software Factory: Managing Software
Development and Maintenance

MANAGEMENT

Planning Techniques for Systems
Management
Strategic Planning for Information Systems
Strategic and Operational Planning for
Information Systems
Microcomputer Decision Support Systems:
Design, Implementation and Evaluation
The State of the Art in Decision Support
Systems
Management Evaluation of Software
Packages
The Management Handbook for Information
Center and End-User Computing
Disaster Recovery: Contingency Planning
and Program Analysis

MANAGEMENT (cont'd)

Techniques of Program and System
Maintenance
The Data Processing Training Manager's
Trail Guide
Telecommunications Planning

TECHNOLOGY

Handbook of COBOL Techniques and
Programming Standards
1001 Questions and Answers to Help You
Prepare for the CDP Exam
1001 Questions and Answers to Help You
Prepare for the CSP Exam
VSAM Techniques: System Concepts and
Programming Procedures
The Library of Structured COBOL Programs:
Concepts, Definitions, Structure Charts,
Logic, Code
How to Use CICS to Create On-Line
Applications: Methods and Solutions
CICS/VS Command Level Reference Guide
for COBOL Programmers
Data Communications: Concepts and
Systems

THE QED EASY LEARNING SERIES

PC Plus
dBASE III PLUS Made Easy
DOS Made Easy
Typing Made Easy
Lotus 1-2-3 Made Easy
Typing Skill Builder
Lotus 1-2-3 Proficiency (Video)
Lotus Macros & Advanced Functions (Video)

THE QED INDEPENDENT STUDY SERIES

Managing Software Development (Video)
SQL As A Second Language
DB2: Building Online Production Systems
for Maximum Performance (Video)

For Additional Information or a Free Catalog Contact

QED INFORMATION SCIENCES, INC. - P.O. BOX 181 - WELLESLEY, MA 02181
Telephone: 800 343-4848 or 617 237-5656

DATA ARCHITECTURE:

THE INFORMATION PARADIGM

W.H. Inmon

QED
Information Sciences, Inc.
Wellesley, Massachusetts

© 1989 by QED Information Sciences, Inc.
QED Plaza
P.O. Box 181
Wellesley, MA 02181

Library of Congress Catalog Number: 88-31280
International Standard Book Number: 0-89435-268-7

Printed in the United States of America
89 90 91 10 9 8 7 6 5 4 3 2 1

Library of Congress Cataloging-in-Publication Data

Inmon, William H.
    Data architecture : the information paradigm / W.H. Inmon.
      p. cm.
    Includes index.
    ISBN 0-89435-268-7 :
    1. Electronic data processing.   2. Information technology.
I. Title.
QA76.I484   1989
005.74—dc19   88-31280
                                                      CIP

To Sarah Annabel Inmon

CONTENTS

Preface   ix

1. The Information Paradigm   1
    An introduction and high-level description.
2. The Information Paradigm—Evolution and
    Formulation   43
    A description of the forces that shape the paradigm
    at work in the industry today.
3. The Information Paradigm—Technical Foundations   89
    A description of some major technical considerations
    of the information paradigm.
4. Conceptual Foundations of the Information Paradigm   135

    An eclectic collection of popular theories that have
    relevance to the information paradigm.
5. Implications of the Information Paradigm   153
    How the information paradigm relates to many
    popular ''saws'' or common wisdoms of the data
    processing community.
6. Specifics of the Information Paradigm   165
    A detailed description of the different levels of data and
    how they interrelate.
7. Migration to the Information Paradigm   187
    A description of a migratory pattern in which
    the organization desires to take a proactive stance.
8. Organizational Implications of the Information
    Paradigm   213
    The information paradigm has a profound effect on
    the organization and organization structure.

9. Economic Considerations of
the Information Paradigm   **225**
There are major perspectives of the information
paradigm other than technical and organizational;
the economic perspectives are described here.

10. Miscellaneous Topics   **247**
Strategic systems and the information paradigm,
methodologies and the information paradigm,
resisting the evolution.

11. Data Integrity and Projection Data   **253**
Data architecture and projection, or future-oriented data;
credibility of processing for planning/budgetary data.

12. A Taxonomy of Data   **267**
All data is not created equal. The best way to create
sectored data is to divide it into historical/projection,
public/private, and primitive/derived sectors.

Index   **279**

PREFACE

One of the curious facets of information engineering is the lack of a paradigm for the ultimate product of the information engineering effort. The focus of most aspects of information engineering is on a very low level of detail. Only very rarely does the information engineer step back and consider the whole that is being built or contemplated.

Contrast the discipline of civil engineering with information engineering. Civil engineers spend much time addressing detailed issues such as strength of materials, material logistics, and costs of construction. But civil engineers also spend considerable time understanding and shaping the final product of their efforts from the broadest perspective. If the civil engineer is building a bridge, at least as much time is spent on the overall shape, solidity, capacity, and usage of the bridge as is spent on such details as what grade of steel, what type of jointing, how deep the foundation is to be. Unlike civil engineers, information engineers spend the vast majority of their time focusing on minutiae, assuming that the final product will be sound if the details supporting the foundation of the final product are sound. Unfortunately, such may not be the case at all.

This book is a description of what the architected, engineered information environment ought to look like, taken as a whole and viewed from a broad perspective. That broad perspective is called, in this book, the information paradigm, which is the foundation of an information systems architecture. The emphasis in this book is not on how to create the components that support the information paradigm. That subject is amply covered in two of the author's previous works, *Information Systems Architecture* (Prentice-Hall) and *Information Engineering for the Practitioner* (Yourdon Press), as well as in numerous other works. Instead, this book discusses what the information paradigm is, what a data architecture is, how the information paradigm evolved, and what the implications of the information paradigm are. The reader will find that there is tremendous worth in understanding the general architecture to which the world of information technology is evolving. The vision of what the ideal architecture for today's and tomorrow's systems can be is an invaluable tool in the following ways:

- Evaluating existing systems and opportunities in light of the paradigm;
- Deciding upon support tools for different activities that are appropriate throughout the paradigm;
- Positioning the organization to support components of the paradigm that are not in place.

This book is for anyone interested in the use, control, and future of information technology. Certainly included in this list are data processing managers, top corporate managers interested in the usage and control of technology, and system developers. But the list of interested parties extends well beyond classical data processing personnel. Equally relevant parties include hardware and software vendors, venture capitalists, academics, and students of information technology. In short, anyone interested in information technology—where we have been, where we are going, why the evolution is occurring, and what the general shape of the architecture is after the forces of evolution have done their work—will find this book invaluable.

This book is the fourth of a suite of books by the author. The first book, *Integrating Data Processing Systems: in Theory and in Practice*, describes the problems and challenges facing the data architect who is addressing system integration. The next book, *Information Systems Architecture*, describes the minimum subset of knowledge needed by the information engineer to build an architecture. *Information Systems Architecture* concentrates primarily on data modeling and methodology. The third book in the suite, *Information Engineering for the Practitioner*, describes in much greater detail many of the implications of the earlier books. In the early books the focus on data was shifted to a balanced focus on data and processing and acknowledged the contribution of the early pioneers of information processing. Other major topics were included as well, such as the notion of the difference between primitive data and processing and derived data and processing. In short, the emphasis of *Information Engineering for the Practitioner* is on technique and implementation.

This, the fourth book in the suite, does not emphasize technique at all. Instead it concentrates on the description of the information paradigm and the implications (and advantages) of focusing on a comprehensive vision of information technology. If there is a single raison d'etre for the book, it lies in the attempt to understand information technology as a whole. The very nature of much of information technology is introspection, and there is no question that such analysis bears much fruit. But at some point a complete diet of nothing but introspection leads to a severe case of myopia. At such point, the broad horizons depicted by the information paradigm are worth contemplating, so as to ensure that the deeply introspective exercises that technicians regularly engage in are properly directed.

The author acknowledges *many* early contributors whose work, in one place or another, added to or accelerated the overall evolution of the information paradigm. The profound influence of such pioneers as Amdahl, Chen, Codd, Constantine, Date, DeMarco, Dykstra, Finklestein, Ganes, Hopper, Jobs, Martin, Myers, Orr, Sarson, Warnier, Wozniak, Yourdon, *et al.*, is recognized. In some part, either large or small, all of the above materially contributed to the evolution of the information paradigm.

The author wishes to thank the several reviewers who have made very valuable contributions:

David Dodge, American Management Systems
Newall Hall, Aetna Casualty Insurance
Claudia Imhoff, American Management Systems
Margot Levy, American Management Systems
Mike Loper, American Management Systems
Nancy K. Mullen, Arthur Andersen and Co.
Alan Pitt, American Management Systems
Cass Squire, American President Line
John Zachman, IBM Corporation

Many thanks to the following people for their help in the physical preparation of this book:

Carol LaRocque
Shirley Mahorney
Carol Snyder

1 THE INFORMATION PARADIGM

*T*he information paradigm was formed in the crucible of inexorably advancing technology, the demand for systems and the cost of building and operating those systems. The information paradigm— data architecture—is the result of an evolution and, in some ways, needs no explanation because many of the components that survived or were shaped by the evolution are familiar. The forces of evolution, like a glacier grinding rocks beneath its awesome weight of ice and snow, stretch technology, stretch costs, and stretch the number and types of systems that are constantly being produced. The result is an architecture—described in terms of data, but applicable well beyond the narrow confines of just data—that fits the generic information needs and budgets of the enterprise in an efficient and effective manner. That data architecture is the paradigm for information systems and technology for stable, effective systems.

The first chapter describes what the information paradigm is and how its components interact. The second chapter describes the evolution that formed (is forming) the information paradigm. Subsequent chapters describe various aspects of the information paradigm, such as its theoretical underpinnings and its technological foundation.

This book is for anyone interested in data base, including but not limited to data processing managers, data base administrators, data administrators, chief information officers, and system developers. The implications of the information paradigm are great. The forces that are pushing the world of data processing toward the architecture are even greater. In a word, the information paradigm is a framework. That framework affects *everyone*—from the technician to the end user—who is using the computer in today's corporate world.

The book is written so that only a mildly technical background is required. Some minor points will be appreciated only by a technician, but the vast majority of the rest is for a wide, nontechnical audience. The manager looking for strategic direction will find the book especially useful.

THE INFORMATION PARADIGM—A DATA ARCHITECTURE

The architecture represented by the information paradigm is characterized by data that is divided into different "levels," or categories. For organizations that are just beginning to feel the forces of evolution at work in their domain, the distinctions between the different levels of data will be blurred. For organizations that have felt the forces of evolution at work for a longer period of time, the distinctions between the different levels of data are much clearer. Indeed, the evolutionary maturity of an organization insofar as data architecture is concerned is characterized by how distinct the different levels of data are. The more mature the organization, the more distinct the levels.

The information paradigm, in its most simplistic form, is shown in Figure 1.

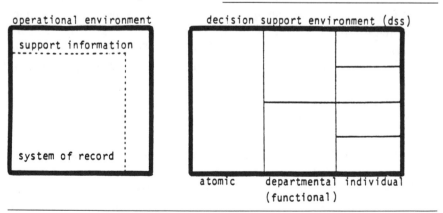

FIGURE 1 The information paradigm.

Figure 1 shows that the two major divisions of the information paradigm are between operational and decision support systems. Operational systems are primarily transaction-oriented and are used to run the day-to-day activities of the enterprise at a detailed level. Decision support systems are those that are used in the management of the enterprise. The domain of decision support systems is very broad, including such activities as end user computing, ad hoc reporting, trend analysis, heuristic spread sheet analysis, projections, and so forth.

The operational domain is divided into two categories—the system of record and supporting (i.e., nonsystem of record) information. The dss (decision support systems) domain is divided into three major subdivisions: atomic, departmental, and individual information processing. Each of the major subcategorizations of the information paradigm will be described.

In many organizations dss analytical processing or end-user computing is not taken as seriously as "real" data processing. The fact that end-user computing arrived much later on the scene than more traditional forms of computing and that end-user computing is a whole different mode of processing fosters this attitude.

But in many ways end-user computing and analytical dss processing represent the culmination of years of more traditional processing. In many cases end-user computing draws sweeping conclusions from otherwise detailed data that is used for day-to-day control of the operations of the organization.

Those who belittle the role of end-user computing and analytical processing just do not see the larger picture that is emerging in the modern corporation.

THE STAGES OF END-USER COMPUTING*

In 1979 *Harvard Business Review* published one of the most widely read articles in data processing. In "Managing the Crises in Data Processing," the author, Richard Nolan, suggested that there were different evolutionary stages through which a data processing organization passed. He described six of these

stages: initiation, contagion, control, integration, data administration, and maturity. Distilled as they were from observations of many DP shops, Nolan's six stages of data processing growth have long since gained wide acceptance and have assumed the status of fundamental truth.

As fourth generation technology turns the DP world into a DP/user world, there is reason to suppose that the user is embarking on the

*By W.H. Inmon, *Information Center Magazine*, January 1985. Reprinted with permission.

same evolutionary path that data processing has spent the last three decades trodding. Users are demanding control of their own destiny, and in doing so they are turning back the clock on themselves, re-creating the data processing environment of a much earlier stage.

There are three forces that seem to be driving the user through the evolutionary stages: the need for rapid system development, the costs associated with system development and operation, and the need for consistency of data in a varied and dispersed user environment.

Must the users go back to the initial stages and start over, recapitulating the history of data processing? The answer is "probably yes." The users of today show all the signs of entering the stages of initiation and contagion. But there are some major differences between today's user-controlled environment and the infant world of DP as it existed in the 1950s and 1960s.

One major difference is in the technologies and the power of the processing that is available today. Under any measure, today's tools are vastly more powerful than yesterday's. In terms of power, there is no comparison between assembler languages and fourth generation languages. In terms of capabilities, there is no comparison between the 64K machine of 1965 (which was a wonder then) and the multi-megabyte machine that is available today. In terms of capacity and cost, there is no comparison between a stack of punched 80-column cards and photo-optical storage. And so the comparison goes.

But the difference in power doesn't mean the user-driven world of today is qualitatively different from the data processing world of a generation ago. It probably just means the users will go through the six stages faster. The real forces of evolution will become apparent to the end user much more quickly than they ever were to the early DP shops. The early DP shops had quite a struggle with their tools, so much so that the forces of evolution were not obvious and often took extended periods of time to manifest themselves.

OTHER DIFFERENCES

The second major difference between today's emerging user environment and yesterday's DP environment is the *type* of need facing the end user. The end user purportedly has a need for decision-support type systems. In contrast to the traditional kind of highly specified, slow-to-develop, and inflexible DP systems of yesterday, the end-user systems are generally small, quick to construct, and easy to change.

The differing needs translate to differing functions. While yesterday's DP systems were designed to *run* the company, modern end-user systems are designed to *manage* it. It is the classical difference between decision support systems and operational systems. And when the user wishes to write operational systems with fourth generation tools, that leads to a whole different set of problems (which will be considered later in this article.)

The different functions argument complicates the analogy in that the forces of evolution are decelerated *at the micro level*, but they are accelerated *at the macro level*. We can explain the complication with an example. Suppose there is a single user (*i.e.*, the micro level) developing decision support systems. These systems might be critical to the user's work, but they are not sensitive to the *operations* of the company, so there is only minimal pressure to build them quickly. The user might be writing a system to compare this year's account activity to last year's. As important as the comparison is, the company won't cease to operate if the system takes more than a week to create. Cutting back on the pressure to create systems fast means cutting back on one of the pressures that drive an organization through the six stages.

But from a macro level (given that *all* departments are building decision support systems) the pressure to move to the higher stages

(such as that of data administration) will be greater than anything that was ever put on DP. When upper management asks three or four related departments for information on which to base a decision and three or four very disjointed answers are returned, upper management will see the need to resolve differences between departments. The resulting pressure for integrated decision support systems will drive the users to move to higher stages much earlier in the development process.

Another difference between the two environments is in their orientations toward technology. The DP world of yesterday was (and still is) very technically oriented. At the heart of the DP department are operating system technicians, network technicians, data base technicians, operations technicians, and the like. Without these technicians, the DP world would not turn. But today's user-friendly environment has gotten away from this orientation. Even in cases where "user friendliness" is more fancy than fact, there is no doubt that today's user environment is much simpler, cleaner, and easier to manage than yesterday's DP environment. Taking away the technicians in a sense means taking away an obstacle between the user and the systems the user wishes to create. There is no doubt that this will greatly accelerate the users' progress through Nolan's stages.

Perhaps the most profound difference between the two environments is in the amount of budgetary control. In yesterday's DP environment, it was DP that bought equipment and software, and it was DP that operated as a service organization. In most shops, the user considered DP services and equipment to be a free resource. To this day, many users still have not made the connection between the bottom line of profitability and the DP resources they consume. But as control of systems is passed to the user, the responsibility for the budget is passed along as well. Most microprocessors and fourth generation software are being sold directly to the user, not to DP. At long last, the dollar is coming directly out of the user's pocket. This encourages the user to see the relationship between the purchase of a PC and upgrading the office carpeting. The shift of budgetary responsibility for computing services will help accelerate the user through Nolan's stages.

There are shops in which DP is still paying, even in the user-controlled environment. In these organizations, the evolutionary forces won't be as strong. In fact, the strategy of DP funding user-controlled systems is probably a negative force for everybody concerned.

THE EXPERIENCE BACKLOG

"Backlog" has become a rather unpleasant word to data processing professionals, but in the development of user-controlled systems, there is a good backlog. The backlog of data processing experience available to the fledgling world of user-controlled systems is the final difference between the old environment and the new. In the early days of DP, everything was brand new. There was no previous experience on which managers, technicians, or anyone else could rely. Patterns were hard to recognize, trends were not apparent, and sound practices often could not be distinguished from unsound ones. The criteria for success were not yet recognized, and the result was a very strange set of priorities in many cases.

But in today's world (for the user and DP alike) there is a basis for comparison. That the experiences of the past three decades have not been lost gives us hope that it might be easier for user-controlled computing to get to the higher stages. The user should be able to avoid grossly incorrect decisions without having to learn by actually committing them first. They have already been committed many times in the past, as almost any data processing professional can painfully testify.

Some of the differences between the two environments will accelerate the users through the initial stages but will not mitigate passage through the later ones. As noted here, the "user friendly" tools and the lessening dependence on technicians will probably tend to rush the user through initiation and contagion, but it is doubtful whether these advances will accelerate the user through the stages of control and integration. In the stages of control and integration, the dominant forces have to do with organizational discipline and don't relate very closely to technology. Today's powerful technology will bring the realization into focus much more quickly than in DP's evolution, but control and integration are political problems and will require political solutions.

THE ISSUE OF CONTROL

In fact, the issue of control is particularly complicated by another difference in the computing environments. Where DP has always tended to be centralized, modern user-controlled computing is by definition decentralized. Control is difficult in any case; in a decentralized environment, the problem is magnified. To make matters worse, the decentralization of the user systems is along departmental—and therefore political—lines. Political boundaries have traditionally been the most difficult over which to exert discipline.

If there's an advantage to any of this, it's that users can no longer blame DP for not producing systems. When upper management *does* turn its hand to the issues of control and integration, the users won't be able to cloud the issue (as has often been done in the past) by pointing to DP as some kind of culprit.

Of course, every organization will find its own way through the six stages, and one of the factors affecting the individual speed is the evolution of the organization's DP department. If the company's DP department is still in the early days of control, then it is unlikely that the end user can evolve any further than DP. (In this case, DP might well *be* the culprit holding up end-user evolution.) The nature of the end-user system is decision support, and such systems normally depend on operational data. If the operational data is uncontrolled and unintegrated, then the end user may have a very shaky foundation on which to operate. In this case, the end user may well be a significant force in the evolution of DP. But we can hope that most DP shops have evolved beyond the early stages.

Putting aside the question of how fast user-controlled computing is going to move through the stages, there are interesting questions that arise as a result of contemplating the future of these systems. What about the continuing evolution in today's DP shop? Is it time to consider seventh and eighth stages? What about companies that do not shift budgetary control for computing to the users? What about companies that allow end users to build operational systems? Let's look at these questions.

Today's DP shop is not going to cease existing (or even cease evolving) just because there is a spread of user-controlled computing. In fact, the need for DP services will continue to grow. But DP will be doing primarily operational activities. The line between operational and decision support systems will become more clear over time. The evolutionary pressures will continue to operate on each side of the line, although they may be relaxed in DP temporarily when decision support systems depart its domain.

THE ALL-IMPORTANT BUDGET

In the shift of budgetary control we have a more immediate question. It is natural for the user to assume responsibility of the budget for computing services as the user takes control of them. In those organizations where—as a result of inertia or lack of planning—DP is still saddled with buying the users' hardware and software while the user controls the environment, DP will be placed in an untenable position, worse than anything it has endured in its evolution to date. But DP's position isn't the only thing at stake.

In order for the user to mature, there must be realization that services and equipment have a price tag attached. As long as DP is paying that price, the user will never make the connection and will be lacking the feedback essential to effective management. Budgetary responsibility should follow control of the environment into the hands of the user.

Parenthetically, there is one type of company (becoming, thankfully, increasingly rare) that will probably not evolve at all. That company is the one with the "infinite budget" approach to DP. In the infancy of DP (Nolan's "initiation" stage), many companies required what seemed to be never-ending budget increases. As long as DP was establishing itself within the company, there was an open-handed attitude toward the budget, and it was necessary. As DP grew up, part of the maturing process consisted of cost-justifying its operations. In many smaller and marginally profitable companies, this maturation occurred quickly, as it had to. But in larger companies (especially those that were highly profitable), there remained an open-handed attitude toward the budget.

Among regulated companies, there were even some that sought to *increase* DP spending (*i.e.*, make it less efficient) in order to raise the regulated prices at which the company operated. In these cases, data processing has always operated as if there were no end to the budget available. For one reason or another, such organizations have little incentive to mature, and there is no reason to believe their end users will mature any more quickly than their DP departments.

Finally, we have the question of users trying to build operational systems with fourth generation tools. And the evidence indicates that in every case the result has been a spiraling of the hardware costs that is unparalleled. (See "What Price Relational?" *Computerworld*, November 28, 1983.) When the user attempts to build operational systems with inappropriate tools, the associated hardware costs mount up so quickly that the user invariably changes the focus on the type of system built.

MORE QUESTIONS THAN ANSWERS

Applying Nolan's stages to end-user computing is perhaps more interesting for the questions it raises than the answers it provides. The very natures of end-user computing and traditional data processing are so different that the stages will no doubt have to be modified for end-user computing. But even the most casual observation reveals that end users are going through the stages of initiation and contagion right now, and they are going through them quite rapidly. It is the control stage where we will see whether the model has to be changed significantly for end-user computing. As I noted, there are political considerations here that promise to make "control" a very difficult stage for this kind of computing.

"Integration" and "data administration" will likewise differ significantly from the classical data processing experience. But these stages are still far enough away that it would be difficult to say what they might be like. And that realization points to some of the fascinating questions that will come up in the next couple of years. Is it necessary for end-user computing to even go through the stages? Can the end user "leap frog" from one stage to another based on the fact that DP has already grappled with so many of the growth questions? Is the evolution in organizational computing merely a change in control within organizations or is it symptomatic of a more profound change? Does the end-user revolution promise a more clear delineation in the roles of DP and the user? What lies beyond maturity for both DP and users? How will the separate evolutions of DP and end-user computing affect each other?

The answers to some of these questions might well create the "fundamental truths" of end-user computing.

OPERATIONAL SYSTEMS—THE SYSTEM OF RECORD

The system of record is the repository of operational data, in which detailed information that is accurate up to the second about the customer and the activities of the customer that are relevant to the day-to-day running of the enterprise are nonredundantly stored. Consider a simple example. Suppose a customer of a bank deposits his or her paycheck. The system of record in this instance would typically include the name, address, and social security number of the customer, the amount, date, and location of the deposit, the current balance of the account, and so forth. All of the detailed, up-to-the-second information about the customer is found in the system of record.

Data is stored in the system of record nonredundantly. If there were multiple occurrences of the same data within the system of record, there would be potential for problems. Suppose a bank stores the same information relating to a social security number in two places in the bank's operational systems for a single account. Suppose the up-to-the-second account balances relating to the social security numbers are not the same (admittedly a mistake). Then the processing that occurs related to the account may be incorrect. For example, interest paid to the customer's account may be incorrectly transmitted to the IRS. The result will be problems for the customer, the bank, and the IRS. At the point that an enterprise does its day-to-day business, there is need for accurate, detailed, nonredundant up-to-the-second information. The system of record, then, is that repository of information.

The concept of the system of record requires that every piece of detailed information have a singular (i.e., nonredundant) existence. If there is ever a conflict in the values for an occurrence of data, the system of record provides, at a detailed level, a basis for reconciliation. In short, all detailed occurrences of data outside of the system of record will reconcile to the system of record.

Supporting Operational Data—Non–System of Record

Most of the information in the operational environment of the enterprise, including data and processing, is contained in the system of record. But there are other legitimate components of the operational environment that are not part of the system of record. One such component is the transaction processing front end of an operational environment.

Take, for example, a banking environment that has an ATM (Automated Teller Machine) component. Figure 2 illustrates the typical relationship between the bank's front end (i.e., ATM) processors and the large background processors.

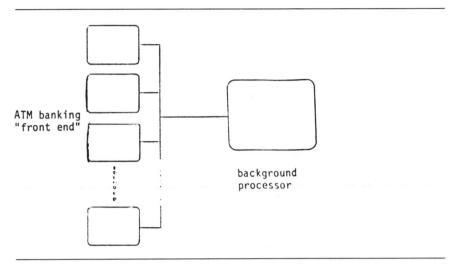

FIGURE 2 Relationship between front end processors and background processors.

Consider where the system of record resides in Figure 2. It resides inside the background processor. Once an account's balance is changed inside the background processor, the balance is effectively changed for the bank, but not until then. But what about the data in the systems at the front end? That data found in the transaction processing front end is not part of the system of record, although it is closely related to the system of record and directly serves it. When a single ATM retrieves a customer's balance, issues money to the customer, and reduces the customer's balance accordingly, the system of record still remains in the background processor! At the completion of the transaction in the ATM, the notification of the activity will be sent to the background processor and the appropriate balance will be changed or posted for change. The front end, then, is not part of the system of record but is nevertheless part of the operational environment.

Now, consider another type of supporting operational system that is not part of the system of record. Suppose an insurance company has three offices: one in Dallas, one in Los Angeles, and one in New York. The insurance company "domiciles" a policy according to geographic location. For example, a policy holder in Houston will have his or her policy domiciled and serviced out of Dallas, a policy holder in San Francisco will have her policy serviced out of Los Angeles, and so forth. Figure 3 shows the simple distributed system.

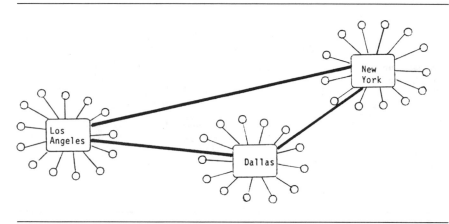

FIGURE 3 A simple distributed system.

Suppose a policy holder from San Francisco is on business in Dallas and has an accident. The policy information is sent from Los Angeles to Dallas, where the claim is serviced. The system of record remains at the domicile—in this case, in Los Angeles. But the servicing of the claim is done in Dallas. The information that is sent from Los Angeles to Dallas is sent outside the system of record but remains in the operational environment. Distributed data is often transported outside the system of record but still remains inside the operational environment. This is another example of a supporting operational system that is not part of the system of record.

Data in the system of record may include data that is widely shared, data that is used privately, or data somewhere in between. For example, a customer file is typically widely shared, whereas a preferred loan account is used by only a few people. And a customer's payment record may be used by more than a few users. Nevertheless, all of those occurrences of data would belong in the system of record environment.

Data Ownership

Of course, data "ownership" should be decided at the outset, either by default or by explicit documentation. Data ownership—on an element by element basis—is the proclamation of who can create, update, and delete data. Under normal circumstances one, and only one, operating department owns any given occurrence of data.

For example, the loans department is solely responsible for the establishment and administration of loans. But on other occasions, the same data is "owned" under different circumstances by different operating departments. The loans department may establish a loan and give it active status. But a separate delinquency department may have the authority to change the status of a loan to "bad," "overdue," or "nonperforming." However, for a given piece of information at any moment in time, one and only one operating department will be in charge of the accuracy or ownership of data.

Each data element in the system of record is owned. Ownership outside the system of record may or may not be formally established, since the content of the data cannot be changed outside the system of record.

Another type of data found in the operational environment is "high probability" data. Typically some archival data will have a high probability of access.

For example, a bank may choose to have the last two months worth of checking activity kept online. When a customer has a query as to his or her balance, the query can be immediately answered from operational systems. But a historical record of checks (even a two-month old historical record) is a type of data that is fundamentally different from a customer's current balance or a customer's current address. High probability archival data, then, is another type of data found in the operational or production environment.

ATOMIC DSS INFORMATION

The second major division of the information paradigm is the dss (decision support systems) environment. There are three levels of data in the dss environment: atomic data, departmental data, and individual data. The first level of information in the dss environment is the atomic* level. The atomic level dss data is detailed data that is stored as of some moment in time, and is usually fed from data from the system of record. Time variancy of data—either directly or indirectly—is reflected at the atomic level. When data is "time variant," each data element has a value as of some moment in time. Some examples of time variant data are the date a customer opened an account, the date a check was cashed, the date a premium was billed, the date a stock was sold, the date an accident happened, and so forth. Atomic dss data is as granular as data in the dss environment can become. It is nonredundant with other atomic data, and the structures of the atomic level are oriented toward the major subjects of the enterprise. There is, of course, some amount of redundancy of data between the atomic and the operational or production environment. All of the atomic dss data can be considered archival (although there are some major differences between classical unarchitected archival data and atomic dss data, as will be discussed later).

As an example of atomic dss data, consider an insurance company that historically stores claims in an atomic dss data base. Such information as date of claim, amount of claim, policy (or policies) linked to claim, settlement, circumstances, other insurees, linked claims, etc., are all stored at the atomic level. Most claims that have been filed but haven't been settled remain in the system of record because there is a high probability of access. And for six months after settlement, the claim may remain in the system of record because there is a good chance the most recent claim information will be accessed.

Eventually, the claim flows from the system of record to the atomic data base as the probability of its access lessens. Note that in the system of record, claim information may be physically scattered in several locations—by agent, by regional office, by policy, etc. But as the data flows to the atomic level, it is gathered and stored according to its major subject, as shown by Figure 4.

The flow of data from the system of record or operational environment to the atomic level occurs on an as-needed basis. If the information in the system of record is actively useful for decision support, then it will flow as soon as it becomes established in the system of record. If, on the other hand, the information in the system of record is only casually

---

*"Atomic" refers to the fine degree of granularity of the data. Other names for Atomic data are foundation data, reports data, an "information warehouse", and "information factory", et al.

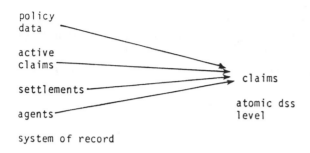

```
policy
data
active
claims
                                    claims
settlements
                          atomic dss
agents                    level

system of record
```

FIGURE 4 When the information is established in the system of record, it is "fed" to the atomic level periodically.

relevant to the decision support environment, then the flow to the atomic level may be correspondingly relaxed.

Before information is purged from the system of record environment, a decision must be made on whether to actually discard the data or to place the data at the atomic dss level.

Departmental Dss Data

The next level of dss data is departmental. The departmental dss level of data is the place where each department—accounting, marketing, engineering, actuarial, etc.—keeps its own dss data, peculiar to its needs, that it gets from the atomic dss data base. Among different departmental dss data bases, there is normally a high degree of redundancy of data.

Data at the atomic dss level is very detailed. As data flows from the atomic to the departmental level, the derivation of data—the transformation from detailed to derived data—is accomplished. The result is that departmental data is summarized or otherwise refined.

The term "departmental" may well be a misnomer for many organizations. Instead, the term "functional" may be used where there are many different departments doing dss analysis. In smaller organizations that have only a few departments, the term "departmental" may be an adequate term to describe mid-level dss data.

One example of departmental data is marketing data that is collected periodically from the atomic data base. On a monthly basis, detailed sales information is collected. From the detailed data, monthly sales by zip code, product line, geographic region, sales district, and so forth, are tabulated and stored at the departmental level. Each month's tabulation is stored by month, so that several years of summarized sales by month are collected departmentally. The same detailed data at the atomic level can be accumulated into multiple stores of data at the departmental level.

A characteristic of departmental data is that departmental-level reports are produced on a regularly scheduled basis. Indeed, much departmental data has the characteristic of regularity of processing.

Individual Dss Data

The last level of dss data is the individual dss data level. At the individual dss data level comes much of the autonomy of processing inherent to the end user computing environment. At the individual dss level, analyses are created, heuristically and quickly, from the departmental data or, on occasion, from the atomic data. The processing done at this level is very individualistic and is almost totally derived. Very little primitive data is found at this level; so there is little or no scheduled processing of data at the individual level.

As an example of the processing done at the individual dss level, an analyst may create a trend analysis of sales by different geographic areas and compare the trends to each other, looking for patterns of differentiation. Upon detecting a trend, the analyst examines other data looking for confirmation.

PRIMITIVE/DERIVED DATA

The information paradigm's most fundamental delineation of data is between primitive and derived data. Primitive data describes a single entity, such as a customer or single event relating to the operation of the enterprise. Derived data relates to multiple entities, such as customers and/or multiple events relevant to the enterprise. The existence of a primitive data element depends directly upon the existence of a single occurrence of the entity or an event. For example, the age, sex, and bank balance of a customer are all primitive pieces of data. If the customer goes away (or if the customer has never existed), then these pieces of information go away from the system of record.

The existence of derived data depends on the existence of multiple occurrences of an entity (or multiple subjects of the enterprise) or multiple events. For example, the average account balance of a bank's customers for a month might be a derived data element. If any customer goes away, there is still an average account balance.

To what extent data is primitive and to what extent data is derived depends upon the eye of the beholder. Data that is derived to a shop foreman may well be primitive to a plant manager. This anomaly points out the need for a careful definition of the scope of integration for a system and the ensuing identification of the audience for whom the scope of integration is built. Confusion as to who is using what data shows up in the architecture.

In most cases, derived data is calculated from primitive data or from other derived data. As an example of primitive data, consider the claim made against a car insurance policy. An accident occurs on December 14 at Main and Broad Streets. The policy holder's name is Maryce Jacobs. The car Maryce was driving is a 1986 Trans-Am, which is covered by policy 12459-01. The estimate of damage is $2,500. Maryce was not hurt, nor was the other party in the car hurt. Snow and ice were a mitigating factor. All of the pieces of information relating to the accident are classified as primitive data or primitive information.

As an example of derived data, consider the analysis of an actuarian at an insurance company, whose job is to determine rates for policies. Based upon the history of claims made in cold climates (i.e., where there is winter ice and snow), rates for New England are higher than rates in Texas. Based upon all claims submitted, rates for females are lower than rates for males. And based upon all claims that are known, across the industry, rates for teenagers are higher than rates for nonteens, and so forth. The actuarian accumulates all claims (over a period of time) and derives the cumulative claim information by major categories of information, such as location of policy, domicile, sex of policy holder, age of policy holder, and so forth. In the accumulations of claim information, there are many forms of derived information or derived data.

The information paradigm separates primitive and derived data as shown in Figure 5.

The system of record (and most other operational data) and the atomic level of dss data contain primarily primitive data. Departmental and individual dss data contain primarily derived data.

The derivation of data (i.e., the transformation of data from its primitive state into its derived state) occurs as data goes from the atomic level to the departmental level. And a higher level of derivation (i.e., a "second

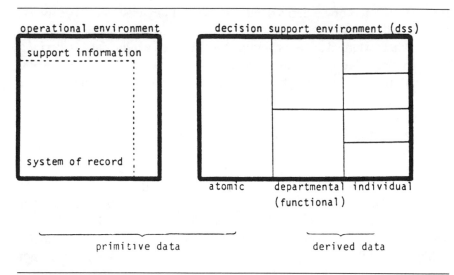

FIGURE 5 The information paradigm separates primitive and derived data.

order'' derivation) occurs as data flows from the departmental to the individual dss level.

Primitive/Derived Differences

The primitive levels of data are distinct from the derived levels of data because of the fundamental differences in the data itself. Although primitive data forms the basis for most derived data, nevertheless, primitive data and derived data are fundamentally different. There are two major ways of perceiving the differences between primitive and derived data: from a theoretical perspective and from a practical perspective.

From a theoretical perspective, consider the primitive data of a retail store's daily sales. Each sale is its own occurrence of primitive data, containing such elements as tax, time of sale, sales amount, and item(s) purchased. Throughout the day, the following occurrences of primitive data are collected as sales are made: Sale #1, Sale #2, Sale #3 . . . and so forth.

Now consider the data element—daily sales total for all stores in the system. Daily sales total is a derived data element because it represents the accumulation of all sales made in a day. In fact, daily sales can be calculated by

DAILY TOTAL SALES = SUM (SALE 1, SALE 2, SALE 3, . . . SALE n)

Of course, there is a close relationship between daily total sales and any given sale. But despite the close relationship, the two data elements are not, in fact, the same thing.

There is a train of thought that suggests that all derived data is redundant because derived data is transformed from one or more occurrences of primitive data. But derived data is inherently redundant in other ways as well.

Suppose that daily total sales by geographic district and daily total sales by product line are to be calculated, as well as daily total sales. Any given sale will contribute to daily total sales, to one geographic calculation of daily total sales, and to one (or more) product lines of daily total sales. Consequently, the three data elements—daily total sales, daily total sales by geographic location, and daily total sales by product line —are redundant because they represent nothing more than a different summation of the same primitive data.

Primitive/Derived Differences—Practical Considerations

There are many practical reasons as well as theoretical reasons why primitive data differs fundamentally from derived data. Some of these differences are:

- Level of detail—primitive data is detailed; derived data is summarized and highly refined.
- Performance—primitive data is required instantaneously (or at least very quickly); derived data is required casually—on the half hour, daily, etc.
- Usage structure—the usage of primitive processing is highly structured; the usage of derived data is highly unstructured.
- Availability—primitive data needs to be continuously available for long periods of time; derived data need be available only periodically.
- Organizational usage—primitive data is used clerically, or at the point where the customer meets the enterprise; derived data is used managerially, or at the point from which the enterprise is directed.
- Concurrency—primitive data measures the most current value of data; derived data measures trends and the change of data across time.
- Static nature of data content—the contents of primitive data are dynamic, constantly changing; the contents of derived data are static, frozen as of some moment in time.

▪ Definition of data—the definition of primitive data is static, or at least fairly stable; the definition of derived data is dynamic, constantly changing.

▪ Amount of data used in normal processing—primitive processing is characterized by the frequent access of limited amounts of data; derived processing is characterized by the infrequent access of large amounts of data.

▪ Algorithmic stability—the algorithms used in primitive processing are essentially stable; derived processing is based on algorithmically dynamic usage of data that is often heuristically derived.

▪ Infrastructure—the primitive infrastructure is geared to high performance, high availability, and data and transaction integrity; the derived infrastructure is geared to autonomy of processing, speed and ease of system construction and speed and ease of system maintenance.

▪ Community of users—primitive data and processing are aimed at a wide community of users, i.e., all the personnel interactivity with the customers of the enterprise; derived data and processing are aimed at increasingly private audiences, the personnel making managerial and enterprise directing decisions.

▪ Data update—primitive data can be updated on a field-by-field basis; derived data is normally accessed and manipulated.

▪ Data management—primitive data is managed in its entirety—a bank for example, must keep track of *all* operational customers; derived data is managed by selective subsets—the manager of marketing does analysis by looking at selected subsets of the population, subsets of time, subsets based on geography, etc.

▪ Philosophy—primitive data and processing are used to run the day-to-day operations of the enterprise; derived data and processing are used to manage the enterprise.

For these reasons—both theoretical and practical—the information paradigm mandates that there be a separation of primitive and derived data.

DATA THAT IS BOTH PRIMITIVE AND DERIVED— TRANSITION DATA

There is some data that, at the same time, is both primitive and derived. Fortunately, there is not a lot of this "dual personality" (or transition) data. The transition data generally appears as (very important) parameters that are created or otherwise established in the derived environment and are used to profoundly shape the business of the enterprise at a detailed level. As an example of transaction data, consider the rates of interest a bank pays on its deposits. The rates are calculated from or, at the least, influenced by derived data. As such, they can be considered to be derived. (Certainly in the eyes of the vice president in charge of marketing, the rates are derived.)

But at the same time the rates are primitive, in that when a teller opens an account or accepts a deposit, the rates apply to an individual customer as of a moment in time. And, certainly, the rates have a profound effect on the bank's business. If the rates are set too low, the bank will attract few depositors. If the rates are set too high, the bank will attract many depositors but will have its margin of profitability reduced. Nearly all organizations have some form of "transition" data that is neither exclusively derived nor primitive. Interestingly, transition data is usually very sensitive to the running of the enterprise.

One of the interesting observations about primitive and derived data is that the algorithmic calculation of data has nothing to do with whether it is primitive or derived. In general, derived data *is* calculated, but primitive data is calculated as well. For example, consider two common calculated values that are kept online: a customer's bank balance and the number of seats that are available on an airplane flight. Both numbers are calculated and both numbers are kept online, accurate up to the second. A bank balance depends upon the existence of a single customer for its existence, and the available seats on an airplane flight depend upon the existence of an airplane flight for its existence. Both are online, high-performance, *calculated* pieces of primitive data.

As a rule, derived data is not kept online unless there is a high probability of its access.

Another Perspective

There is another perspective of primitive and derived data and the relationship between primitive and derived data and operational, atomic, departmental, and individual data, as shown by Figure 5-a.

In Figure 5-a, it is seen that as a shop first builds systems, it encounters much primitive data. As time passes, derived data is collected, to the point of overwhelming primitive data. The fundamental relationship between the levels of data is depicted as well.

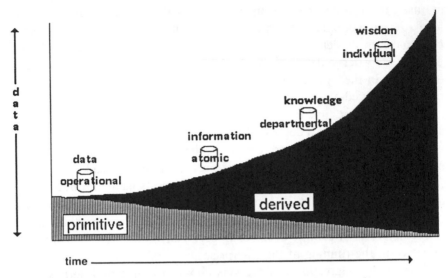

In the early stages of computing, there is much primitive data in a
shop. As a shop matures there is much more derived data and much
less primitive data.

(Courtesy of Duane Hufford and Col Wayne Byrd, U S Army)

FIGURE 5-a In the early stages of computing, there is much primitive
data in a shop. As a shop matures, there is much more derived data
and much less primitive data. (Courtesy of Duane Hufford and Col.
Wayne Byrd, U.S. Army)

Primitive data supports operational processing and is just plain "data."
Atomic data supports information and is a combination of derived and
primitive data. Departmental data is a basis of knowledge and is almost
entirely derived data. And individual data is the foundation for wisdom,
which is almost exclusively derived data.

The information cycle

The flow of data goes (in normal cases) from the primitive to the derived
environment, as depicted by Figure 6.

If the information environment is considered in isolation, then the flow
is unidirectional and is as shown in Figure 6. But Figure 6 is only a
smaller part of a larger cycle. Figure 7 illustrates the larger information
cycle.

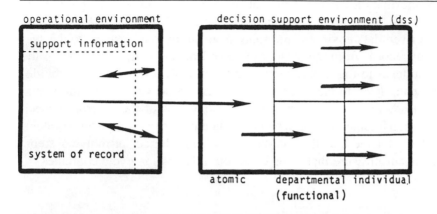

FIGURE 6 The normal flow of data in the information paradigm.

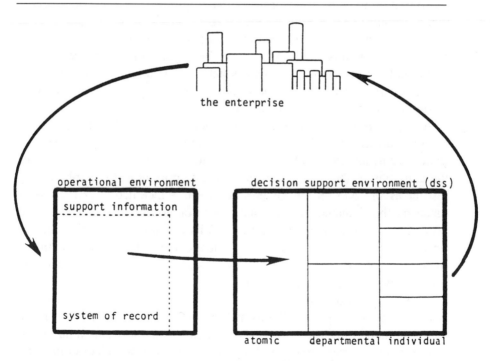

FIGURE 7 The information cycle and the information paradigm.

The information cycle shows that operational systems manage and are fed by the activities of the enterprise. In turn, the primitive data feeds the derived data environment, going from supporting systems to the system of record, from the system of record to the atomic level, from the atomic level to the departmental (or functional) level, and from the departmental level to the individual level. But processing at the individual level leads to results that influence the business of the enterprise (such as the transitional or dual personality data of a bank—its interest rates). Once the business of the enterprise has been altered, primitive systems once again measure that change and the information cycle continues.

PRIVATE SYSTEMS/PRIVATE DATA

At first glance, it is a temptation to state that all data and all systems of a corporation must fit the information paradigm. But such is not the case. Only "public" data need fit the information paradigm. Public data is data that is relevant to multiple functional units of the enterprise. Usually, it relates to the mainstream business of the organization. The reverse of public data is private data, which is data that is directly relevant to, at most, one functional unit of the organization and generally not directly related to the mainstream business of the organization.

As an example of private data, consider the financial management of a public utility. The financial manager (among other things!) sets and trades securities on a daily basis (i.e., stocks, bonds, etc.). Of course, the activities of the financial manager are important to the public utility insofar as the bottom line of profitability is concerned. But the trades made by the financial manager have little or no direct influence on the service provided by the public utility, on its day-to-day activities, and so forth. Therefore, financial activities independent of the mainstream of the utility may be considered private data and not subject to the discipline imposed by information paradigm.

Another form of private data is classical, individual data. An office worker may store personal information in his or her electronic filing cabinet. Such items as the worker's calendar, frequently called numbers, family anniversaries, and birthdays may be kept in the electronic filing cabinet and are not subject to the discipline of the information paradigm.

Generally speaking, whether data is public or private is an obvious issue. If there is a question, the corporate data administrator should make the determination.

THE CONCEPTUAL FOUNDATION

At the heart of the information paradigm is the conceptual foundation of data as it relates to the enterprise. In some cases, the conceptual foundation consists of a data model. In other cases, the conceptual foundation is a data and process model. In any case, primitive information (and/or primitive processing) is separated from its derived brethren, and a primitive model is created. Of course, every time a derived unit of information or processing is encountered, its primitive basis is identified and placed in the conceptual model if it is not already there.

For example, the derived data element Monthly Payroll is removed from the conceptual foundation. But the primitive basis of Monthly Payroll—employee #1 pay, employee #2 pay, etc., is included in the primitive conceptual model, if it has not already been included. Figure 8 shows how the conceptual model relates to the information paradigm.

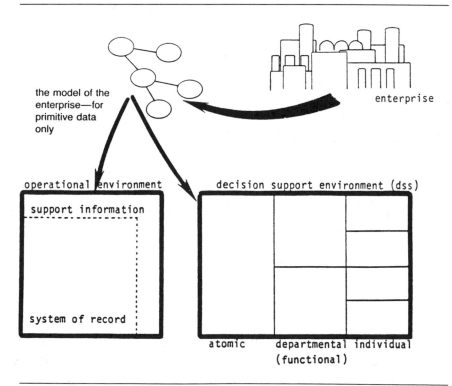

FIGURE 8 How the conceptual model relates to the information paradigm.

The primitive conceptual model needs to contain *all* the primitive information that is to be in the paradigm. But there is no need to capture all the derived data that will be represented (or that will be derivable) by the information paradigm. Only the most obvious, most important pieces of derived data need be captured. Indeed, the processing at the derived level is such that much processing is heuristically done, and the analyst cannot predict what will be derived in advance. As long as there is a sufficiently detailed foundation of primitive data, then the analyst doing decision support processing will suffer few restrictions in doing heuristic dss processing.

Different Levels of Dss Data

The information paradigm illustrates three levels of data: atomic, departmental (or functional), and individual. And for most organizations, three layers appear to be optimal. But there is nothing magical about this number. Depending upon the size and complexity of the organization, different levels of dss data may suffice, as shown by Figure 9.

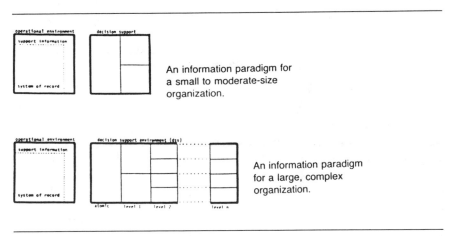

An information paradigm for a small to moderate-size organization.

An information paradigm for a large, complex organization.

FIGURE 9   Different levels of dss data.

In any case, there will be a need for atomic data and operational data, even for the smallest organization. And for large, complex organizations, there may be a need for multiple layers of dss data.

VARIATIONS OF THE INFORMATION PARADIGM

The information paradigm, as presented, fits the needs of the generic organization. But, depending on the business of the organization, there may be variations of the paradigm. Several variations will be discussed.

A large financial firm does much of its prospecting for customers through demographic analysis of data bases leased or rented externally. Thus, the foundation of dss processing is not restricted to operational data. External data plays a big role in dss processing, as shown by Figure 10.

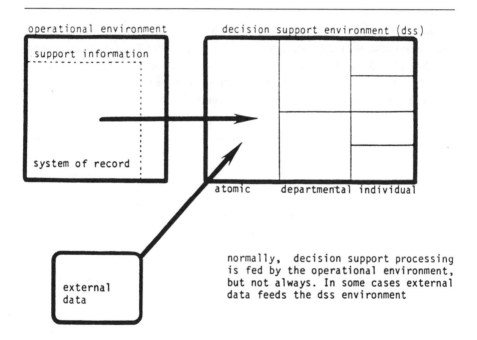

FIGURE 10 Normally, but not always, decision support processing is fed by the operational environment. In some cases, external data feeds the dss environment.

The external data is received and loaded into an atomic base. At that point, it is processed in a manner indistinguishable from that of other data. Atomic data serves as a public source of data, then, in that a company's operational data and external data can reside in an atomic data base. An advantage of the information paradigm in the face of external data is that *all* dss users can access the data from a common source. With atomic dss data bases, there is a need to bring external data into the organization in one and only one place.

A disadvantage of external data is that, unlike normal operational data, if errors are detected, there is (usually) no opportunity to correct the data. Instead, invalid external data is merely discarded. Contrast the disposal of incorrect external data with the detection of incorrect data in the operational environment. In the operational environment, when there is incorrect data, it is corrected at its source, and the cause for incorrectness is remedied.

Another variation of the information paradigm is found in organizations that do no operational processing. An example of this type of organization is illustrated by a state education agency that must measure various and sundry aspects of the local school districts. The organizational dynamics of such a state agency are shown by Figure 11.

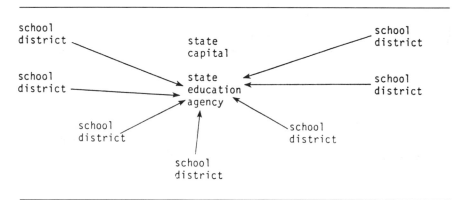

FIGURE 11 Each school district acts as its own operational environment. The state agency is fed atomic data from the various school districts.

Figure 11 shows that each school district is responsible for the monitoring and administration of its own schools, teachers, and facilities. Periodically, however, the school districts must report on different aspects to the centralized state agency. The state agency then compiles information representing the entire state.

In this example, there is effectively no operational environment, at least from the perspective of the state agency. (Of course, each local school district is really its own operational environment.) The information paradigm for the state agency, then, looks like the one depicted in Figure 12.

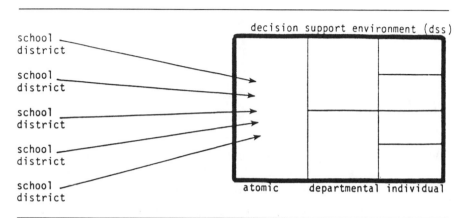

FIGURE 12 The information paradigm for the state agency.

One of the major issues of the arrangement shown in Figure 12 is that of the discipline required to achieve uniformity and consistency of data as the data enters the atomic level. In the variation shown in Figure 12, it is absolutely mandatory that a subject-oriented data model be constructed and adhered to rigorously.

A third variation of the information paradigm is illustrated by a ticketing agency for local sporting and entertainment events. The systems built for the ticketing agency do nothing more than price, allocate, and issue tickets for an arena or auditorium. They represent, in essence, system-of-record processing exclusively. The system(s) are shown by Figure 13.

There is no (formal) back end decision support processing in the sports and entertainment booking systems. Of course, decisions are made as to what events are to be scheduled in the arena or auditorium usually on the basis of the popularity of the event. But there are no formal, systemic feedback loops from the system of record to the decision makers.

The variations of the information paradigm presented show that not

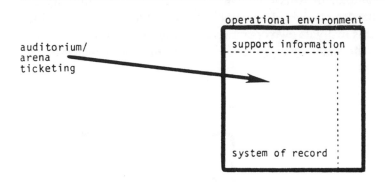

FIGURE 13   Example of system-of-record processing.

every processing environment directly supports the paradigm. Instead, there are "subsets" of the paradigm. But the variations reinforce the foundation rather than disenfranchise them.

Of course, even for the "standard" data processing organization, there is no "enforcer" waiting to discipline the organization if it does not adhere to the information paradigm. Instead, the forces of evolution tend to act in the role of enforcer. The more the organization deviates from the paradigm, the more the forces of evolution will serve to correct the variance.

ARCHIVAL DATA

The role of archival data has been mentioned in the discussions of various components of the information paradigm. But a separate discussion of archival data is warranted because of its importance.

Archival data fits into the information paradigm in several places, depending upon the probability of access of the data. Figure 14 shows the fit of archival data.

Figure 14 shows that archival data with a very high chance of access may be stored in the system of record, that archival data with a fair chance of access will be stored at the atomic level, and that summarized archival data will be stored at the departmental and individual level. Once the probability of access drops to near zero, then archival data will either be purged entirely or be kept in a "dead letter file" in the eventuality of some future unforeseen need for it.

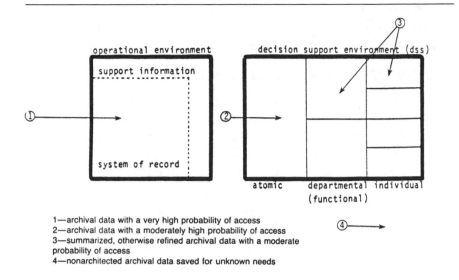

FIGURE 14 Archival data in the information paradigm:

As an example of the positioning of archival data, consider the following account activities for a bank. For each customer, the previous 30 days of account activity information is stored in the system of record. This allows the customer to have rapid access to data should there be a need for it. Furthermore, there is relatively little account activity data over a 30-day period, and the odds are good that if a customer wants to examine previous records, the records desired will be from the past 30 days.

Periodically, the system of record is "scrubbed," and the 30 days worth of activity data is sent to the atomic level. At the atomic level, account activity for the previous three years is collected. There is (obviously) much more data at the atomic level than at the system of record level, and, correspondingly, the probability of access is lower.

Departmental processing periodically sums up atomic data into summaries. A typical summary is net account activity by month by domicile. Although much primitive data goes into the monthly accumulation, the storage of the data at the derived departmental level requires relatively little storage.

Finally, after three years of existence at the atomic level, the detailed data is either purged entirely or removed to a separate media, such as microfiche.

The different levels of dss data that have evolved have not done so accidentally. The following discussion will address some of the major functions served by the levels of data.

CREDIBILITY OF DSS PROCESSING

In the first days of computers, the concept of master files arose. As master files proliferated, there soon appeared major problems with the redundancy of data. Shortly thereafter, the data base concept supplanted the master file concept. The data base concept required that a single source of data serve all processing needs, as shown by Figure 15.

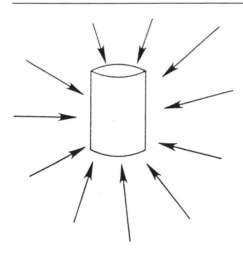

FIGURE 15 Data base — a single source of data serving all needs — a 1960s concept.

But very quickly there arose a need to access data in a manner unsuited to data base. The structure of data bases simply could not change as fast as the need for the data changed. In short order, "extracts" of data were done so that data would be available in a form accessible to users. The generic "extract and load" philosophy is depicted by Figure 16.

As long as there were few users doing dss processing, there was little difficulty with the extract approach depicted by Figure 16. But in the face of much dss processing, there arose a problem with its credibility.

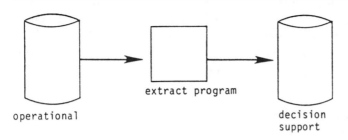

FIGURE 16 The "extract and load" philosophy — an early acknowl-
edgement of the differences between primitive and derived data.

Figure 17 illustrates the origins of the lack of credibility of the dss
environment.

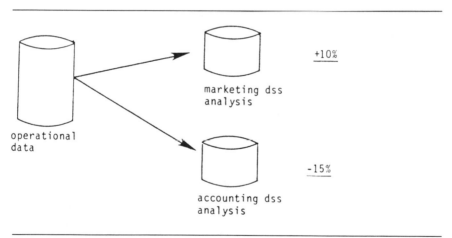

FIGURE 17 The analysis of the marketing and accounting departments
vary dramatically.

The scenario depicted in Figure 1.17 shows that management has asked
marketing to research a problem, and marketing has responded with a
value of + 10 percent. A similar question is researched by the accounting
department, and accounting responds with a value of − 15 percent. Management is concerned because the answers are not remotely the same.
Credibility of the entire process of dss analysis is at stake.

If marketing and accounting were operating from different sources of data, then the differences might be easily explained. Instead, they claim to operate from the same source of data.

Upon investigation, it is determined that there are four primary reasons why the discrepancy of values has occurred. The four reasons are:

1. Timing
2. Algorithmic extract differences
3. Complexity due to generations of extracts
4. Uncontrolled sources of input into the dss process

Regarding the first reason—timing—it is discovered that marketing has extracted their data on Sunday evening and accounting has extracted theirs on Wednesday afternoon, as shown by Figure 18.

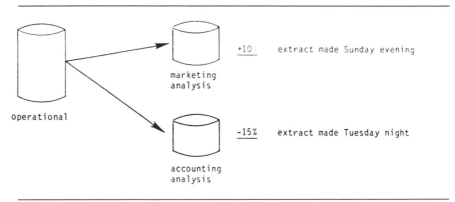

FIGURE 18 One of the reasons for the discrepancy of dss data is the difference in the timing of the extract.

There is no reason to expect that the operational base of data has remained the same from Sunday to Wednesday. Why, then, is there an expectation that data selected at different times—even if from the same sources—will be the same?

The second reason for the difference of opinion between the marketing and the accounting dss analysts occurs because the marketing analyst has selected all accounts with a balance greater than $500 and the accounting analyst has selected all accounts who have been with the bank since 1980. The difference in the extract algorithms is shown by Figure 19.

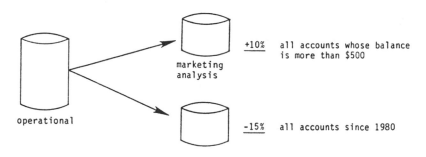

FIGURE 19 The extract algorithms have selected entirely different populations for the analysis of data — another reason for the discrepancy of dss data.

There simply is no strong correlation between the populations of data selected for each dss analysis. The length of time a customer has been with the bank and the amount of money in a customer account is coincidental. It should be no surprise that very different conclusions were drawn from an analysis of two distinct populations.

The third—and probably the most pervasive—reason for the difference in results is that there are generations of extracts in the dss world. One extract—from the operational to the dss world—does not accurately portray reality. In fact, there is usually a series of extracts, an intermediate number of extracts, especially where personal computers are used.

Finally, the fourth reason for lack of credibility compounds the difficulties, in that uncontrolled sources of data coupled with indeterminate levels of extracts create a dss environment where the sources of data cannot be reconciled.

The simple operational-to-dss extract that has been shown is not really representative of the dss environment. Instead, the dss environment is better depicted by Figure 20.

In Figure 20 there are many (indeterminate) generations of extracts complicated by many uncontrolled sources of data. The ability of the analyst to actually determine the common source of data is circumscribed. The ability to *ever* reconcile the differences of opinion is questionable.

Unlike the classical dss environment that has been portrayed, the architected environment—with the operational, atomic, departmental, and individual levels of data—is an environment where differences of opinion,

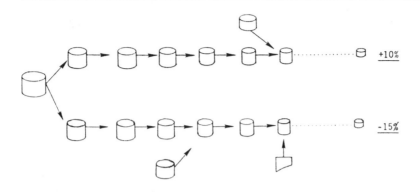

FIGURE 20 Uncontrolled sources of data and indeterminate numbers of extracts and generations of data are other reasons for the discrepancy of dss data.

when they arise, can be reconciled. It is noteworthy that differences of opinion caused by unreconciled data can occur still in the architected environment. However, when differences of opinion occur in the information paradigm, they can be reconciled with a minimum of effort.

The information paradigm addresses the issue of timing discrepancies—the first reason for lack of credibility—in that the atomic level of data provides a foundation that can be used for reconciliation. Each element of data in the atomic environment has associated with it some moment in time. When timing is a problem and there is an atomic data base, reconciliation occurs by merely doing dss processing from the appropriate time variant snapshot of data. In other words, when dss processing is a problem because of timing of extracts, then one or more extract has been done with an inappropriate time variant snapshot of data. Figure 21 shows how snapshots of data can be used to reconcile timing problems.

The ease of resolution of timing difficulties with atomic data bases is contrasted with resolution from operational data. Operational data is dynamic and constantly moving. Trying to reconcile two extracts made at different times from a constantly changing foundation is *very* difficult to do. But with atomic data—which is essentially a frozen set of snapshots—there is no problem with reconciling time differences.

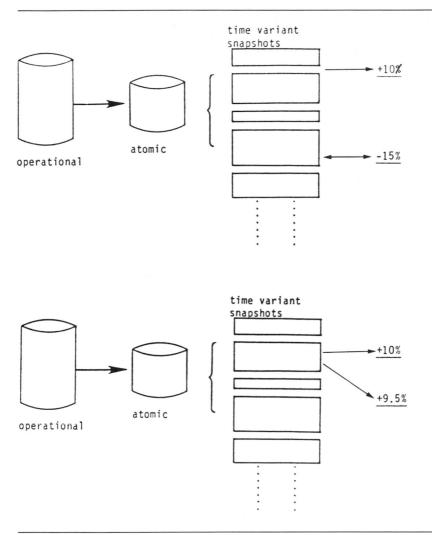

FIGURE 21 Resolution of time variancy of data for dss analysis is simplified with atomic data bases in that, when analysis is being done on snapshots of data that are inconsistent, reconciliation of data consists of doing analysis from the same snapshot of data.

The second reason for lack of credibility of dss processing is extract algorithm differences. Figure 22 shows the *worst* case of algorithmic reconciliation in the information paradigm.

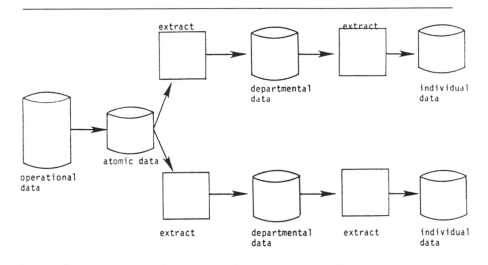

FIGURE 22   In the architected environment, there are, *at most*, four extracts that must be analyzed if the reason for discrepancies of data is algorithmic extract inconsistencies.

There are *at most* four extract algorithms that must be compared and reconciled. The four algorithms are the two that flow data from the atomic to the departmental level and the two that flow data from the departmental to the individual level. Two of those algorithms—those that control the flow of data from the atomic to the departmental level—are very public, stable algorithms. The result is that if differences of opinion arise because of extract algorithm differences, then a finite amount of resources is required for resolution.

The third reason for lack of credibility of dss processing is the generations of extracts. In the information paradigm indeterminate levels of extracts simply are not valid.

Also, the atomic data base provides a foundation for external sources of data, should there be a need for them. With a common source of data at the atomic level, there is no need for uncontrolled sources of data.

In short, discrepancies of data can occur in the information paradigm, but when they do occur, resolution is a very manageable, finite process.

But the information paradigm sets the stage for more than just credibility of dss processing. The speed with which departmental processing can be constructed—from scratch—once the atomic foundation is in place is blinding. Assuming that the atomic foundation has been laid, it is not unusual for departmental processing to be created in one or two week's time.

Figure 23 shows that the construction of independent departmental processing can be created very quickly.

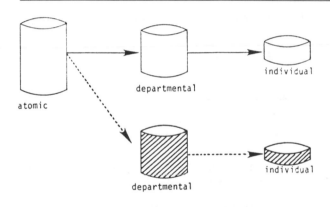

FIGURE 23   Once the foundation of atomic data is laid, new departments and new individual analyses may be created quickly and independently.

Another major advantage of the information paradigm is the speed with which data may be disseminated within the architecture. The time from when an event occurs and is known to the operational system to when the data is available for departmental processing may be as short as 24 hours, even for very large volumes of data. Figure 24 shows the speed with which data can flow within the information paradigm.

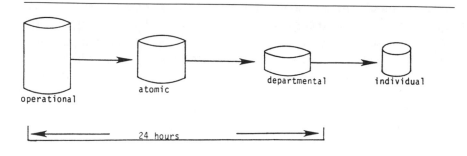

FIGURE 24 The time from entry into the system until the transaction is available to the full spectrum of dss analysts is as short as 24 hours, even for very large institutions.

Another very significant advantage of the information paradigm is the enhancement of availability and performance of operational systems. The removal of bulk amounts of data that has a moderate to low probability of access from the operational environment does the following:

- Makes online data base recovery quicker and easier, enhancing availability,
- Makes data base reorganization faster and simpler, enhancing performance,
- Removes much unnecessary processing from the operational environment, freeing up machine cycles for higher levels of performance.

There are, in short, very powerful incentives for evolving to the information paradigm.

SUMMARY

This chapter has introduced the notion of the information paradigm. The information paradigm consists of four major components: operational data, atomic data, departmental data, and individual data.

Operational data is detailed, up-to-the-second data with a high probability of access. Atomic data is archival data at a detailed level with a moderate probability of access; atomic data forms the foundation for all dss processing. Departmental data is data that relates to the specific analytical needs of the department; it is usually processed on a scheduled basis and involves time variant summarized data bases. Individual data is data that is used in ad hoc processing, usually at the PC level. An essential part of the operational environment is the system of record. The system of record is nonredundant where the definitive current value of data resides.

There are three types of data in the architecture: primitive, derived, and transitional. Primitive data is detailed data that directly relates to one occurrence of the major entities of the enterprise. Derived data is data that relates to two or more occurrences of the major entities of the enterprise. Derived data normally has primitive data as its basis. Transitional data, which is only a small fraction of the total data of the enterprise, has characteristics of both primitive and derived data.

The information cycle is the flow of information from the operational to the atomic to the departmental to the individual level. The decisions made by the enterprise are shaped at the departmental and the individual levels and are measured at the operational level.

There are many variations of the information paradigm and the information cycle. In some environments each of the levels of data is formally represented, and in some environments, one or more levels are informally represented.

One of the major reasons for existence of the information paradigm is the credibility of processing that is possible within the infrastructure of the different levels of data.

2 THE INFORMATION PARADIGM— EVOLUTION AND FORMULATION

*T*he beauty of its blue green ice belies the awesome creeping power of the glacier. Ask an artist what he or she sees when looking at a glacier and the reply is shapes and colors that occur nowhere else in nature. But ask an engineer what he or she sees, and the reply is an enormous machination capable of shaping the earth to its own form. Slow as it may be, the glacier evolves steadily, predictably, and powerfully with a force that alters all that is in its way.

The information paradigm—moving with the deliberate force of a glacier—did not appear suddenly and mysteriously. Instead, it was created over several decades as a result of an evolution and as a response to several powerful forces that were interacting all at once. This chapter will discuss the forces that shaped the evolution of the information paradigm.

FORMULATION CRITERIA

The forces of information technology and usage that shaped the evolution of the information paradigm are the needs for:

- High performance,
- High availability,

- Speed of application development,
- Speed and ability to do application maintenance,
- Accuracy of data and credibility of decision support processing,
- Autonomy of decision support processing,
- Graceful migration of nonarchitected systems to the paradigm,
- Global representation of the business needs of the enterprise.

The result of the forces of information technology and usage at work is a stretching of data. The content and structure of data at any moment in time will not suffice at a later moment in time.

High Performance

System performance is perhaps the most important and, historically the first, factor in the shaping of the information paradigm. Data that cannot be accessed in a timely manner is worth very little, especially in transaction processing systems where the interaction between the enterprise and the customer directly depends on the timeliness of the data. The stretching of data that is at the heart of the evolution of the information paradigm appears unequivocally as the issue of performance.

Fast system performance depends on careful application construction and execution. The free-form, wholesale access and manipulation of data that is typical in the decision support environment is the very antithesis of the disciplined processing that occurs in a high-performance environment. Trying to do analytical decision support processing on transaction-oriented systems, where there is any significant volume of either decision support processing or transaction processing greatly limits the performance potential. In other words, high-performance transaction processing cannot reside on the same processor that is doing decision support processing.

Performance is measured in two ways depending on the processing nature of the environment being evaluated. In the batch environment, performance is measured in terms of throughput—the time from the moment of job submission until the results are returned—both on the average and in the worst case for a batch job. In the online environment, performance is measured in terms of transaction response time—the length of time a transaction is in route through the system and in execution— both for the average transaction and for the worst case.

The information paradigm accommodates high performance—both batch and online—in that the separation of the operational environment from the dss environment separates two operationally incompatible modes of processing. The result of the separation is a beneficial effect to performance. Separating operational and dss data and processing allows online, transactional processing to proceed unimpeded. The smooth uninterrupted flow of online, operational transactions results in optimal online performance. Figure 25 illustrates the relationship between performance sensitivity and the information paradigm.

Performance is an issue in the dss environment as well, but the criticality of performance is not nearly the issue that it is in the operational environment. The nature of the dss environment is such that the decisions made or influenced by dss processing are not decisions that normally require split-second processing and access to data. Decision support analyses that complete on the half hour, half day, or overnight are the rule and are quite acceptable. In the normal case, the marginal benefit of completing a dss process at 10:00 A.M. or 10:05 A.M. is nil.

Another perspective of performance and the information paradigm is in the difference in the way data is fundamentally accessed in each environment. Figure 26 shows the difference in the fundamental mode of access of data.

Generally speaking, operational data is accessed randomly and in small quantities. For example, when a bank account has a withdrawal processed against it, only a small amount of data (which is randomly accessed) is needed to process the transaction. But the access and amount of data used in dss processing is quite the opposite. In dss processing, it is normal to access very large amounts of data per processing request in a sequential

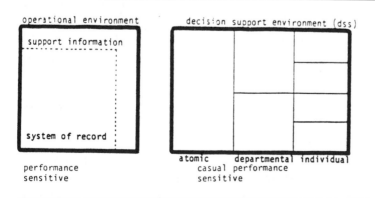

FIGURE 25   The relationship between performance sensitivity and the information paradigm.

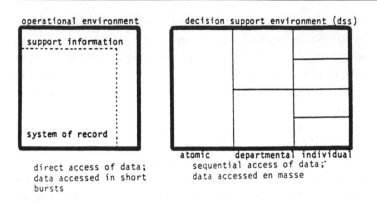

operational environment

support information

system of record

direct access of data;
data accessed in short
bursts

decision support environment (dss)

atomic   departmental individual
sequential access of data;
data accessed en masse

FIGURE 26 The difference in the fundamental mode of access of data.

manner. A simple example of dss processing data en masse is the request to determine the average account balance for all accounts for a bank on a given day. The resources required for accessing large amounts of data preclude high performance.

As an example of an environment not yet aligned with the information paradigm, and how the need for high performance leads to the information paradigm, consider a manufacturing environment where assembly routing and completion processing data are mixed freely with material requirements analysis. Throughout the day, assembly lines complete an order or receive unassembled goods for the satisfaction of an order. Detailed transactions are entered into the system for the activities of assembly management and control. The transactions trace the flow of activities to and from the different assembly lines, and control what is to be manufactured and what is to be routed. When the system slows down, the flow of manufacturing slows down as well. When order analysis—"what if" processing—occurs that projects the impact of potential new orders or modifications to manufacture of existing parts, the system virtually stops while the analysis is being done.

When the system is split into operational and dss components, however, performance does not suffer. When the systems are split, both assembly routing and material analysis can be done at the same time. The split of processing is done for reasons of performance and pushes the systems a significant step closer toward the information paradigm.

High Availability

System availability has influenced the evolution of the information paradigm, in that there are very different availability needs for operational data than there are for decision support data. Operational data needs to be available a large percentage of the time; decision support data needs to be available only selectively. *All* of the data in an operational environment needs to be available, whereas only subsets of data typically need to be available for the decision support environment. Operational data is available across a wide network, while decision support data is available to only selected groups of individuals. The differences between the availability needs for the different types of data are such that, for reasons of availability alone, there is a natural division of data.

Availability of data is measured by the amount of time data is unavailable when, in fact, it should be available to the user of the system. When operational data is unavailable during the time that it ought to be available, then one or more day-to-day functions of the enterprise are disabled. The consequences of operational unavailability are severe because operational systems are where the enterprise meets the customer.

But dss unavailability is normally a much less consequential event. When dss data is unavailable, decisions are only delayed until the data becomes available. Of course, if the dss outage is extremely long, then there may be some substantial consequences to the enterprise. But, generally speaking, the immediacy of making long-term decisions based on dss processing is such that reasonable delays in dss processing have only a small bearing on the direction taken by the enterprise.

The information paradigm supports the differences in availability requirements in the dss and operational environments in the same way that performance was supported: by separating operational and dss data in the information paradigm:

- Operational availability is enhanced because operational data can be designed with a high orientation to production availability with no regard for dss data availability needs.
- Dss data is physically stored separately from operational data, presenting the operational designer with the fewest constraints. In other words, if dss and operational data were mixed and there was a need for high availability, the options of the designer would be limited because of the bulk of the data to be managed. Separating the data reduces the bulk, thus giving the designer multiple options.

As an example of the forces of availability at work in an environment not yet evolved to the information paradigm, consider a manufacturing environment where inventory is kept. The inventory system is available 24 hours a day—the same hours that the manufacturing facility is up and operating. The inventory of *all* of the parts in the shop is available. An engineering department tries to use the existing operational data for dss analysis but quickly runs into problems. While the online system is up and running, the engineering dss analyst cannot access the bulk of data that is needed. Unfortunately, since the online system runs 24 hours a day, effectively the engineer has no time in which dss analysis can be done.

Some of the other problems that the engineering department faces are that not all parts need to be analyzed and that more than just current inventory value is needed for dss analysis. The engineering department decides to periodically extract its own sets of data and put the data in an environment that can be easily and conveniently manipulated. The engineering department, then, has evolved towards the information paradigm because of the difference in its availability needs for dss processing and the availability needs of the operational environment.

Speed of Development

The speed and efficiency of application development is greatly enhanced by the information paradigm, although at first glance the enhancement is not obvious. Before a discussion of development efficiency ensues, it is worthwhile to note at which level of the data architecture application development occurs. Traditional application development occurs at the operational level. Certainly, there exist applications in the dss world, but dss applications tend to be constantly changing and are usually quickly and heuristically constructed. Oftentimes in the dss world, the systems that are built are called end user applications and are fundamentally different from structured, operational applications. The very term "application" carries with it a connotation of structured usage of data that is typical of the operational environment, not the dss environment.

The compelling need for speed of application development is manifested in the information paradigm in two places: in the form of nonredundancy of the system of record, as shown by Figure 27, and in the dss environment when end user systems are developed autonomously.

Figure 27 shows that data is nonredundant in the system of record (and is organized around the major subjects of the enterprise). Because the system of record data contains nonredundant data and code, system-of-

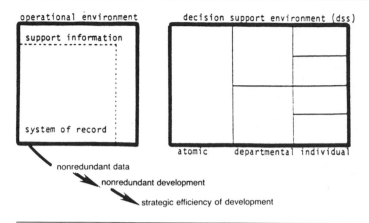

operational environment   decision support environment (dss)

support information

system of record

atomic   departmental   individual

nonredundant data

nonredundant development

strategic efficiency of development

FIGURE 27   Data is nonredundant in the system of record.

record applications need to be developed only once. The result is a *strategic* economy of consolidation, where development is strategically very efficient because development needs to occur only once.

To appreciate the effect of nonredundancy of operational data, consider development prior to the information paradigm. In this world, applications were built one at a time, around a limited set of requirements. The result was that application-by-application development produced enormous amounts of redundancy of data and processing that required enormous amounts of redundant development, as shown by Figure 28.

With redundancy of data comes redundancy of development, and the implication of redundancy of development is the wholesale inefficiency of application development.

But the information paradigm holds other implications for application development as well. By separating primitive data from derived data, the application developer building system-of-record-applications has the smallest, simplest set of requirements possible, thus streamlining the application development process.

In addition to the economies gained by nonredundant development of systems, there is the freedom gained by separating dss systems from operational systems. When dss systems are separated from operational systems, the end user has full license to do his or her own thing in the dss environment. The atomic-level data is "reusable" and satisfies a multitude of requirements. The requests for dss processing that can be done by the end user simply never enter the queue for operational de-

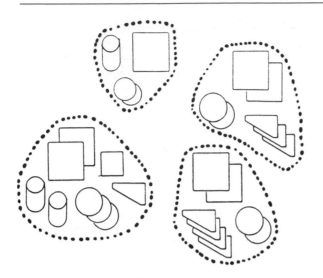

FIGURE 28 Prior to the information paradigm, application-by-application development was the norm, and redundancy of data and processing was rampant.

velopment. The development backlog for operational systems then, is relieved of what has classically been considered a second-class citizen —the request for the development of many dss processes.

As an example of an unarchitected environment and the need for quick system development, consider an environment that is being built an application at a time. If five redundant applications are built and there is much overlap between applications, and if 500 programmer-months are required per application, then by going to the information paradigm, approximately 4 × 500 programmer/months could be saved. In actuality, because the overlap between applications is not perfect, something less than 4 × 500 programmer-months will actually be saved. By going to the information paradigm, where there is nonredundancy of operational processing, many programmer resources will be freed up for other work.

In line with the nonredundancy of data is the notion of reusability of data. The atomic data base—the heart of the architecture—is almost perfectly suited for reusability. And reusability of data is, strategically, one of the keys to success. Reusability of data and code is one of the transformations that an organization must make in order to advance beyond systems development practices of the 1960s.

Speed and Ability to Do Maintenance

As the efficiency of development goes (in terms of reduction of the total amount of development to be done), so follows maintenance. The information paradigm addresses the issue of application maintenance by effectively reducing the amount of development that needs to be done in the first place. It follows that since there is a minimum amount of application code that needs to be developed, there also is a minimum amount of application code that needs to be maintained.

But the information paradigm is doubly beneficial for maintenance. Since the information paradigm mandates nonredundant data in the system of record, there is no need for synchronization of redundant elements of data, and the absence of code needed for synchronization greatly simplifies applications requirements. The simplification of processing reduces maintenance requirements accordingly.

In addition to reducing maintenance by reducing redundancy, the information paradigm also significantly enhances the maintenance profile by separating primitive from derived data. Primitive data is essentially stable data, and derived data is constantly changing. When the two types of data are locked together, the constant change of derived data causes entire systems to be in a permanent state of upheaval. But when the environments are separated, the derived environment can change independently of the primitive environment.

An example of how the forces of maintenance push processing toward the information paradigm is a manufacturing environment where customer order data is stored with summary order data and order history data. One day, the marketing analyst decides that customers could best be served by dividing them into classes of data, such as preferred customer, regular customer, and so forth. Determining the class of a customer requires looking at the order history for number of orders, size of orders, and so forth. Unfortunately, the system has been written so that no customer classification has been anticipated. The analyst puts the request for system change on the development queue and is told that there is a two-year backlog.

The analyst then decides to create his or her own separate dss history file so that customers—at least informally—can be categorized. The historical file can thus be created and maintained quickly and independently. The analyst has taken a step toward the information paradigm because of the forces of maintenance.

The information paradigm is the handiwork of a long evolutionary process. The most remarkable thing about the evolution is that it is so widespread and so predictable, over so many diverse organizations. Large organizations and small organizations, banking and insurance organizations, manufacturing and service organizations, public and private organizations are all experiencing and witnessing the evolution.

Any discussion of the evolution of data processing *must* pay homage to the pioneering work done by Richard Nolan and as published in the Harvard Business Review. The article which is included is one of a series of articles written by Nolan and is a classic in its own right. Anyone discussing the topic of evolution of data processing should be aware of the work done by Nolan.

MANAGING THE CRISES IN DATA PROCESSING*

A momentous change is taking place in the mission and function of corporate computing activities

Now that the experiences of many companies with advanced data processing (DP) systems can be analyzed, fresh and important observations can be made for the guidance of policy-making executives. For one thing, we can see the outlines of both the past and future, with six stages of DP growth standing out. Although no companies have yet entered stage 6, a few are approaching it, and a great many have entered the intermediate stages. Stage 3 produces a notable jump in already rapidly increasing computer costs; stage 4 features the rise to control of users of DP programs; and stages 5 and 6 feature the development and maturity of the new concept of data administration. For DP managers and program users, this evolution has significant implications. Planning, control, operations, technology, and costs —all are affected profoundly. Using the benchmarks described in this article, managers can see where their organizations stand in the evolutionary process. Turning to the guidelines described at the end, they can better understand how to manage the growth that lies ahead of them.

Mr. Nolan is chairman of Nolan, Norton & Company, Inc., Lexington, Massachusetts. Formerly he was associate professor of business administration at the Harvard Business School, where he taught courses in control and data processing and did extensive research in this field. He is the

*By Richard L. Nolan, *Harvard Business Review*, March–April 1979. Reprinted with permission.

author or coauthor of a series of earlier HBR articles, including "Controlling the Costs of Data Services" (July–August 1977), "Business Needs a New Breed of EDP Manager" (March–April 1976), and "Managing the Four Stages of EDP Growth" (January–February 1974, with Cyrus F. Gibson).

The member of the corporation's steering committee did not mince words:

"I'm telling you I want the flow-of-goods computer-based system, and I am willing to pay for it. And you are telling me I can't have it after we have approved your fourth running annual budget increase of over 30%. If you can't provide the service, I'll get it outside. There are now reliable software companies around, and my people tell me that we should take seriously a proposal that we received from a large minicomputer vendor."

The reply of the vice president of information services was not well received:

"I'm at the edge of control. It isn't any longer a question of financial resources. My budget has grown from $30 million in 1975 to over $70 million in 1978. The technology is getting ultracomplex. I can't get the right people fast enough, let alone provide suitable space and connections to our sprawling computer network."

On returning to his office, the vice president knew that the steering committee member would be going ahead with the minicomputer. There was no way that the corporate technical staff could provide the flow-of-goods functions for the money or within the time frame that the minicomputer vendor had promised. Something was not right, even though he could not put his finger on it.

The vice president mused at the irony of it all. Five years ago he was brought in to set up a corporate computer utility after a similar period of poorly understood growth (that growth had been the undoing of his predecessor). Now key questions were being asked about a similar growth pattern of the data processing (DP) budget, and he did not have the answers. He wished he did!

The plight of the vice president of information services is not singular. The rapid growth in DP services that many companies experienced in the mid- to late 1960s is occurring again in numerous companies. The resurgence is confusing.

The senior managements of some of these companies thought that the DP control structures put in place during the 1970s, such as charge-out, project management, and consolidation of computing activities under tight budgetary control, would contain any future budget growth. Nevertheless, the annual DP budget growth rates are exceeding 30%. Further, just the annual budget *increments* are equal to the total size of the budgets four or five years ago. The confused top executives of these companies are searching for answers to what underlies this growth. Is it good? Will it stop? What are the limits?

The answers are not obvious, but a probing of the status of the DP activities in different companies and of the current technological environment sheds light on the situation and provides insights into the management actions that are needed to prepare for and manage the growth.

SIX STAGES OF GROWTH

Studies I have made during the 1970s of a series of companies—3 large corporations early in this decade, 35 companies several years ago, and then a large number of IBM customer concerns and other corporations since then—indicate the existence of six stages of growth in a company's DP function. These stages are portrayed in *Exhibit I*.

The scheme shown in this exhibit supersedes the four-stage concept I described in HBR in 1974.[1] The four stages described then continue to be valid, but the experience of recent years reveals a larger and more challenging picture.

---

1. See my article, written with Cyrus F. Gibson, "Managing the Four Stages of EDP Growth," HBR January–February 1974, p. 76.

This exhibit shows six stages of DP growth, from the inception of the computer into the organization to mature management of data resources. Through mid-stage 3, DP management is concerned with management of the computer. At some point in stage 3, there is a transition to management of data resources. This transition involves not only restructuring the DP organization but also installing new management techniques.

To understand the new picture, one must look at the growth in knowledge and technology, at organizational control, and at the shift from computer management to data resource management. I will consider each of these topics in turn.

Burgeoning of Knowledge

Organizational learning and movement through the stages are influenced by the external (or professional) body of knowledge of the management of data processing as well as by a company's internal body of knowledge.

The external body of knowledge is a direct response to developments in information technology. It is concerned with developments in the theory of DP management as well as with the collective documented experiences of companies. The internal body of knowledge, however, benefits from the external body of knowledge but is primarily

Exhibit I
Six stages of data processing growth

Growth processes

| | Stage I
Initiation | Stage II
Contagion | Stage III
Control | Stage IV
Integration | Stage V
Data administration | Stage VI
Maturity |
|---|---|---|---|---|---|---|
| Applications portfolio | Functional cost reduction applications | Proliferation | Upgrade documentation and restructuring of existing applications | Retrofitting existing applications using data base technology | Integration of applications | Application integration "mirroring" information flows |
| DP organization | Specialization for technological learning | User-oriented programmers | Middle management | Establish computer utility and user account teams | Data administration | Data resource Management |
| DP planning and control | Lax | More lax | Formalized planning and control | Tailored planning and control systems | Shared data and common systems | Data resource strategic planning |
| User awareness | "Hands off" | Superficially enthusiastic | Arbitrarily held accountable | Accountability learning | Effectively accountable | Acceptance of joint user and data processing accountability |

Transition point

Level of DP expenditures

experiential—what managers, specialists, and operators learn firsthand as the system develops.

It is important to realize how greatly DP technology spurs the development and codification of an external, or professional, body of knowledge. For this reason a company that began to automate business functions in 1960 moved through the stages differently from a company that started to automate in 1970 or 1978. The information technology is different, and the extent of professional knowledge on how to manage the DP technology is much greater in the latter years. Not only is the external body of knowledge more sophisticated, but the information technology itself is more developed.

Control & Slack

Organizational learning is influenced by the environment in which it takes place. One possible environment is what might be called "control"; a second might be called organizational "slack," a term coined by Richard M. Cyert and James G. March.[2]

In the *control* environment, all financial and performance management systems—including planning,

budgeting, project management, personnel performance reviews, and chargeout or cost accounting systems—are used to ensure that DP activities are effective and efficient. In the *slack* environment, though, sophisticated controls are notably absent. Instead, incentives to use DP in an experimental manner are present (for example, systems analysts might be assigned to users without any charge to the users' budgets).

When management permits organizational slack in the DP activities, it commits more resources to data processing than are strictly necessary to get the job done. The extra payment achieves another objective—nurturing of innovation. The new technology penetrates the business's multifunctional areas (i.e., production, marketing, accounting, personnel, and engineering). However, the budget will be looser, and costs will be higher. Management needs to feel committed to much more than just strict cost efficiency.

The balance between control and slack is important in developing appropriate management approaches for each stage of organizational learning. For example, an imbalance of high control and low slack in the earlier stages can impede the use of information technology in the organization; conversely, an imbalance of low control and high slack in the latter stages can lead to ex-

2. Richard M. Cyert and James G. March, "Organizational Factors in the Theory of Oligopoly," *Quarterly Journal of Economics,* February 1956, p. 44.

Exhibit II
Optimum balance of organizational slack and control

Stages	Organizational slack		Control		
	Computer Data		Computer Data		Objective of control systems
Stage 1	Low		Low		
Stage 2	High		Low		Facilitate growth
Stage 3	Low Low		High Low		Contain supply
Stage 4	High		Low		Match supply and demand
Stage 5	Low		High		Contain demand
Stage 6	High		High		Balance supply and demand

plosive DP budget increases and inefficient systems.

Exhibit II shows the appropriate balance of control and slack through the six stages. In stage 3 the orientation of management shifts from management of the computer to management of data resources. This shift, associated with introduction of the data base technology, explains the absence of entries in the computer columns after stage 3.

Shift in Management Emphasis

In stage 2 more and more senior and middle managers become frustrated in their attempts to obtain information from the company's computer-based systems to support decision-making needs. *Exhibit III* helps to explain the root of the problem. The exhibit is based on a fictional corporation that represents a kind of composite of the organizations studied. The spectrum of opportunities for DP equipment is called the "applications portfolio."

The triangle illustrates the opportunities for cost-effective use of data processing to support the various information needs in the organization. Senior management predominantly uses planning systems, middle management predominantly uses control systems, and operational management predomi-

Exhibit III
Applications portfolio late in Stage II

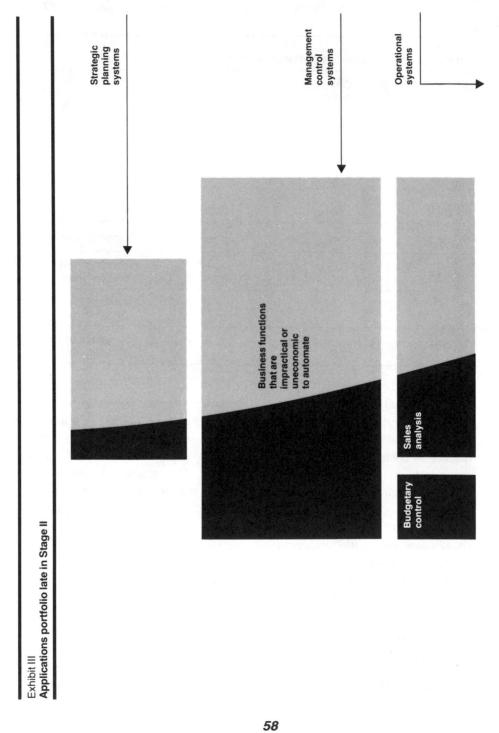

Strategic
planning
systems

Management
control
systems

Operational
systems

Business functions
that are
impractical or
uneconomic
to automate

Sales
analysis

Budgetary
control

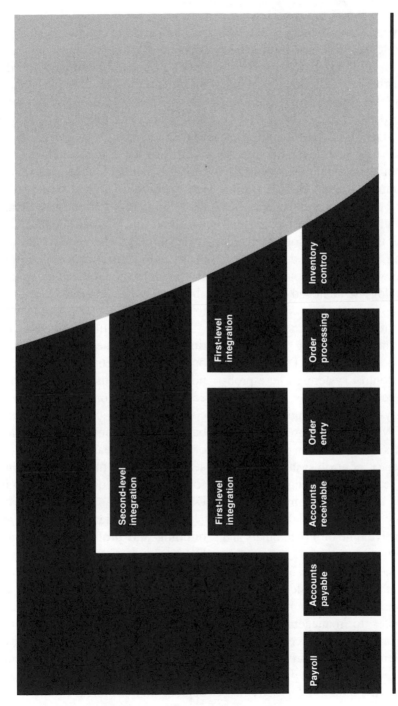

Second-level integration

First-level integration

First-level integration

| Payroll | Accounts payable | Accounts receivable | Order entry | Order processing | Inventory control |

Note: An example of first-level integration is a purchase order application that uses order processing and inventory status information. An example of second-level integration is a vendor payment application that uses accounts payable and purchasing information.

59

nantly uses operational systems. At every level there are information systems that are uneconomic or unfeasible to automate, despite managers' desires for faster and better data.

In stage 1 in this organization, several low-level operational systems in a functional area, typically accounting, are automated. During stage 2 the organization encourages innovation and extensive application of the DP technology by maintaining low control and high slack. While widespread penetration of the technology is achieved by expanding into operational systems, problems are created by inexperienced programmers working without the benefit of effective DP management control systems. These problems become alarming when base-level systems cannot support higher-level systems—in particular, order processing, production control, and budgetary control systems. Maintenance of the existing, relatively poorly designed systems begins to occupy from 70% to 80% of the productive time of programmers and systems analysts.

Sometime in stage 3, therefore, one can observe a basic shift in orientation from management of the computer to management of the company's data resources. This shift in orientation is a direct result of analyses about how to put more emphasis, in expanding DP activities,

on the needs of management control and planning as opposed to the needs of consolidation and coordination in the DP activities themselves. This shift also serves to keep data processing flexible to respond to management's new questions on control or ideas for planning.

As the shift is made, executives are likely to do a great deal of soul searching about how best to assimilate and manage data base technologies. The term "data administration" becomes common in conferences, and there is much talk about what data administration controls are needed.

But there is little effective action. I believe there is little action because the penetration of the technology is obviously low at its inception, and a combination of low control and high slack is the natural balanced environment to facilitate organizational learning. However, at the same time the seeds are being sown for a subsequent explosion in DP expenditures.

Stage 3 is characterized by rebuilding and professionalizing the DP activity to give it more standing in the organization. This stage is also characterized by initial attempts to develop user accountability for the DP expenditures incurred. Usually these attempts take the form of chargeouts for DP services. Unfortunately, both the conceptual and technical problems of implementing user accountability lead to confusion and alienation; real gains in accountability are not made. Nevertheless, the trends of DP charges in user budgets are rarely reversed.

Consequently, during stage 3 the users see little progress in the development of new control systems while the DP department is rebuilding, although they are arbitrarily held accountable for the cost of DP support and have little ability to influence the costs. Even the most stalwart users become highly frustrated and, in a familiar phrase, "give up on data processing."

Explosive Growth

As stage 3 draws to a close, the DP department accomplishes its rebuilding and moves the data base and data communication technologies into several key application areas, such as order entry, general ledger, and materials requirements planning. In addition, the computer utility and network reach a point where high-quality services are being reliably provided to the users. When these accomplishments are realized, a subtle transition into stage 4 takes place.

Just when users have given up hope that data processing will provide anything new, they get interactive terminals and the various supports and assistance needed for using and profiting from data base technology. Already they have benignly accepted the cost of DP services. Now, with real value perceived, they virtually demand increased support and are willing to pay pretty much whatever it costs. This creates DP expenditure growth rates that may be reminiscent of those in stage 2, rates one may have thought would not be seen again.

It is important to underscore the fact that users perceive real value from data base applications and interactive terminals for data communication. In a recent study of one company with more than 1,500 applications, I found that users ranked their data base and interactive applications as far and away more effective than users of conventional or batch technology ranked their applications. This company has been sustaining DP expenditure growth rates of about 30% for the past four years. More important, the users of the new applications are demanding growth to the limits of the DP department's ability to expand.

The pent-up user demand of stage 3 is part of the reason. But a more important part of the reason is that the planning and control put in place in stage 3 are designed for *internal* management of the computer rather than for control of the growth in use of it and containment of the cost explosion. *Exhibit IV* shows the typical pattern of starting and de-

Exhibit IV
Growth and maturation of data processing planning and control

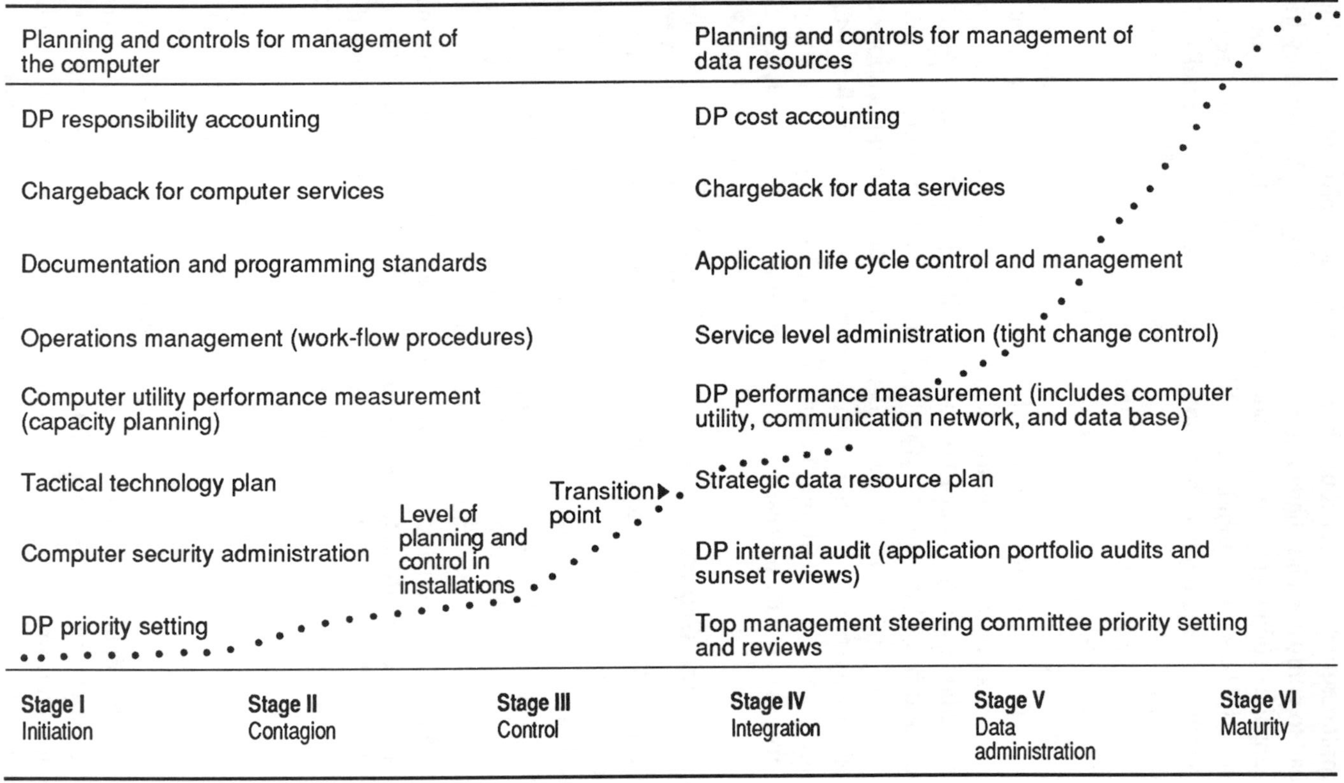

Planning and controls for management of the computer

Planning and controls for management of data resources

- DP responsibility accounting
- Chargeback for computer services
- Documentation and programming standards
- Operations management (work-flow procedures)
- Computer utility performance measurement (capacity planning)
- Tactical technology plan
- Computer security administration
- DP priority setting

- DP cost accounting
- Chargeback for data services
- Application life cycle control and management
- Service level administration (tight change control)
- DP performance measurement (includes computer utility, communication network, and data base)
- Strategic data resource plan
- DP internal audit (application portfolio audits and sunset reviews)
- Top management steering committee priority setting and reviews

Level of planning and control in installations

Transition ▶ point

Stage I	Stage II	Stage III	Stage IV	Stage V	Stage VI
Initiation	Contagion	Control	Integration	Data administration	Maturity

veloping internal and external (that is, user-managed) control systems. Late in stage 4, when exclusive reliance on the computer controls proves to be ineffective, the inefficiencies of rapid growth begin to create another wave of problems. The redundancy of data complicates the use of control and planning systems. Demands grow for better control and more efficiency.

In stage 5, data administration is introduced. During stage 6, the applications portfolio is completed, and its structure "mirrors" the organization and the information flows in the company.

IDENTIFYING THE STAGE

How can executives determine what stage of development their corporate data processing is in? I have been able to develop some workable benchmarks for making such an assessment. Any one of the benchmarks taken alone could be misleading, but taken together these criteria provide a reliable image. I will describe some of the most useful benchmarks so management can gain a perspective on where it stands and on what developments lie down the road. For a visual portrayal of the benchmarks, see *Exhibit V*.

It is important to understand that a large multinational company may have divisions simultaneously representing stages 1, 2, 3, 4, and perhaps 5 or even 6. However, every division that I have studied has its DP concentrated in a particular stage. Knowledge of this stage provides the foundation for developing an appropriate strategy.

First-level Benchmarks

The first step is to analyze the company's DP expenditure curve by observing its shape and comparing its annual growth rate with the company's sales. A sustained growth rate greater than sales indicates either a stage 2 or 4 environment. Then, analyze the state of technology in data processing. If data base technology has been introduced and from 15% to 40% of the company's computer-based applications are operating using such technology, the company is most likely experiencing stage 4.

In the light of International Data Corporation's research on the number of companies introducing data base management systems technology in 1977 (shown in *Exhibit VI*), I believe that roughly half of the larger companies are experiencing stage 3 or 4. This is further corroborated by evidence that 1978 saw the largest annual percentage growth in the total DP budgets of U.S. companies—from $36 billion to an estimated $42 billion, or a 15½% increase.

Exhibit V
Benchmarks of the six stages

First-level analysis	Tracks rate of sales growth.	Exceeds rate of sales growth.	Is less than rate of sales growth.	Exceeds rate of sales growth.	Is less than rate of sales growth.	Tracks rate of sales growth.
DP expenditure benchmarks.						
Technology benchmarks.	100% batch processing.	80% batch processing. 20% remote job entry processing.	70% batch processing. 15% data base processing. 10% inquiry processing. 5% time-sharing processing.	50% batch and remote job entry processing. 40% data base and data communications processing. 5% personal computing. 5% minicomputer and microcomputer processing.	20% batch and remote job entry processing. 60% data base and data communications processing. 5% personal computing. 15% minicomputer and microcomputer processing.	10% batch and remote job entry processing. 60% data base and data communications processing. 5% personal computing. 25% minicomputer and microcomputer processing.

Level of DP expenditures

Second-level analysis

	Stage I Initiation	Stage II Contagion	Stage III Control	Stage IV Integration	Stage V Data administration	Stage VI Maturity
Applications portfolio.		There is a concentration on labor-intensive automation, scientific support, and clerical replacement.		Applications move out to user locations for data generation and data use.		Balance is established between central-ized shared data/common system applications and decentralized user-controlled applications.
DP organization.		Data processing is centralized and operates as a "closed shop."	Data processing becomes data custodian. Computer utility estab-lised and achieves reliability. ◀ Transition point			There is organizational implementation of the data resource management con-cept. There are layers of responsibility for data processing at appropriate organ-izational levels.
DP planning and control.		Internal planning and control is installed to manage the computer. Included are standards for pro-gramming, responsibility accounting, and project management.		External planning and control is installed to manage data resources. Included are value-added user chargeback, steering committee, and data administration.		
User aware-ness.	Reactive: End user is superficially involved. The computer provides more, better, and faster information than manual techniques.		Driving force: End user is directly involved with data entry and data use. End user is accountable for data quality and for value-added end use.		Participatory: End user and data process-ing are jointly accountable for data quality and for effective design of value-added applications.	
Level of DP expenditures ▶						

65

Exhibit VI
Data base management software installed and projected to be installed on IBM medium- to large-scale computers in the United States

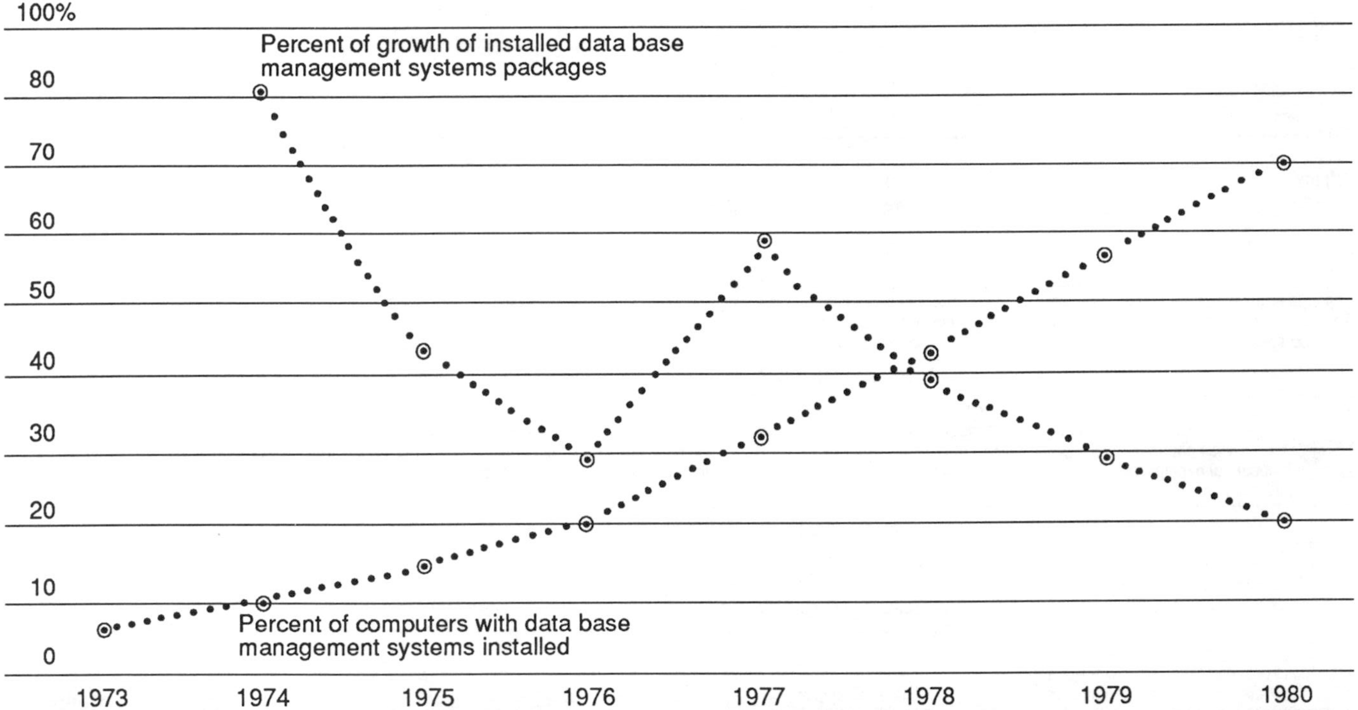

Percent of growth of installed data base management systems packages

Percent of computers with data base management systems installed

100%
80
70
60
50
40
30
20
10
0

1973   1974   1975   1976   1977   1978   1979   1980

Source: Richard L. Nolan, "The New EDP Economics," presentation at the International Data Corporation Conference, San Francisco, April 3, 1978.

As shown in *Exhibit VI*, about 55% of IBM installations in 1979 will have data base technology, compared with only about 20% in 1976. I feel that this means the explosive stage 4 in DP expenditures can be expected in the next two to five years in most companies; the increases may be somewhat moderated by continuance of the impressive technological advances that have improved prices and equipment performance.

Second-level Benchmarks

The second step is to focus on the four growth processes shown in *Exhibit V*. Each major organizational unit of the company, such as a subsidiary, division, or department, should be listed. Then the growth processes associated with each organizational unit should be identified. For example, a decentralized subsidiary generally has all four growth processes, from expansion in the applications portfolio to an increase in employees' awareness of DP potentials and functions (see the left-hand side of *Exhibit V*). However, a division using the services of a corporate computer utility is likely to have only two of the growth processes—expansion in the applications portfolio and in user awareness.

Next, identify the stage (see the bottom of *Exhibit V*) of each of the growth processes associated with the organizational unit. Use growth as an example in the applications portfolio. The approach used for this process is similar to that for any of the processes. The procedure is as follows:

1. Define the set of business functions for the organizational unit that represents cost-effective opportunities to apply DP technology. I call this the "normative applications portfolio." It represents the business functions that would be receiving DP support if the company had achieved stage 6 maturity. *Exhibit VII* portrays such a scheme.

2. Taking each function in turn, indicate for each set of systems the support that data processing gives to the function in the organization. Ask, "What is it doing for our business?" I suggest doing this by shading the space for the function on the normative applications portfolio; use a ten-point scale to shade the function at 10%, 40%, 80% or whatever amount seems appropriate. Looking at all the shaded functions as a whole, judge the level of support given the system as a whole.

3. Then, match the support given the system as a whole with the benchmarks shown to the right of *Exhibit VII*. For instance, 80% support of operational systems, 20% support of management control systems, and just a faint trace of sup-

Exhibit VII
Investment benchmarks for DP applications

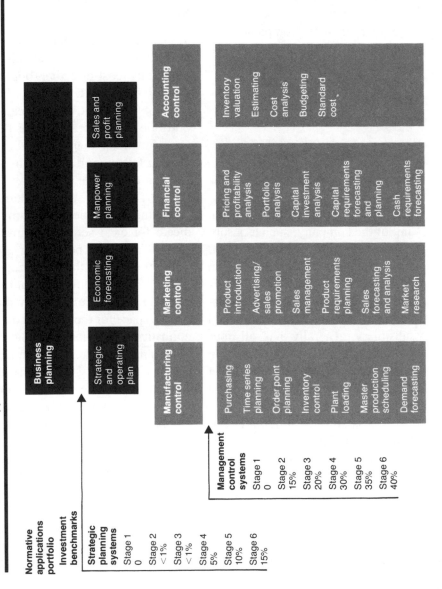

Normative
applications
portfolio

Investment
benchmarks

**Business
planning**

| Strategic and operating plan | Economic forecasting | Manpower planning | Sales and profit planning |

**Strategic
planning
systems**

Stage 1
0

Stage 2
<1%

Stage 3
<1%

Stage 4
5%

Stage 5
10%

Stage 6
15%

Manufacturing control	**Marketing control**	**Financial control**	**Accounting control**
Purchasing	Product introduction	Pricing and profitability analysis	Inventory valuation
Time series planning	Advertising/ sales promotion	Portfolio analysis	Estimating
Order point planning	Sales management	Capital investment analysis	Cost analysis
Inventory control	Product requirements planning	Capital requirements forecasting and planning	Budgeting
Plant loading	Sales forecasting and analysis	Cash requirements forecasting	Standard cost
Master production scheduling	Market research		
Demand forecasting			

**Management
control
systems**

Stage 1
0

Stage 2
15%

Stage 3
20%

Stage 4
30%

Stage 5
35%

Stage 6
40%

**Operational
systems**

Stage 1
100%

Stage 2
85%

Stage 3
80%

Stage 4
65%

Stage 5
55%

Stage 6
45%

Manufacturing	Marketing	Distribution	Finance	Accounting	Personnel	Administration
Facilities and environmental protection and control	Order release	Distribution center operation	Cash management	Billing and accounts receivable	In-house education	Library services
Testing and quality control	Order tracking and inquiry	Shipping document preparation	Tax and government reporting	Credit	Government reporting	Stockholders relations
Machine control	Order processing	Vehicle scheduling	Auditing	Payroll	Employee services	Legal
Plant maintenance	Order entry	Freight routing and tracking		Asset accounting	Wage and salary administration	
Time reporting	Dealer/branch/operations	Freight bill rating and audit		Accounts payable		
Receiving		Distribution planning		General ledger		
Stores control						
Material movement control						
Plant scheduling						

port for strategic planning systems would show the organization to be at stage 3.

4. Next, look for matches and mismatches between DP investment and the key functions that contribute to the company's return on investment or profitability. For example, if the company's business is manufacturing, and if half of the DP system investment goes to support accounting, a red flag is raised. The possibility of a mismatch between expenditure and need should be investigated.

After the functional assessment, one should conduct a technical assessment of the applications. The technical assessment gets at the concern of whether the DP activity is using current technology effectively. Benchmarks used include individual system ages, file structures, and maintenance resources required.

Again using a scheme like that described for *Exhibit VII*, compare the support given by data processing to the different corporate functions with the technical assessment. Are the DP systems old, or are the file structures out of date, or are there other shortcomings indicating that up-to-date technology is being neglected? Such neglect may be the result of managerial oversight, of a shortsighted desire to make a better annual profit showing, or of other reasons. In any case, it means that a portion of the company's assets are being sold off.

During the definition and assessment of the applications portfolios for a company, a DP "chart of accounts" is created. The business functions identified in the applications portfolio are the "objects of expenditures." Creating the chart of accounts is an important step in achieving the level of management sophistication required to effectively guide this activity through stages 4 and 5 and into the stage 6 environment.

So much for the applications portfolio analysis. Using the same sort of approach, management can turn next to the other growth processes shown in *Exhibit V* for second-level analysis. When the analysis is completed, management will have an overall assessment of the stage of the organization and of potential weaknesses in its ability for future growth.

If complete analyses of this type are made for all important organizations—divisional and functional—of the company, management will have a corporate-wide profile. *Exhibit VIII* is an example. Such a profile provides the foundation for developing an effective DP strategy.

GUIDELINES FOR ACTION

In most sizable U.S. corporations, data processing is headed for an extremely rapid growth in the next five years. This growth is not necessar-

Exhibit VIII
One company's stage analysis

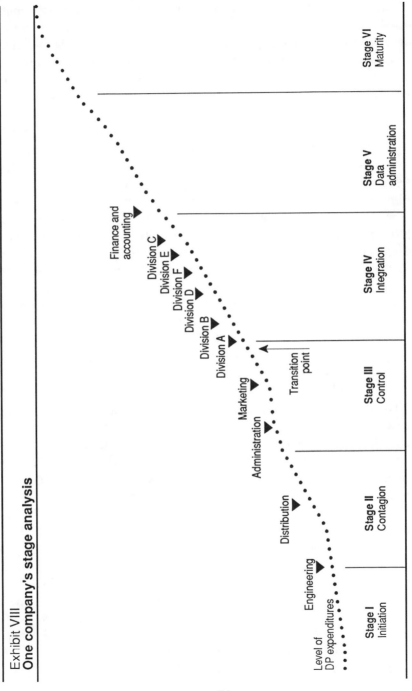

ily bad; in fact, I believe that if the growth can be managed, it will be the most cost-effective growth experienced to date. Here are five guidelines for managing the growth successfully.

1. Recognize the fundamental organizational transition from computer management to data resource management.

With the introduction of data base technology in stage 3, an important shift in emphasis occurs—from managing the computer to managing the company's data resources. Obviously, this transition does not occur all at once. It appears first in the analysis of the late stage 2 applications portfolio and is a result of the requirement to restructure it so that applications can be tied together efficiently.

The transition also becomes apparent during the implementation of controls. Difficulties with chargeout systems that are computer-oriented cause management searches for alternative ways to achieve user accountability. This often leads to the conclusion that the user can be accountable for the functional support, but data processing must be accountable for management of shared data.

The key idea is to recognize the importance of the shift in management emphasis from the computer to data and then to develop applications and planning and control systems to facilitate the transition. Applications should be structured to share data; new planning and control systems should be data-oriented.

2. Recognize the importance of the enabling technologies.

The emerging information technologies are enabling companies to manage data economically. It is important to emphasize the word *economically*. What companies did only a few years ago in establishing large central DP utilities is no longer justifiable by economic arguments. Data resource management changes the economic picture.

Data base and data communication technologies are important from an organizational standpoint. Sprawling DP networks are enabling new approaches to management control and planning. We can now have multidimensional control structures such as function (e.g., manufacturing, marketing, and finance), product, project, and location. Managers and staff can be assigned to one or more of the dimensions. Through shared data systems, senior management can obtain financial and operating performance reports on any of the dimensions in a matter of hours after the close of the business day, month, quarter, or year.

Last but not least, developments

in on-line terminals, minicomputers, and microcomputers are opening up new opportunities for doing business at the operational level. Airline reservation systems, for example, no longer stand alone in this area; we now can include point of sale (POS) for the retail industry, automated teller terminals (ATMs) for the banking industry, and plant automation for the manufacturing industry.

3. Identify the stages of the company's operating units to help keep DP activities on track.

A basic management tenet is: ''If you can't measure it, you can't manage it.'' The applications portfolios of a company provide data processing with a chart of accounts. In the past, management lacked a generic and meaningful way to describe and track a DP activity—that is, to locate it in relation to the past and future. However, there is now a generic and empirically supported descriptive theory of the evolution of a DP activity—the stage theory. One can use this theory to understand where the company has come from, which problems were a result of weak management, and which problems arose from natural growth. More important, one can gain some insight into what the future may hold and then can try to develop appropriate management strategies that will accomplish corporate purposes.

4. Develop a multilevel strategy and plan.

Most DP departments have matured out of the ''cottage industry'' era. They have reached the point where they are woven into the operating fabric of their companies. There are many documented cases of the important impact that a computer failure of mere hours can have on a company's profitability.

Nevertheless, many DP departments continue to hold on to the cottage industry strategy of standing ready to serve any demands that come their way. This can have a disastrous effect when stage 4 begins to run its course. The extent and complexity of corporate activity make it impossible for data processing to be ''all things to all users.'' Consequently, decisions will have to be made on what data processing will be—its priorities and purposes; when, where, and whom it will serve; and so on.

If the DP management makes these decisions without the benefit of an agreed-on strategy and plan, the decisions are apt to be wrong; if they are right, the rationale for them will not be adequately understood by users. If users do not understand the strategic direction of data processing, they are unlikely to provide support.

Development of an effective strategy and plan is a three-step process. *First*, management should determine where the company stands in the evolution of a DP function and should analyze the strengths and weaknesses that bear on DP strategies. *Second*, it should choose a DP strategy that fits in with the company's business strategy. And *third*, it should outline a DP growth plan for the next three to five years, detailing this plan for each of the growth processes portrayed in *Exhibit V*.

It is important to recognize that the plan resulting from this three-step process is, for most companies, an entry-level plan. Thus the plan cannot and should not be too detailed. It should provide the appropriate "blueprint" and goal set for each growth process to make the data processing more supportive of the overall business plan. It should also be a spark for all those in DP activities who want to make their work more significant and relevant to corporate purposes.

5. Make the steering committee work.

The senior management steering committee is an essential ingredient for effective use of data processing in the advanced stages. It provides direction to the strategy formulation process. It can reset and revise priorities from time to time to keep DP programs moving in the right direction.

From my observation, I think that the steering committee should meet on a quarterly basis to review progress. This would give enough time between meetings for progress to be made in DP activities and would allow the committee to monitor progress closely. Plan progress and variances can make up the agenda of the review sessions.

A manufacturing environment that is being run from a single data base is an example of the forces of credibility and accuracy of data. The data base contains, among other things, information about the rejection rate of goods supplied by a shipper. Management asks the engineering organization to analyze the amount of rejects and the effect on the manufacturing process. Engineering replies that there is a high rate of rejection, which costs around $10,000 per day. Management then asks the accounting department for its assessment of the situation. Accounting analyzes its data and states that no more than $500 per day is being lost in rejects. Management is perplexed. Is the rejection rate a problem or not? Who is to be believed—the engineering department or the accounting department?

In actuality, the engineering analysis used data from the end of the month (which happened to be a bad month). The accounting analysis used data retrieved from the next month (which was an unusually good month). Even though engineering and accounting used data from the same data base, they did not use data from the same base at the same time. To resolve the problem, a "foundation" of dss data is needed, and part of the foundation is the time stamping of data. Once the data is time stamped and exists independently of the operational environment, reconciliation can be done, and the engineering and accounting departments can use the same basis of data.

The recognition of the need for foundation data is a step towards the information paradigm.

Autonomy of Processing

The possibilities for and appeal of autonomous processing of data are such that autonomy of processing is a very powerful force that will not be denied. Autonomy of processing is an issue primarily in the dss environment. The essence of much of end user computing is heuristic, iterative analysis of derived data. Heuristic analysis cannot be accomplished effectively or efficiently if there are barriers to resources—hardware, software, data—that inhibit processing. The information paradigm provides the analyst with a very high degree of autonomy at the individual dss level, and to a lesser extent, at the departmental dss level, as shown in Figure 29.

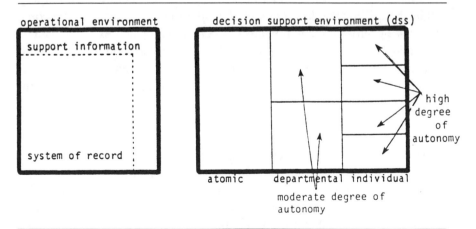

FIGURE 29 The autonomy of end user computing and the information paradigm.

The end user at the individual level experiences very little inconvenience or awkwardness because of the information paradigm. In fact, because of the orderliness of data, locating and using data is actually streamlined by the information paradigm.

For example, an end user marketing analyst wishes to access the orders that have been made for high-volume parts over the past four years. Unfortunately, the applications that process orders have only six month's history. In addition, for those orders that are kept, there are stringent requirements that restrict access to the data. The analyst can get at order data only on Sunday evenings when the system is being used lightly. In order to do his or her own processing, the marketing dss analyst decides to create a historical data base.

The need for autonomous processing—the freedom to do processing individually—has pushed the analyst toward the information paradigm.

Ability to Migrate from Nonarchitected Systems to the Paradigm

The state of the world is such that many older systems have not been built in accordance with the information paradigm. Fortunately, conformance to the information paradigm is not a binary proposition. Once the data model is built, manifesting the paradigm is a task that can be accomplished a step at a time.

For a typical migration from the unarchitected environment to the information paradigm, consider how the system of record can be initially established. Upon the development of a blueprint for the system of record, the existing environment is analyzed. Once analyzed, existing data is identified that can be used in place to form the foundation for the system of record. Then, as the existing environment ages and changes, it is replaced in accordance with the blueprint. Figure 30 shows that the form and structure of the system of record have been identified and that certain components of the existing environment fit the system of record with no further change.

As an example of the need for an architecture that can be developed gracefully, a step at a time, consider a manufacturer who has a collection of application systems. The manufacturer designs an architecture that meets all of the company's needs; however, it must be built all at once. Regardless of *any* other aspects of the architecture, the costs and risks associated with a one-time-only wholesale replacement of existing systems preclude the implementation of the architecture.

As an alternative, the manufacturer investigates the information paradigm, which can be implemented gracefully, a step at a time, with no wholesale upheaval of existing systems. The need for migration to an architecture in a graceful fashion leads the manufacturer to the information paradigm.

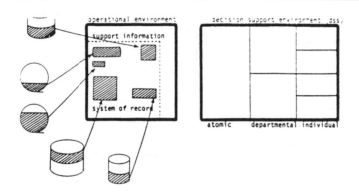

FIGURE 30 Initially, the existing environment is analyzed to determine what fit there is between the information paradigm and the system of record.

Global Representation of the Enterprise

Because the foundation of the primitive environment is a subject orientation of data, it is natural to represent the needs of the organization globally, not on an application-by-application basis. Figure 31 shows the relationship between the information paradigm and the global model of the organization.

The information paradigm, then, is shaped by each of the criteria identified. In short, the information paradigm is a product of *all* the shaping factors, interacting at the same time. Figure 32 illustrates where within the information paradigm each of the forces that shape the paradigm is satisfied.

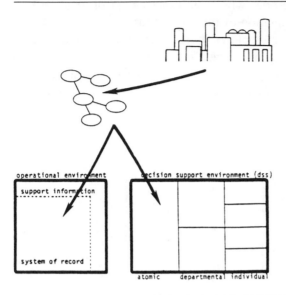

FIGURE 31 The enterprise is modeled conceptually, and the high-level model forms the basis for the design of the system of record and the atomic level of data (i.e., primitive data).

EVOLUTION TO THE INFORMATION PARADIGM

[Any discussion of evolution of stages of data processing growth must acknowledge the pioneering work of Richard Nolan, as published in the Harvard Business Review. The stages presented in this book parallel, to some extent, the evolution first recognized by Nolan. However, an attempt has been made to:

- Describe the forces that shape the evolution,
- Describe detailed attributes of each stage,
- Identify the data architecture—the information paradigm—that results from the evolution.]

The information paradigm has evolved over a long period of time as the result of many diverse pressures. The evolution is depicted by Figure 33.

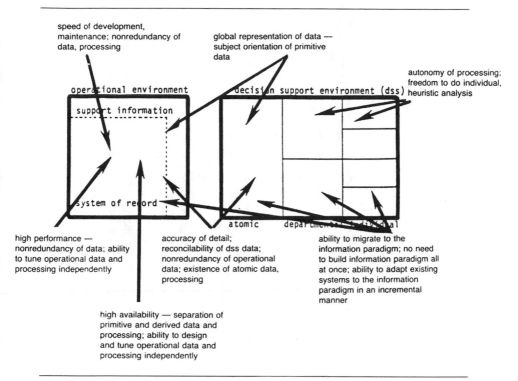

FIGURE 32 Where within the information paradigm each of the forces that shape the paradigm is satisfied.

Figure 33 should be read merely as a sequence of events, not as a cause-and-effect schematic, even though some events most likely have occurred in a cause-and-effect fashion.

The Evolution

In the early dawn of automation, there was automated data processing, or ADP. Automated data processing was dominated by punched cards, paper tape, and mechanical devices. The primary usage of ADP was for the replacement of existing operations. ADP usually could improve the efficiency of manual operations, and at that time, the techniques of systems analysis and design were typified by mimicking existing manual operations with automated tools. The programming language of the day

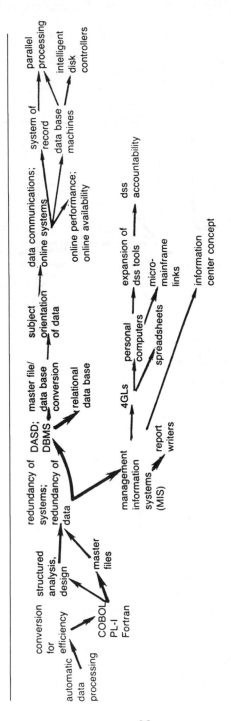

FIGURE 33 A progression of some of the major developments of information technology and usage — note that the events are chronologically arranged and may or may not represent a cause-effect relationship.

was Assembler. Soon the tedium of creating code in Assembler increased to the point that the production of code became the bottleneck in the development process. Shortly thereafter, early languages such as COBOL and Fortran appeared, and later PL-1. Concurrent with the transition from assembler to COBOL and Fortran was the transition of automated processing (i.e., mechanical processing) to electronic processing, as transistors began to replace vacuum tubes and card sorters.

The mechanical act of producing code ceased to be an impassable barrier, and with the usage of COBOL and PL-1, the next barrier appeared—coping with the complexity of establishing requirements and converting those requirements to code. In response to these barriers to development, there arose structured programming, soon followed by the disciplines of structured analysis and design. Concurrently with the establishment and growth of the structured movement came the storage of data on magnetic tape files and the further refinement of electronic processing. (In fact, the electronic miniaturization of computer processing was just beginning, and the transition from vacuum tube to transistor to semiconductor was paving the way for increases in speed of processing by orders of magnitude.)

As structured analysis and design blossomed and application systems were being developed with ever-increasing speed, master files attached to each of the applications began to blossom. In short order, the number of master files and the complexity of flowing data from one master file to the next swamped the programming development resource, in terms of both building new systems and maintaining existing systems. With the advent of master files and the explosion of applications came the redundancy of data and the redundancy of processing inherent to the application-by-application development practice of the day. And, at about the same time, an entirely new need for data and processing was recognized—the need for MIS (Management Information Systems).

The problems presented by redundancy of data and redundancy of processing were nontrivial. The complexity of the problem and the need to protect existing investment—in both applications and technology—as much as possible fashioned an environment in which a whole new approach to technology was required. From those problems sprang the concept of data base and the storage medium—DASD (Direct Access Storage Devices).

Data base was supported by a DBMS (Data Base Management System), which allowed the programmer to access data directly on DASD without requiring a whole, deep level of technical knowledge about DASD. Shortly after the appearance of DASD and DBMS, master files were converted to data bases. And almost concurrently, it was recognized that the mechanical conversion of master files to data base did not achieve the consolidation of data and processing that was at the heart of the problems of redundancy.

In response to the need for consolidation, relational data base and data normalization arose, leading to the conclusion that a subject orientation of data did, in fact, analytically address the major problems of massive redundancy. At the same time, as data base grew, the technology of online processing appeared. It was a short step from using DASD with a DBMS to the technology of teleprocessing monitors and online access and update of data. And as soon as online systems began to be built, the issues of online response time and availability arose. Concurrent to the advent of high-performance online systems was the notion of the system of record, requiring absolute accuracy, integrity, and nonredundancy of detailed data. As fast as online processing grew, the demands for more processing power led to the inevitable splitting of the workload across multiple machines and then to the notion of data base machines.

In a parallel track, stemming from the first desire for MIS systems, arose report writers designed for quick, read-only access of data. From the origins of report writers came 4GLs (Fourth Generation Languages). In the same genre, personal computers and spreadsheet processing appeared. The popularity of spreadsheets and decision support processing led to an expansion of dss tools and the usage of the micro-mainframe link, which in turn led to the crisis in credibility of dss processing, in which the need to do dss processing at all was questioned if, in fact, the results of dss processing could not be believed. The credibility crisis provided strong motivation for the different levels of dss data: the atomic level, the departmental level, and the individual level.

One of the interesting questions an organization can ask is, "Is the evolution that has been described inevitable?" In other words, once an organization finds its place in the evolution that has been described, can it use the evolution to predict future trends? The answer is yes. As long as the forces are at work that push the organization through the phases of evolution, then the organization *can* use the evolution that has been described to anticipate future trends.

Of course, the forces at work in an organization vary in terms of forcefulness and immediacy, so that the rate at which an organization

STAGE 1

STAGE 2

STAGE 3

General description: ADP
  Hardware: card sorters,
  keypunch
Software: Autocoder, ASM
  Common media: cards, paper
  tape, reports, collaters
  Notable milestones: existence
  of automation, mimicking of
  existing systems, emphasis
  on efficiency

General description: ADP,
  electronic processing
  Hardware: IBM 1401, 1130,
  other ADP gear
Software: ASM, Fortran
  Common media: cards, paper
  tape, some mag tapes,
  reports
Notable milestones: transistors
  to semiconductors,
  condensed storage on mag
  tape

General description: advent of
  masterfiles
Hardware: IBM 1401, 360/20
Software: DOS, COBOL,
  FORTRAN, MFT, MarkIV
Common media: cards, tapes,
  reports
Notable milestones: migration
  to mag tape and master files,
  birth of report writers, speed
  of CPU and main memory
  increases greatly due to
  miniaturization

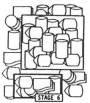

STAGE 4

STAGE 5

STAGE 6

General description: master file
  explosion
Hardware: IBM 360/xx
Software: MVS, COBOL, PL-I
Common media: mag tapes,
  reports
Notable milestones: advent of
  multiple master files,
  redundancy of data
  (wholesale maintenance
  backlog is born, origins of
  structured techniques

General description: explosive
  system growth
Hardware: IBM 360/xx
Software: MVS, IMS, Total,
  System2000, COBOL,
  MarkIV, VM
Common media: mag tape,
  DASD, reports, limited CRT
  usage
Notable milestones: system of
  record born, subject
  orientation of data as a
  concept, extension of
  structured techniques, further
  explosion of master files,
  relational data base concept
  and normalization, advent of
  MIS systems (dss
  predecessor)

General description: online
  processing
Hardware: IBM 370, Amdahl
  V-5, V-6
Software: IMS/DC, CICS, ACP,
  MVS, Total, 4GLs, VM,
  Model 204, ADABAS
Common media: terminals,
  disks, printers
Notable milestones: building of
  systems of record, MIS to
  DSS transformation, direct
  end user involvement born,
  issue of online performance
  'raised, data communications
  grows explosively

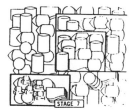

STAGE 7

General description: full-bore
  online processing, dss
  processing
Hardware: Tandem, IBM 370/
  30xx, PC
Software: MVS, IMS/DC, CICS,
  VSAM, VM, A 4GLs, Lotus 1-
  2-3, ADR Datacom DB, Mant
Common media: DASD,
  reports, limited mag tape

Notable milestones: front end
  systems, growth of
  uniprocessors (toward
  upward limit), system of
  record establishment, much
  direct end user involvement,
  information center
  organization born

FIGURE 34 Another perspective of the evolution of the information paradigm from that of the organization.

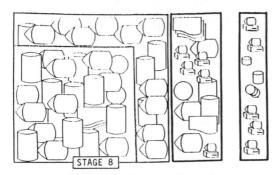

General description: mature operational processing, formative dss
    processing
Hardware: IBM 308x, Amdahl 58xx, PC-XT, AT
Software: MVS, IMS, DB2, CICS, TSO, VSAM, VM, ACP(TPF), 4GLs,
    PC spreadsheet extensions
Common media: DASD, reports, limited mag tape
    Notable milestones: micro-mainframe links, accountability — cost
    justification of data processing and end user computing,
    dissatisfaction with integrity of dss environment, integration of
    operational/dss processing, elevation of the data administration
    function

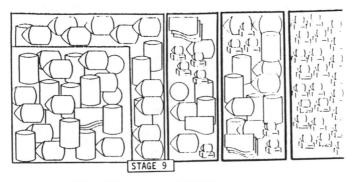

General description: fully mature environment
Hardware: IBM 309x, Amdahl 58xx, PC's, Teradata
Software: MVS, IMS, DB2, CICS, TSO, VM, VSAM, ACP(TPF), 4GLs,
    PC software explosion
Common media: DASD, reports, limited mag tape
Notable milestones: separation of dss levels of data, information,
    development of back end systems (data base machines, intelligent
    disk controllers), continued parallel growth to meet workload
    demands, continued emphasis on cost justification, strategic use of
    systems, advent of artificial intelligence

FIGURE 35   Another perspective of the evolution of the information par-
    adigm from that of the organization.

evolves may vary from that in other organizations. But the general direction of the evolution is constant.

Another perspective of the evolution of the information paradigm from that of the organization, as it grew with technology and information systems, is shown by Figures 34 and 35.

Figure 34 and Figure 35 are presented in terms of IBM and IBM-compatible technology because IBM is the dominant manufacturer in the marketplace. It has a full line of products, and its products represent the evolution being depicted. These figures are drawn in full awareness of other vendor's products, and they neither endorse IBM's products nor reject non-IBM products.

[There is little significance attached to the numbering of the stages seen in Figure 34 and Figure 35, other than the fact that the stages occur sequentially.]

How the Forces Shape the Evolution

The first phase of the evolution depicted in Figure 34 shows that the automation of manual processes was the first stepping stone—the genesis—of the information paradigm. As technology and the uses of technology progressed, the need for MIS processing and the system of record became apparent at about the time that data base began to become a reality. As data base processing progressed to online data base processing, the importance of the system of record came into focus.

The rise of the personal computer and the concurrent popularization of fourth generation languages triggered the use of end user computing and decision support processing (whose predecessors were MIS systems). It is noteworthy that as system of record processing and decision support processing grew, other forms of processing were slowly squeezed out.

Of special interest is at what point in the evolution the shaping criteria influenced the information paradigm. The need for high performance and high availability was a shaping factor as online processing became a reality. The need for rapid application development was a shaping factor throughout—in the move from Autocoder to Fortran, in the genesis of the structured approach, in the advent of 4GL technology, and so forth. Each of these advances increased the power of the code and, hence, speeded the rate at which systems could be developed.

The burden of maintenance appeared during the era of explosive master file growth (and to some extent, never disappeared). Maintaining redundant processing of master file systems was one of the primary motivations for going to data base.

The accuracy of data became an issue as master files proliferated. Soon data bases (under DBMS and on DASD) replaced master files. But the technology of data base did not address the issue of consolidation of data. The notion of consolidating data bases into the major subjects of the enterprise led to the system of record, which unlocked the true potential of data base.

The proliferation of undisciplined dss systems led directly to the need to introduce discipline and the resulting levels of dss processing. The inconsistency and incongruity of a plethora of dss systems mandated credibility, which led to the different levels of data.

The backlog of system requests, coupled with the tools for development, led to the autonomy of dss processing. Unrecognized (for the most part) at the time was the fact that dss processing was a different form of processing than classical data processing systems.

Once the different components of the information paradigm were recognized, the next problem was reconciliation of the existing, nonarchitected environment with the information paradigm. Fortunately, the nature of the information paradigm is such that it can be built a step at a time.

The final criterion is the need to represent globally the needs of the organization. The global needs of the organization are manifested in the subject orientation of the system of record and in the deliberate separation of primitive and derived data.

Shift from Efficiency to Effectiveness

An interesting shift in emphasis has occurred during the evolution of the information paradigm. The earliest motivations for building systems were for the sake of efficiency. Automation was a cheaper and faster means of doing existing work, and manual systems were replaced, on a wholesale basis, by automated systems in the name of efficiency. But as the size of systems progressed and technology matured, the emphasis has shifted from efficiency of processing to effectiveness of processing. The general thrust of dss processing is toward the effective use, not necessarily the efficient use, of computers.

An example of the effective use of computers is the personal computer. The personal computer is used heavily for calculations over a short period of time; then it sits idle, waiting for the next task. In general, the total capacity of the personal computer is barely tapped. It is thus used inefficiently but (hopefully!) not ineffectively.

Another interesting observation concerning the information paradigm is that different organizations are at different stages in the evolution. One company does not march in lockstep—from one stage to the next—with other companies. Instead, each enterprise marches at its own pace and in response to its own stimulus. What is surprising is the uniformity of the information paradigm, given that each enterprise responds to its own stimulus independently of any other enterprise. The most rational reason for the uniformity of the evolution is that the same forces must be acting on different organizations although at different rates.

Some of the external forces that indirectly affect the rate at which the information paradigm evolves within an organization are:

- Advancements in technology. Until technology exists that provides a basis for processing, the information paradigm cannot advance. For example, early MIS processing was a nascent form of dss, but dss did not blossom until personal computers and 4GL technology were available. Early MIS technology simply did not lend itself to powerful and flexible uses.
- Awareness of costs of processing. In the early stages of evolution, there was little real emphasis on costs. But as the computer budget began to appear as a significant part of the operating budget, attitudes and spending habits changed. The result was that mature systems not only had to perform but perform efficiently. In general, the more awareness there is of costs, the more acceleration there is through the stages of the information paradigm accelerates.
- Relationship of data processing to the mainstream business of the organization. In some organizations, data processing is a back office activity, removed from the mainline business of the organization. In other organizations, data processing is close to the bottom line of the business. In general, the closer data processing is to the mainline business of the enterprise, the faster the evolution occurs.

SUMMARY

The information paradigm is the result of many powerful factors interacting at once. The shaping factors are:

- High performance, high availability. By separating primitive and derived data, performance and availability are greatly enhanced because machine cycles and units of DASD are freed.
- Speed of development. Speed of development is enhanced in that atomic data is "reusable" and provides an immediate basis for dss development.
- Speed of maintenance, speed of maintenance is enhanced in that highly volatile data—dss data—is removed from highly stable data—operational data.
- Accuracy of data/credibility. Accuracy/credibility of data is enhanced in that the atomic environment provides a basis for reconciliation of dss processing, and the system of record provides a foundation for operational reconciliation.
- Autonomy of dss processing. The richness of data available at the atomic level and the departmental level provides the individual analyst with more data than was ever before available.
- Migration from existing systems. The architecture can be achieved a step at a time, using existing nonarchitected systems as a basis.

3 THE INFORMATION PARADIGM— TECHNICAL FOUNDATIONS

*T*he speed of a glacier hides the mechanics—the dynamics—of the tremendous force of the glacier at work. Indeed, the speed of a glacier seems to suspend in time the mighty forces of water, ice, gravity, and mass, so that the grinding and shoving against granite is done almost in a dreamlike state. Fortunately, the mechanics of the evolution of the information paradigm are more tractable. The technical foundations of the information paradigm, not surprisingly, are uniquely adapted to the different criteria that have shaped each part of the paradigm. This chapter will discuss, component by component, the hardware and software foundations of the information paradigm.

In the operational arena, the emphasis of hardware and system software is on high performance and high availability. High performance and high availability are achieved by:

- faster, bigger processors,
- separation of the workload over multiple smaller processors,
- usage of software capable of sustaining high performance.

In the decision support arena, the emphasis of hardware and software is on autonomy of processing. The first level of dss processing—the atomic level—centers around hardware capable of providing a centralized foundation for dss processing. The next level of dss processing uses hardware that is capable of serving a wide variety of departmental needs. Finally, the third level of dss processing, the individual level, focuses on only ad hoc reporting. Underlying the hardware is the data communication that allows data to flow from one level of the architecture to another.

OPERATIONAL HARDWARE—SYSTEM OF RECORD

At the heart of the operational environment is the system of record. The hardware needed to support the system of record is high-performance, high-availability hardware. There are two common hardware configurations for the system of record that are capable of high performance and high availability: a centralized configuration and a decentralized configuration. As an example of the system of record in the centralized and the decentralized environments, consider the policy information for an insurance company with offices in New York, Dallas, Los Angeles, and Chicago, and with headquarters in Hartford, Connecticut. A typical centralized hardware foundation for the insurance company is shown by Figure 36.

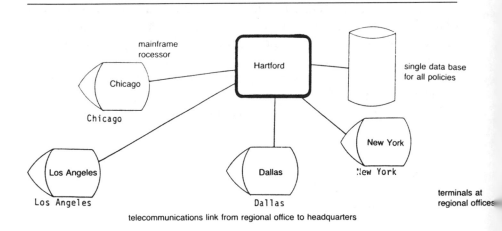

FIGURE 36 A mainframe processor forms the backbone of the centralized system of record.

In Figure 36, a single mainframe processor serves the system of record for the entire insurance company. Note that there is a single physical data base (with the characteristic nonredundant, detailed, subject-oriented data) attached to the mainframe. Each regional office is served by a telecommunications link and terminal access to the mainframe. The system of record exists as a single, centralized data base in this configuration.

The centralized configuration shown in Figure 36 is common (perhaps the most commonly occurring configuration) and serves the needs of many organizations. When higher levels of performance are needed, the hardware is upgraded to a larger, faster processor.

But suppose the processing needs of the system of record are such that a single mainframe processor will not suffice either technically or economically. A variation of the centralized approach is a hybrid configuration that can be called the "distributed centralized" approach. In the distributed centralized approach, the operational workload is distributed over multiple centralized (tightly coupled) processors. Figure 37 shows a typical distribution that might be done for the insurance company.

Figure 37 shows that there is a single occurrence of data for any given policy, even though different types of policies are physically scattered over different data bases. The system of record is realized through the existence of several physical data bases. The processing is still centralized, and to a policy holder or agent in Dallas (or any other regional office!), there is no difference between this configuration and the one described in Figure 36. Note that the split of data by type of policy is hardly the only way that data could have been split across the different processors. Some other criteria that might be used for the distribution of data include:

- By policy range. All policies from 0000 to 2499 are in one data base, policies from 2500 to 4999 are in another, policies from 5000 to 7499 are in another, and policies from 7500 to 9999 are in another data base; for example.
- By marketing division. Upscale policies are in one data base, commercial policies in another, and regular (i.e., nonupscale, noncommercial policies) in another.
- By date of issue. Policies issued prior to 1979 are in one data base, policies issued from 1980 to 1983 are in another, and policies issued after 1984 are in yet another data base.

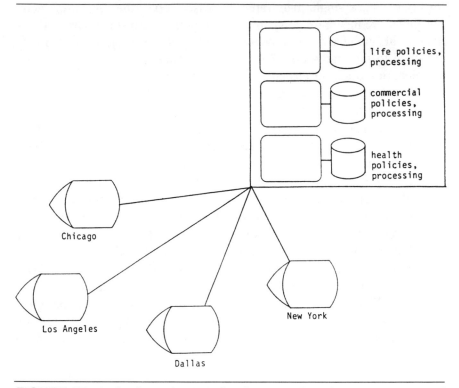

FIGURE 37 A distributed, centralized approach to the management of the system of record.

There are, in fact, a practically infinite number of combinations of ways that data can be split to accommodate the distribution of a workload over tightly coupled processors. But the splitting of data must be done with care because of its far-reaching implications. Some of the implications are:

▪ Can the split be easily extended? Chances are good that if the data needs to be split once, it will need to be split again. Any plan for the division of data must be extensible.

▪ Can the split apply across the organization, to all types of data? It does an organization no good to need to split a workload and have one type of data split one way and another type of data split another. For example, the distribution of a workload in an insurance company where policies are split by policy number range and claims are split chronologically will produce, at best, awkward results.

The splitting of the operational workload can be done either at the application or at the system level, assuming that the operating system and DBMS are amenable. The migration from the configuration shown in Figure 36 to the configuration shown in Figure 37 is not a trivial task. Once the application design and code are determined, rethinking a major split is a complex and usually enormous task. As a consequence, if there ever needs to be a split for workload distribution, the seeds should be laid in the application at the initial moment of architecture.

The ability to split data is important because when data can be split, the workload can be divided over multiple processors. The level of performance and availability that can be achieved is not constrained, for all practical purposes.

A final note about workload distribution in a centralized environment is that the system of record remains the same, in concept, regardless of the physical landscape.

Distribution of Data

The second common configuration for the system of record is distribution of processing to a decentralized environment (classical distributed processing) where processors are not tightly coupled, as shown in Figure 38.

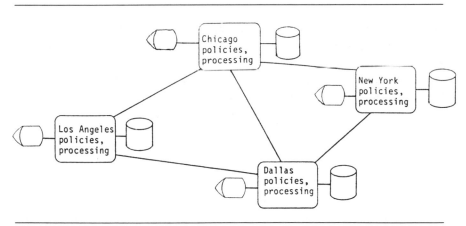

FIGURE 38 The system of record in a distributed environment.

Figure 38 shows that data (i.e., data that forms the basis of the system of record) exists nonredundantly in multiple locations. The system of record for Los Angeles policies exists in Los Angeles, and nowhere else, for example. In some ways the configuration shown in Figure 38 is merely an extension of the configuration shown in Figure 37, except that the split of data is done geographically, the processing and data are executed at geographically separate locations, and the processors are loosely coupled. But the concept of the system of record remains the same.

Most of the same considerations hold for distributed processes that hold for "distributed centralized" processing, such as:

- If geographical division is done once, it is likely to be done again.
- If some types of data and processing are geographically split, then all data and processing need to be geographically split.

Of interest are the differences between the configurations shown in Figure 36 and Figure 38, the classical centralized and classical decentralized configurations respectively. Some of the major differences are:

- Data transmission for normal processing. In the centralized environment all detailed processing must be transmitted from the region to the host, and these normal transmissions may be very numerous. In the case of decentralized processing, normal requests and processing are satisfied locally, using minimal transmission resources.
- Data transmission for abnormal processing. An example of abnormal processing is the case where one region accesses data outside its control. In the case of centralization, the transmission resources required for abnormal processing are no more than those for normal processing. In the case of decentralized processing, abnormal processing usually will require significant transmission resources.
- Reliability. The centralized configuration has the disadvantage that a failure of the central component effectively disables the entire network. The decentralized configuration has the advantage that failure of any node (or region, in the example shown) affects only a part of the network.
- Performance. The centralized configuration has the disadvantage that once capacity of the largest available centralized processor is exceeded, Draconian measures are required. The distributed configuration has the advantage that when any one processor's capacity is exceeded, the workload can be split over more processors. In addition, when a distributed node has its capacity exceeded, the ability to upgrade to a large processor for that node is usually a viable option.
- Version control. Version control for both system and applications software is almost a nonissue in the centralized configuration, since there is only one environment to be maintained (and hence only one version of

software to be controlled). But for the decentralized configuration, version control is a large issue. The programs controlling one node need to be synchronized and compatible with the programs serving other nodes, and the coordination and control of software over nodes of a network are nontrivial.

- Operation costs. In a centralized environment, operations of the computer environment can be consolidated. In a decentralized environment, many operations must be repeated.

- Processor costs. Generally speaking, the cost per unit of power of centralized computing is less than the cost per unit for decentralized computing. (See Chapter 9 in *Technomics—the Economics of Technology and the Computer Industry*, Dow Jones-Irwin, 1986, for an in-depth discussion of this controversial topic.)

With the advent of personal computing and the autonomy of processing that became available to end users came the notion that personal computers could do anything. While personal computers are very versatile and powerful, and while personal computers provided the catalyst for the unleashing of dss analytical processing, there are limitations to what personal computers can do and should be asked to do. The article— THE EVERLASTING MAINFRAMES—provides a sobering balance to the perspective that personal computers are going to replace mainframes on a wholesale basis.

THE EVERLASTING MAINFRAMES*
How large computers survive DDP

The campaigns of the small-computer "revolution" have been highly publicized over the last few years, from the traditional 16-bit minicomputer to the supermini, the personal computer and the supermicro. Much less documented, but in many respects equally dramatic—and certainly with as much long-term

*By Donald R. Powell, *Computerworld*, June 1983. Copyright 1983 by CW Communications/Inc. Reprinted with permission.

significance—has been the remarkable resilience of the large mainframe.

A few years ago, a new direction in computing technology was heralded: Distributed data processing using powerful minicomputers was about to turn the conventional DP world upside down. Given the prevailing mood among users, the future of the large-scale mainframe looked uncertain. However, structural forces already at work in the industry by 1976 would substantially alter the course of the DDP revolution.

The huge installed base of large computers and the investments in software to run them were important moderating influences. Users could not readily convert their applications to small systems, no matter how attractive, thus creating great demand for improved large systems. In addition, few DP organizations could accept the loss of control over their function that many advocates of DDP suggested. Nor could DP countenance the duplication of effort that resulted from unregulated small-computer deployment.

Early attempts at replacing large-scale systems with small ones resulted, in most cases, in many smaller management problems replacing one big one. It turned out that most of the problems of managing computers were intrinsic to the technology and not the result of overcentralization, as had been widely suggested.

Of even more significance, however, was that for the first time in years, there was some real competition in the large-system market. Traditionally, users were so committed to the architecture of their installed systems that there was little competition between vendors. The advent of the plug-compatible CPU manufacturers dramatically changed that environment. Amdahl Corp. made its first volume ship-ments in 1976 and by the end of the year had achieved significant market impact. These first Amdahl systems clearly showed that major innovations in performance, price and technology were possible in the production of large computers.

In addition, it was obvious that the Japanese computer manufacturers would soon be in a position to exploit the same advanced technology as Amdahl.

IBM responded quickly to the new level of competition. In 1977, it introduced the 3033, which provided twice the performance of the 370/168 at about the same price. This announcement brought to light a startling fact: There was indeed elasticity of demand in the market for large computers.

Previously, it had been assumed that this market size was determined by the basic requirements of the small number of very large organizations and was thus quite stable. The overwhelming flood of orders for the 3033 showed that this was not the case: at lower prices, a much larger volume of systems would be sold, allowing, in turn, even lower prices. Elasticity in the marketplace had been assumed for years in pricing minicomputer systems, resulting in low unit prices, and the recognition of elasticity as a factor in the large-system market was a fundamental change in the way these computers were produced and priced.

The cycle of lower prices and higher volumes was repeated several times during subsequent years as IBM made frequent price reductions and product announcements. Each IBM announcement was followed closely by equivalent announcements from Amdahl and National Advanced Systems, Inc. (NAS), the other two competitors in the market for large 370-type computers. In late 1981, IBM introduced the 3081K, a system with nearly six times the processing power of a 168, at a lower price than the older machine.

Table 1 traces the hardware evolution of large systems since 1970 in terms of millions of instructions per second (Mips) and "dollars per Mips," which is the purchase price of the CPU, memory and channels, divided by the number of Mips. Throughout this discussion, Mips is considered to be based on commercial mixed work loads, with the 370 instruction set. Scientific work loads or different instruction sets and architectures can produce Mips rates that vary by factors of two, three or more for systems with equal throughput.

Table 1 shows the two distinct periods of large-system evolution: negligible change between 1970 and 1976, followed by dramatic improvements between 1976 and 1982. Both Amdahl and NAS now offer systems larger than the 3081K, with equivalent or better levels of price/performance, and several Japanese manufacturers are selling highly competitive systems, some as fast as 50 Mips. Most other mainframe vendors (notably Control Data Corp. and Sperry Corp.) have also introduced powerful new large systems that are fully competitive with the 3081.

The advent of the plug-compatible vendors brought about the competitive pressure for improved hardware, but in addition, user demand and IBM's need for additional revenue sources in the face of falling hardware prices combined to spur the development of more efficient large-system software. In 1977, along with the 3033 announcement, IBM introduced a substantially improved, independently priced version of its primary operating system for large CPUs. MVS (Multiple Virtual Storage).

TABLE 1. Hardware Evolution

Year	System	Mips	Dollars per Mips
1970	370/166	1.8	$2,475,000
1976	370/168	2.5	$2,240,000
1982	3081K	14.0	$ 315,000

MVS/SE provided significant performance improvements over the "public-domain" version of MVS, particularly in interactive environments. In 1981, another MVS version (MVS/SP 1.3) again improved performance, also with emphasis on interactive work. These improvements have been brought about by redesign and recoding of many MVS components and, in some cases, by microcode assists.

TSO (The Time Sharing Option), a subsystem of MVS, is the most widely used time-sharing software on large computers. It is in use on about 70% of large 370-type systems, according to a recent survey by International Data Corp.

Table 2 (on In Depth/6) is an attempt to quantify the performance impact of operating system evolution since 1970. The table shows the "path length" (number of CPU instructions required) per transaction for an average TSO work load in a business environment. The work load is assumed to consist of interactive program development, application execution and general time-sharing functions in a variety of computer languages. Also shown is the nominal capacity of a 2.5-Mips processor (the approximate speed of a 370/168 or 3033S), expressed as the maximum number of concurrent terminal users that could be supported, assuming that the CPU is the limiting resource in the configuration. The performance shown in Table 2 for MVS/SP Version 2 is an estimate only, based on design changes that have been announced.

The capacities shown in Table 2 assume very active terminal users and a moderately heavy work load. Care should be exercised in comparing these numbers with other environments, particularly in using the number of terminal users supported, by itself as a measure of system efficiency, a common mistake. One of the main goals of interactive system designers is to

TABLE 2. Software Evolution

Year	System	Path Length	Users per 2.5 Mips
1970	OS/MVT	420,000	110
1972	OS/VS2, Release 1	700,000	65
1974	OS/MVS, 2.0	975,000	45
1975	MVS 3.0	800,000	60
1976	MVS 3.7	600,000	75
1977	MVS/SE 1.0	450,000	100
1980	MVS/SP 1.3	390,000	115
1982	MVS/SP V2, TSO "E"	375,000	120

reduce the number of users supported on a given hardware configuration by providing facilities that are powerful and easy to use, thereby allowing users to express their work requirements as quickly as possible.

Restrictive designs can reduce the load per user, but do not necessarily increase system efficiency. Only if expected work load, availabvle facilities, terminal activity rate and system response time are held constant (as has been done in Table 2) is the number of concurrent users a meaningful measure of system performance.

General-purpose operating systems typically exhibit average path lengths of 300,000 to 500,000 instructions per time-sharing transaction for commercial work loads. The most efficient operating systems dedicated to time-sharing are normally in the lower part of the range, while more generalized, portable operating systems are usually near the high end. There is little evidence to support the frequently voiced opinion that small-computer operating systems are generally more efficient than the equivalent large-system software.

The impact of the various stages of large-computer software evolution can clearly be seen from Table 2. In particular, the increase in CPU path lengths resulting from virtual storage operation is evident during the early 1970s. Since 1976, the additional cost of virtual storage has gradually been eliminated; the current MVS version is now twice as efficient in interactive environments as the pre-1976 software and nearly three times more efficient than the initial release of MVS. And other large-system vendors as well as IBM have reoriented their systems software for more effective interactive operation. As a result, interactive use of large computers is increasing industrywide by more than 50% per year.

The combined impact of improved software and more cost-effective hardware has been a dramatic reduction in the hardware costs of interactive processing on mainframes. The reduction, of course, excludes support costs, which have risen with inflation and are now substantially larger than hardware costs for all computers, large and small.

To quantify the impact of recent large-system evolution, the purchase price of the hardware needed to support one interactive workstation has been estimated and is shown in Table 3 (on In Depth/8). It has been assumed in this table that no more than half the workstations would be in use simultaneously, based on a ratio of one workstation per two computer users, with 1.5 hours of use per user per day, with allowance for peaks. Three costs are shown in Table 3: CPU costs, which

TABLE 3. Large-System Cost per Workstation

Year	System	CPU Costs	System Costs	Workstation Costs
Environment: dedicated interactive work load				
1976	IBM 370/168	$49,000	$52,900	$58,900
1982	IBM 3083E	$ 3,500	$ 5,700	$ 7,700
Environment: mixed batch/interactive work load				
1982	IBM 3083E	$ 1,300	$ 2,600	$ 4,600
Environment: mixed work load, PCM hardware, limited-function				
terminal				
1982	Amdahl 5850	$ 1,000	$ 2,300	$ 3,600

include the costs of the central processor, main memory and I/O channels; system costs, which include CPU costs (as above), along with 20 million characters of on-line storage per workstation, access to high-speed tapes and printers and basic operating system costs; and full workstation costs, which include the previous costs along with a display terminal with full-screen capability and communications control function.

Table 3 shows that between 1976 and 1982, CPU costs per workstation on mainframe systems have declined by a factor of 14 and full workstation costs by a factor of 7. In monthly terms, the hardware-related costs for interactive computer use now represent less than 10% of the salary and overhead expenses associated with a typical computer user, and many large organizations now plan to provide personal workstations for each user-interactive facility at the same cost or less than

other system alternatives, even in dedicated interactive environments. In addition, modern mainframe systems are much more effective than small computers in support of mixed work loads consisting of both batch and interactive processing. Mixed work loads allow for significant further economies. The peak loads experienced by interactive systems typically last for only a short period, so dedicated interactive machines cannot normally use more than 20% of the capacity of a given processor on a 24-hour basis. Computers supporting mixed work loads often achieve utilization levels of 60% or more, resulting in much lower unit costs for all types of work.

In a mixed work-load environment, the CPU costs of supporting time-shared operation of large mainframes—a matter of concern only a few years ago—can be as low as $40 per month per workstation, or about 1.5% of the salary of a typical programmer or other computer user. With plug-compatible hardware and limited-function terminals, full workstation costs can be as low as $3,600.

Although there are no longer economies of scale related to CPU processing, such economies remain in the unit costs of on-line storage, other peripheral equipment, software and support costs. On-line storage, for example, is two to four times less expensive on a large mainframe than on a minicomputer and 10 to 100 times less expensive than on a microcomputer. In many applications, this single cost is the most important to be considered.

The same ratios are evident in software costs. For example, the price of a full-function data base management system is typically 1% to 2% of the hardware cost of a large mainframe, 5% to 15% of the cost of a minicomputer and 20% or more of the cost of a microcomputer. This factor will become increasingly important in system selection in the years ahead.

Also of increasing significance, but often overlooked, is the cost of hardware maintenance. Annual maintenance as a percentage of purchase price is typically 3% to 5% for large mainframes, 7% to 9% for minicomputers and 11% to 13% for microcomputers. Over a five-year useful life, this maintenance increases the effective cost of own-

ership of a microcomputer by 60% or more and a minicomputer by 40%, while the equivalent figure for a mainframe is only 20%.

As a result of these and other factors, most proposed DDP configurations are still not economically attractive unless substantial savings in communications costs are possible. It is not necessarily true, as sometimes assumed, that DDP will always reduce communications costs. If most required computer use is within reasonable physical proximity, communications costs and overheads will actually increase with most implementations of DDP.

For example, the widely discussed architecture of local microcomputers as workstations for interactive processing in mainframe-hosted networks can result in such high volumes of file transfers between processors that communications overheads are greatly increased. In addition, there is often little savings in required host capacity as compared with performing all processing entirely within the host.

Along with the low unit costs of current large systems computing, they continue to have many functional and performance advantages over smaller machines. For example, most small systems have significant limitations on the total on-line storage that can be attached. A 3081-class computer would normally have access to 60 billion to 80 billion characters of on-line storage, with expansion to hundreds of billions of characters possible. By comparison, even the largest minicomputers can support only a few billion characters and microcomputers only a few million.

In many environments, these restrictions can significantly reduce the effectiveness of the smaller systems. Even if 60 billion characters of storage could be included in a network of small computers, the cost of the on-line storage alone in such an environment would usually exceed the complete hardware cost (including CPU, memory and peripherals) of a large system with equivalent capacity.

In many applications, response time can also be far better on a big mainframe than on smaller machines. A basic benchmark, performing a moderate amount of processing or data manipulation, might require 60 seconds of processing time (and also response time) on a dedicated microcomputer. This benchmark might need 3 seconds of CPU time on a supermini and would typically receive 5 to 10 seconds response time on a time-shared system. On a 3081-class machine, such a benchmark would require only one-tenth of a second of processor time and should normally receive almost immediate response.

While it might be generally ac- cepted that large systems can today provide some of the previously outlined advantages, it is often asserted that future small systems will eventually reduce or eliminate these advantages, since the rate of small-computer evolution is so rapid.

It is worth looking at this assertion in more detail, by comparing recent experience in the mainframe industry with that in the minicomputer industry. In 1976, two of the leading minicomputer systems were the Digital Equipment Corp. PDP-11/70 and the Hewlett-Packard Co. HP 3000 Series II. The current successors to these systems, the VAX-11/780 and the HP 3000 Series 44, provide up to twice the CPU performance of the older machines at about the same price.

This nearly two-to-one improvement, while impressive in itself, has clearly not kept pace with the advances in the mainframe industry, where price/performance ratios have improved by a factor of at least six in the same time period. There is no evidence to support the view that small-system evolution is, or will be, more rapid than that for large systems.

MARKETPLACE VERDICT

Technical achievements by themselves are, of course, of little value; the real measure of any product is determined by the marketplace. In

TABLE 4. Large-System Installed Capacity (370-Type Only)

(A) Processing Capacity	
Year	Installed Mips
1976	1,884
1977	2,685
1978	4,230
1979	7,507
1980	11,034
1981	15,062
1982	19,789

(B) Interactive Workstations			
Year	Time-Sharing	Transaction Processing	Total Workstations
1976	50,000	35,000	85,000
1982	850,000	625,000	1,475,000

1976, there was already a substantial installed base of large systems, which many predicted would gradually be replaced by smaller machines. In fact, nothing of the kind has occurred: the response of the marketplace to the new generations of mainframes has been overwhelmingly positive.

Table 4, derived from historical large-system population figures published by International Data Corp., outlines the approximate worldwide installed capacity of large-scale, 370-type computer systems. (A large system is considered to be a 370/165 class machine or larger.)

Table 4 clearly shows that there is little evidence to suggest any trend toward replacement or "offloading" of these large mainframes. On the contrary, the installed base has expanded enormously, with more than 10 times the installed capacity at the start of 1982, relative to 1976. Interactive use has grown even faster; Table 4B indicates that the total number of interactive workstations supported by large systems increased by a factor of nearly 20 in the same six-year period. In addition, shipments of large 370-type systems are expected to exceed 10,000 Mips per year during 1982 and 1983 as volume shipments of the 3081-generation machines begin.

Growth in the market for large computers is not restricted to commercial systems. In the last few years, Cray Research, Inc. and Control Data Corp. have created an entirely new market for high-speed parallel processors for scientific applications. This market is also thriving and allowing the implementation of many new applications that would be completely impractical on smaller computers.

Despite the record of continued large-system market growth, industry analysts often suggest that this market is a low-growth, "mature" segment of the industry. There appear to be several reasons for this misconception. First, the percentage growth of various industry segments is frequently used as the only measure of the strength of that segment. Clearly, it is unreasonable to compare the $18 billion-per-year mainframe industry with the $3 billion-per-year microcomputer industry (based on 1981 shipments) on this basis; growth of "only" 10% in the mainframe market is more in absolute dollar terms than even 50% growth in the microcomputer market. Moreover, growth rates invariably fall as any industry gets larger, as witnessed by the minicomputer industry, which has seen its growth rate fall from 35% to 10% or less as it has grown in size (although it remains less than one-third the size of the mainframe market). Even with infinite demand, it is simply not practical for a $20 billion-per-year

industry to expand revenues 50% annually.

Second, the unit price erosion of mainframes has been severe in recent years. As a result, growth in the dollar volume of shipments has been slower than the growth in Mips, although the value of large systems shipped is now more than double the 1977 levels. The small-system market has had far greater price stability and has thus experienced revenue growth almost in line with increases in shipments, giving that market a high apparent growth rate relative to the mainframe market.

Finally, all mainframes are often grouped together as a single market segment, even though they span more than two orders of magnitude in price and performance. Smaller mainframes, once the largest part of the computer industry, have been relatively unsuccessful during recent years. Prior to the introduction of the IBM 4300 class of machines in 1979, smaller mainframes were not price-competitive with the equivalent minicomputers and, in some cases, were functionally deficient as well. Even today, for example, IBM lacks an integrated, full-function operating system for its smallest mainframes (excluding System/38).

As a result of these factors, there was no growth at all in the market for small mainframes (in the 370/

138 and 148 range) between 1975 and 1980, according to IDC's 1981 *Review & Forecast*. Grouping all mainframes together as a single market segment suggests a lower growth rate for the larger systems than has actually occurred.

Careful analysis of large-system capacity installed, as presented in Table 4, clearly indicates that the market for large mainframes continues to be one of the most rapidly expanding industry segments.

Another source of confusion is that the extent and impact of the implementation of distributed processing are often overstated, particularly in the trade press. As with any popular medium, the trade papers naturally emphasize anything new and unusual; a large user installing a third or fourth 3081 is hardly newsworthy, while the same user acquiring a few minicomputers or microcomputers is often considered worthy of extensive analysis and comment, simply because it continues to be a relatively unusual event.

Also, much of the material in the trade papers is generated by those with a vested interest in selling some product or service, and since there are a great many organizations attempting to profit from small computers and relatively few producing large computers, there is a preponderance of published material advocating small computer use.

According to a recent *Fortune* survey, only about 20% of large-system users implemented distributed processing applications (involving remote processors and data bases) between 1976 and 1980. And of even this 20%, about half indicated that their next major hardware upgrade would be to the central site, rather than at remote sites.

These figures suggest that it is rare for distributed processing to be implemented as an alternative to centralized processing. Distributed applications are normally additions to existing large systems when specific applications merit this design, and they frequently result in increased, rather than decreased, central site capacity.

There has been so little substance behind most of the furor about distributed processing that even IBM may have misjudged the market. In 1979, IBM introduced the 8100 system, designed from the ground up as a distributed processor. This system is often considered a failure in the marketplace, primarily because the market for true distributed processing (cooperative, linked processors) is much smaller than once expected, and there is no indication that this situation will soon change.

Certainly, there is no available evidence to support the view that there is a long-term, historical trend toward replacing large mainframes with distributed small computers.

Today, it is relatively rare to hear industry experts announce the imminent demise of the large mainframe, although there is a lingering suspicion in some minds that this will eventually come to pass.

In summary, a review of industry trends leads to the following conclusions:

▪ Large mainframe computers continue to be the almost universally preferred alternative for large organizations; large systems enforce standardization, allow better management control of the corporate information assets, minimize duplication of effort and, as a result, make the best use of the most critical DP resource—skilled manpower.

▪ Distributed processing represents a significant advance in system design methodology if geographic and application characteristics are appropriate. It is usually an ineffective approach for providing general computing capabilities in large, single-location organizations. True DDP almost always increases the complexity of any given application.

▪ In most environments, large systems provide generally lower cost computing than multiple small systems. In addition, they allow for larger applications to be processed easily and efficiently and allow nondisruptive growth of individual applications.

▪ In many cases, distributed processing is being implemented with small versions of the larger systems. A small mainframe can often provide many powerful and cost-effective networking and distributed processing features, while also providing exact compatibility with large host systems.

▪ Current large systems will continue gradually to add layers of function and areas of application. Large-computer operating systems are often criticized for excessive complexity and lack of the "elegant simplicity" which so delights the academic purists, but economic commitments to these systems are so enormous—in excess of $150 billion invested in MVS applications alone—that wholesale replacement by completely new software is both impractical and undesirable. The evolutionary process for large operating systems is, in many respects, quite similar to that of the human brain, which also consists of multiple layers of progressively higher level functions. That most harsh and impartial critic, natural selection, has already determined the wisdom and necessity of such an evolutionary path.

▪ The integrated processing environments supported by current large systems, consisting of facilities for batch, time-sharing and transaction processing, will continue to be a requirement for the foreseeable future. Although batch processing is now relatively less important than in the past, it continues to be the preferred mode of operation for jobs requiring long running times, large volumes of output or human intervention for such activities as mounting tape or disk volumes. Batch is also the least expensive mode of operation for repetitive "production" work. Full integration between processing modes, including file and program compatibility, results in a conceptually and operationally simpler environment, lower overall costs and higher organizational productivity.

- Small systems can provide significant benefits as centralized processing tools for small organizations. In most cases, the use of several smaller computers would not be considered if a single larger one could be used. Any small business that allowed individual employees to acquire any desired computing equipment would not be in business for long.
- Small-system vendors are rapidly introducing larger versions of their successful minicomputers. HP is now marketing the HP 3000 Series 64, and DEC, the VAX-11/782. These systems both use 32-bit words and offer processing power in the range of the 370/158, which, only

a few years ago, was considered a large "centralized" system.

These powerful systems provide a reasonable growth path for current minicomputer users, since installing multiple small minis is not an acceptable alternative for most users. At the same time, mainframe architectures are being implemented on much less expensive hardware. The "370 on a chip" will arrive within a year or two, allowing the acceptance of industry-standard architectures at all levels of the industry.

- The industry forces that have produced the recent rapid evolution of the large computer will continue for at least the next few years. These forces include intense competition, the rise of the Japanese manufacturers, market elasticity and advances in microelectronics technology.

From a philosophical standpoint, there seem to be two essentially opposing trends that will determine the course of the computer industry over the next few years. One is the increasing desire of many individuals to control their own computing environments.

This trend will lead to some acceptance of "personal" microcomputers in large organizations, particularly those without tight financial controls.

The feelings of personal ownership engendered by these small machines, and the involvement in the details of computer operation that they allow are sources of significant appeal to many potential computer users. Indeed, this is an underlying, though usually unspoken, consideration in much of the discussion about distributed processing. Many people simply enjoy being involved in acquiring and operating computer systems, with as much involvement in technical detail as possible.

However, it is far from certain that there will be a favorable long-term return on investment from corporate expenditures on "personal" applications and systems, particularly when the required functions can often be made available more economically with larger systems that would facilitate sharing of any results achieved. Moreover, it remains to be seen just how much organizational computing can really be construed as "personal."

A number of management concerns result from the proliferation of personal computers in large organizations; among them, fragmentation of corporate information resources, duplication of effort and the potential lack of integrity and complete lack of security of data stored on floppy disks. Also of concern is the possibility that expenditures on microcomputers will lead

corporate management to believe that further expansion of centralized systems is not required. In fact, the applications practical on personal computers are so simple and their effective capacity so small that this would rarely be the case.

This same phenomenon following minicomputer acquisitions has caused serious problems in some organizations in past years. In some cases, these acquisitions were viewed as an alternative to central system expansion, with the result that critical centralized corporate applications were jeopardized by inadequate mainframe capacity.

In spite of any abstract or theoretical advantages of decentralization—and despite the ideological and religious fervor that a desire for decentralization can ignite—everyday business practicalities will continue to dictate a substantial degree of corporate control over information gathering and processing activities. These activities consume inordinate amounts of human and other resources if not managed appropriately. The need for efficient information processing leads directly to the second fundamental trend driving the computer industry in this decade: centralized information resource management.

Centralized control of the data processing function does not mean that end users of all kinds should be denied access to appropriate computing tools, only that these tools should be made available in a way that will most benefit the overall organization—which usually means use of shared, centralized services. There is no question that many DP departments have been remiss in not promoting the direct use of computing throughout their organizations and in not providing sufficient capacity to support such use. Insufficient central-site capacity often leads to pressure for tactical decentralization, even though this might not be an appropriate strategic direction.

In a sense, the ability to centralize, control and therefore share knowledge and tools as "community property" has been one of the most important factors in the cultural evolution of mankind and is no less a requirement in the computer age than any other. The need for control and sharing of resources will lead to ever larger and more powerful central computing facilities.

The environments illustrated in Figure 36, 37, and 38, then, are typical of the hardware that forms the foundation of the system of record and operational processing. Note that the concept of the system of record is independent of its hardware foundation.

OPERATIONAL HARDWARE—SUPPORTING SYSTEMS

A normal part of the operational environment that is separate from the system of record is the supporting systems. Not all operational environments have a need for supporting systems, and some operational environments execute supporting functions in the system of record. Other environments separate the two functions. A typical supporting system is a transaction-gathering "front end," as shown by Figure 39.

Figure 39 shows a typical transaction front end system. The front end serves the purpose of formatting a transaction, doing simple editing, checking for abnormal or special activities and accounts, and so forth. A real-life example of a front end is the ATM environment that sits in front of the bank's system of record of accounts.

Auxiliary data can be stored in each front end processor, such as processing limits, suspended accounts, and so forth. While the data stored

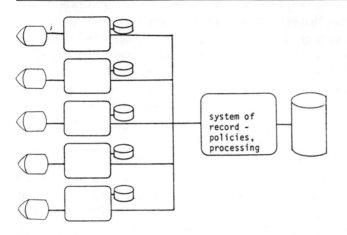

FIGURE 39 A front end to the system of record for gathering, monitoring, editing transactions.

in the front end is valuable and useful data, it should not be mistaken for system of record data.

Another type of supporting system is the back end system. Commonly called a data base machine (or intelligent disk controller, depending upon the definition of a data base machine), the back end system is a device that can enhance the throughput, independence, and availability of data. A typical back end processor is shown by Figure 40.

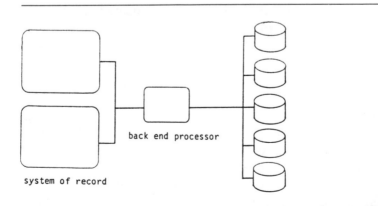

FIGURE 40 A data base machine, or an intelligent disk controller.

It is a temptation to state that the system of record moves to the back end processor when a back end processor is used. Depending on the application, this may or may not be true. While the update and access of data may be shifted to the back end processor, the integrity protection that is available is available at a system level. The system of record usually remains in the host processor, in the application that directs the processing against the back end. As such, the system of record is an application concept rather than a system concept.

DSS HARDWARE—DECISION SUPPORT SYSTEMS

Atomic Level

The primary concern in hardware selection for the atomic level is the management of large amounts of data and the ability to pass and receive data from a diverse number of processors.

The hardware foundation for the atomic dss level is unquestionably centralized, usually in the form of a mainframe. The amount of data to be handled and the amount of processing going into and out of the atomic level is such that anything less than a fair amount of hardware resources will not suffice. Figure 41 depicts the hardware environment appropriate to the dss atomic level.

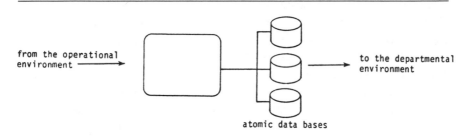

from the operational environment

to the departmental environment

atomic data bases

FIGURE 41   The atomic level of data and processing.

The needs of the dss atomic level are fairly straightforward. Data is periodically (and in large masses) received from the operational environment. In turn, it is periodically (and also in large masses) stripped from the atomic level and sent to the departmental level. Thus, much sequential processing occurs. There is seldom, if ever, any online processing that occurs at the atomic level.

There is no question that the information paradigm predicts a future in which data processing will be done on a wide variety of machines. The question is just exactly how this dispersal of processing power will come about. Some pundits project a future dominated by personal computers. Other see minicomputers leading the way. Still others see a combination of types of processors. The article—HOWE DDP PROPONENTS SAW THE INDUSTRY—is but one opinion as to how processing will be dispersed.

HOW DDP PROPONENTS SAW THE INDUSTRY*

The DDP revolution appeared to be in full swing by 1976. One could not read a trade magazine or attend a conference without hearing another prediction that DDP was the wave of the future.

Even more exciting, the development of the microcomputer was then just on the horizon; it was widely expected to further the revolution by providing an individual computer for every end user. Before long, DDP advocates explained, those huge, obsolete, centralized mainframes would be replaced by economical, efficient mini- and microcomputers, and those elitist computer ''experts'' would be cast out of their raised-floor silicon towers.

It was widely argued in the industry that most data processing problems resulted from excessive centralization and the use of ineffective large-scale computers.

*By David Powell, *Computerworld*, June 1983. Copyright 1983 by CW Communications/Inc. Reprinted with permission.

In particular, it was frequently suggested that large systems were much too inefficient, expensive and unreliable for interactive operation, which was clearly of paramount importance to the industry's future.

JUSTIFYING SMALL SYSTEMS

In some cases, organizations used the perceived trend to smaller systems, by itself, as justification for acquiring minicomputers, regardless of any objective evaluation of alternatives.

In other cases, users bought small systems in order to circumvent the normal budgetary controls which were (quite correctly) applied to the centralized computer services. In some organizations, advocates of moderation in the race to join the DDP stampede were looked on as a little backward.

There was, in fact, considerable evidence to support these ideas. The predominant large-scale system in use in 1976 was the IBM 370/168. The 168 was only 30% more powerful than the 370/165, which had been introduced in 1970, and the cost of the two systems was nearly the same in most configurations. Thus, the hardware price/performance levels of large computers improved only marginally during the early 1970s. In addition, several mainframe vendors introduced virtual storage features during this period. Support for virtual storage enhanced the functional capabilities of the large systems but, in some cases, resulted in significantly higher overhead.

For example, the CPU resources required to support a given interactive work load doubled between IBM's real storage operating system, OS/MVT, and its virtual storage successor, OS/VS2, Release 2.

The result of these factors was that large-system users suffered a net reduction in performance levels during the six years of 1970 to 1976. During this same period, minicomputer technology had made great strides in improved performance, reduced price and enhanced software capabilities.

These small systems had become powerful enough to be seriously considered for many significant applications.

Moreover, it was widely suggested that small systems were evolving rapidly, while large-system evolution had stagnated.

For all these reasons, the future of the large-scale mainframe in the emerging world of DDP looked problematic to some in the mid-'70s. However, mainframe industry forces would soon begin to alter the course of distributed processing, ensuring the continued dominance of large computer systems.

In the eventuality that the atomic level requires more processing power than a single mainframe has been designed for, it is entirely conceivable that a "distributed" atomic environment be created. Such an environment is shown in Figure 42.

Figure 42 shows that policies, claims, and premium atomic data has been spread over three processors. This distribution of data is natural because it aligns nicely with the orientation to subject data. Given the amount of archival data that accumulates at the atomic level, it is not unlikely that some form of distribution will be required, especially as the atomic environment matures and becomes fully populated.

The final hardware criteria for the atomic level is that the hardware be able to accept data from and pass data to a wide variety of hardware devices. The hardware that exists at the atomic level is likely to be interfacing with *many* types of hardware. It would be a mistake to choose

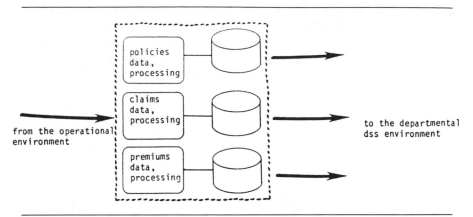

FIGURE 42 A distributed atomic environment.

hardware for atomic processing that was not comfortably conversant with a wide variety of processors.

Departmental Level

The next level of dss information is departmental. As data flows from the atomic level to the departmental level, the transformation from primitive data to derived data occurs. And the singular atomic source feeds multiple departmental sources, as shown in Figure 43.

There are two philosophies in selecting the hardware basis for departmental dss processing. One approach is to allow multiple departments to use the same large processor, usually a mainframe or large minicomputer. Another approach is to give each department its own processor, usually a minicomputer or small mainframe. These two approaches are contrasted in Figure 44.

There are advantages to either approach. When departments share a single large processor, on the occasion when there are spare resources, a department may have available to it an enormous amount of processing power. By the same token, when one department is using a significant amount of processing power, other departments that share the processor may feel irritated because of the negative effects they may experience. And when multiple departments share the same large processor, the resources consumed by the processor are often viewed as "public" money and are not directly allocated backward to any one department.

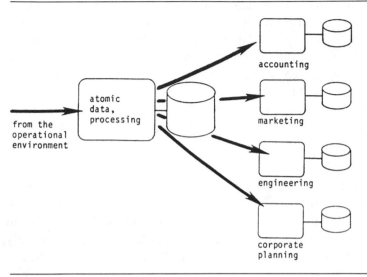

FIGURE 43 Atomic data feeds multiple departmental data base environments.

The other approach is to allow departments to have their own processor. When departments have their own separate processor, there is a feeling of autonomy. One department is *never* frustrated when the processing resources are used by another department. And responsibility for resource allocation is simple and direct—a department pays for its own processor and other resources directly consumed.

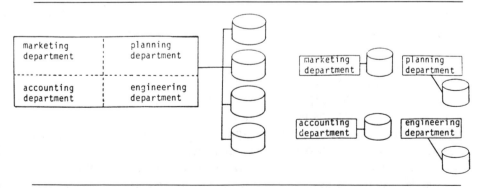

FIGURE 44 Two approaches to hardware at the departmental level.

The processing needs at the departmental level are diverse. For scheduled reports, a fairly large amount of processing power may be required. In addition, it is likely that a large amount of data accumulates at the departmental level over time. It is normal, moreover, to have a fair amount of ad hoc or unscheduled processing occur at the departmental level as well. Certainly individual dss data bases must be fed.

Because of the diversity of requirements, a general-purpose processor, usually with a fair amount of power, is required at the departmental level.

Individual Level

The underlying hardware at the individual level is unquestionably oriented toward individual, highly autonomous nonshared processing. As in the case of departmental processing, there are two approaches. One is to assign many users their own private facilities on a large processor, usually a mainframe. This approach is often called "time sharing." Another is to push users onto their own processors, usually a personal computer or more powerful individual work station.

The issues related to which approach is most advantageous are exactly parallel to those discussed for departmental dss processing. When individual users share a large processor, there is always the question of who pays for the processor. When individuals have their own processors, there is little doubt as to who should pay for it. There are two unique processing needs that arise at the individual level. One is for the storage and management of *many* versions of closely related data, most of which can be considered temporary versions. The other is for the ability to do heuristic, iterative processing.

SOFTWARE

System of Record

The software foundation for the system of record is one that is characterized by teleprocessing monitors and data base management systems. The software has the capability of high levels of performance, usually measured in transactions per second and high levels of availability. Because of the availability needs, logging and backup and recovery are standard features. Processing is typically one record at a time, and the standard languages of COBOL, Fortran, and PL-1 are common. The online day gives way to the "batch window" in the evening, when batch updates, extracts, backups reorganizations, and other utilities are run. The essence of the software found in the system of record is transaction-oriented, procedure-oriented software.

Supporting Systems

Operational supporting, non-system-of-record systems are characterized by a very high transaction processing rate, a limited data base capability, and a somewhat large teleprocessing capability. Record-at-a-time processing is the norm. Base languages might include Assembler. The singular orientation of supporting systems is toward high performance and transaction processing, even with somewhat degraded transaction and data integrity in some cases. Procedural code typifies supporting systems.

Atomic Dss Level

The atomic-level software is characterized by the need for data management and the ability to handle large, bulk volumes of data. Given the number of interfaces flowing into and out of the atomic level, the more common (i.e., the more basic and widely used) the software is, the better. The software needs of the atomic level are very straightforward.

Departmental

Departmental software needs to have a fair amount of logic and calculation capabilities because of the derivation that occurs as the primitive data is transformed to derived data. In addition, some capability for managing bulk data is also required. Set-at-a-time processing is the norm, along with nonprocedural languages. Typical of the software for departmental processing are 4GLs. The teleprocessing needs for departmental processing are limited compared to the same set of needs in the system of record.

Individual

Software at the individual level is oriented, not surprisingly, to very stylistic individualist needs. Spreadsheets, user-friendly languages, and other software tools in support of heuristic processing are the norm. The amount of data managed is much smaller than at other levels. The teleprocessing needs are likewise limited. Nonprocedural languages doing set-at-a-time processing are absolutely the norm at this level.

OTHER PERSPECTIVES

While the technological perspectives of hardware and software are certainly interesting, they are hardly the only ones. Another useful perspective of the underlying technology is the nature of access of data—either direct or sequential. Figure 45 illustrates the differences.

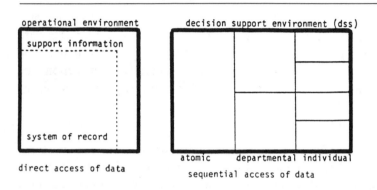

FIGURE 45 A simplified perspective of the underlying access of data in the information paradigm.

Figure 45 shows that operational data is primarily oriented toward direct access of data and that dss processing is oriented toward sequential access of data.

One apparent anomaly is the high-performance, operationally-oriented system-of-record transaction processing environment that, at night, turns into a batch processor doing dss work. Is the computer a direct access processor for system of record processing or a sequential processor? During the day, system of record activity is occurring, and at that time the processor is doing predominately operational processing. But as the online day ends, so ends the system-of-record environment and the processor turns into a dss processor doing sequential processing.

The environments that are being processed, either the system-of-record operational or the sequentially-oriented dss environment, are created by the workload being processed, not by the processor. The same processor can do either system-of-record processing (i.e., direct access processing) or dss processing (i.e., sequential processing), but not both at the same time.

Another distinction is between update and access processing. Typically, during the day, much online update processing occurs. At night, the processing that occurs is access of and manipulation of the dss environment, not the system-of-record environment. After dss extract processing is finished, much sequential manipulation of data, that is, dss processing, calculation, summarization, and so forth, occurs.

Another technical perspective is that of path lengths that are typical of the different environments. A path length is simply the stream of instructions required to execute a transaction or a program. The system-of-record environment is typified by short path lengths. The operational non-system-of-record environment (i.e., the supporting operational environment) is typified by very short path lengths.

The atomic environment is typified by very long path lengths; the departmental environment, by long path lengths. The individual dss environment is typified by moderately long path lengths.

Furthermore, the frequency of execution of the path lengths is very different. System-of-record path lengths are executed frequently; supporting system-of-record operational path lengths are executed very frequently. Atomic path lengths are executed very infrequently; departmental path lengths are executed infrequently. Individual path lengths are executed moderately infrequently. Figure 46 shows the difference in path lengths and frequency of execution.

HARDWARE/SOFTWARE INTEGRATION ACROSS THE INFORMATION PARADIGM

The different hardware/software technology that populates the landscape has been discussed as if each level of data and processing used different, unrelated technology for different levels of the information paradigm. In practice, such *is* often the case, although a case may be made for technological integration. But the differences in processing are, generally speaking, so diverse that no one product line meets all needs. Certain hardware architectures are suited for some types of processing, for example, but not all types.

The issues of hardware integration are most meaningfully discussed from two perspectives: vertical integration and horizontal integration. The vertical perspective refers to the technology within a given level, while the horizontal perspective refers to the technology considered across the different levels.

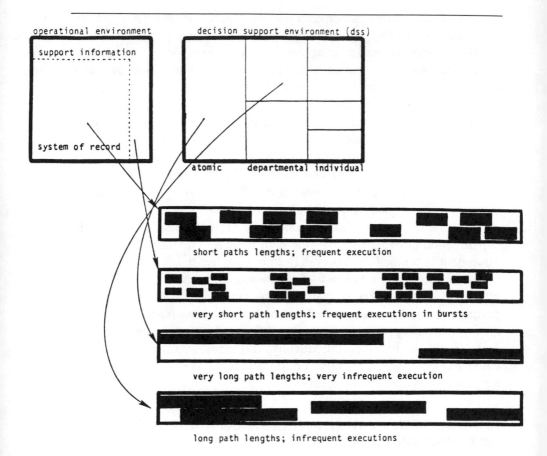

FIGURE 46 The difference in path lengths and the frequency of execution across the information paradigm.

Vertical Compatibility of Technology

There are some strong motivations for vertical compatibility of technology, especially in the system-of-record, atomic, and, to some extent, departmental levels of the information paradigm. When the hardware/software technology within a given level is integrated and compatible, the following results are achieved:

- Skills become transferable.
- Volume discounts may apply.
- Troubleshooting can be focused.
- Support needs can be consolidated.
- Training can be uniform and consolidated.
- Growth within a product line can proceed in an orderly manner.

In short, there are many virtues to vertical technological compatibility throughout the different levels of the architecture.

Horizontal Compatibility of Technology

Horizontal compatibility has advantages. Some of these advantages are:

- The potential for volume discounts.
- Compatibility of interfaces as technology grows.
- Transferability of skills.
- Consolidation of training.

But there are major disadvantages. One disadvantage of a customer choosing a single vendor or a single technology horizontally is that the customer is unable to take advantage of specialized technology that is particularly suited to one level of the information paradigm but not to others. Technology, either hardware or software, that attempts to be all things to all people, all at the same time across the information paradigm, is technology that is second-rate across the board. For each level there will be specific technology that is much better suited for that level than the general-purpose technology.

DATA COMMUNICATIONS

One of the technical foundations of the information paradigm is the ability to communicate from one level of data processing to another. Indeed, without the ability to move data from one level to the next, the architecture could not exist.

Data Flow

There are very different sets of needs for data communications depending on the flow of data from one level to the next.

Operational to atomic flow

The operational to atomic flow is marked by the need to move massive amounts of data from the operational level to the atomic level. Generally speaking, the frequency of the flow is predictable. Also, because the flow is often from a mainframe to a mainframe or from a series of minicomputers to a mainframe, there is little variety in the types of lines needed to connect the different levels of data.

Atomic to departmental flow

The atomic to departmental flow involves less data than the operational to atomic flow. The frequency of the flow is much less predictable, and there is a wide variety of lines that are used in the atomic to departmental flow.

Departmental to individual flow

The departmental to individual flow of data involves much less data than the other types of flows. In addition, the frequency of flow is very irregular. There is a very wide variety of types of communications made at this level.

Atomic to individual flow

Another type of flow is the atomic to individual flow. This flow of data is the most infrequent. It involves only a small amount of data.

The actual technology used to actuate the data communications from one level to the next is not specified by the architecture. Instead, the information paradigm merely specifies how much data is to flow, the frequency of the flow, and the general type of processor found at each end of the flow. Because the information paradigm does not call for a specific type of data communication, there are many technical possibilities at the point of implementation.

Refreshing Data—Operational to Atomic

The simplest strategy to keep data current in both the operational and atomic environments is periodic, massive refreshment of data. While this strategy is appealing from a simplicity perspective, it has *enormous* drawbacks. The machine processes required are more than significant—they are overwhelming. As a result, wholesale replacement of data as a strategy for refreshment is an option that is used for only very small data bases and in only very special circumstances.

A more normal approach is to move only transactions through the operational to atomic interface to refresh data.

One of the major technical considerations is the volume of data that flows throughout the architecture even when only transactions are shipped from one environment to the next. In the simplest case (which requires the most resources), every time a data element changes in the operational environment, a corresponding change must be reflected in the atomic environment. For example, a bank decides to track all transactions related to customer balance. Figure 47 depicts the simple update of transactions in both environments.

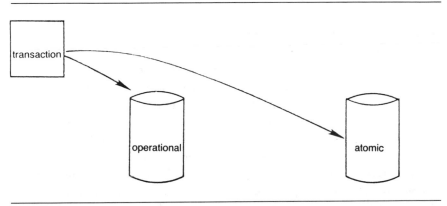

FIGURE 47 Multiple posting of transaction in rapid succession.

Not only is the volume of transactions flowing between the systems an issue, but the timing of the updates is also an issue. At some moment in time, the operational data base will have been updated while the atomic data base will not have been updated. Philosophically, this should not present a problem because atomic data is archival in nature and should not need to be kept in lockstep—up to the second—with operational data.

To ease the burden of keeping data in sync, each operational field may be time stamped with the time of its update. In other words, in the operational environment, as a field has its value updated, the day and time the value is updated is likewise stored. Now the operational to atomic

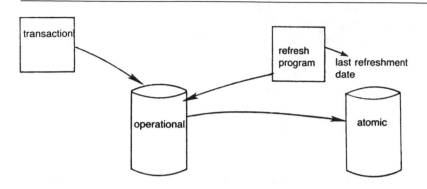

FIGURE 48 Immediate update of transactions to the operational data base, followed by periodic refreshment of atomic data.

refreshment of data can be done on an as-needed basis with no concern for the immediacy of update, as shown by Figure 48.

The scenario in Figure 48 shows that time of update is stored as well as the actual value updated. At a later point in time, a "refreshment" program is run. The refreshment program simply moves all data into the atomic data base that has changed since the last refreshment. The refreshment program first finds out when the last refreshment was run. Then the refreshment program scans the operational data, looking for any dates that are greater than the previous refreshment. When a date is encountered that is greater than the previous refreshment date, the updated value is shipped to the atomic data base. As an example, in a working environment, the previous refreshment date was July 10, 1987. The refreshment program then encounters update dates of July 11, July 12, and so forth. All data transacted after July 10 is shipped to the atomic data base.

The date-of-update technique gets around the issue of immediacy of update (as found in Figure 47). But for all practical purposes, the technique is inefficient. For example, does every field that is to be updated have its own date of update? If so, much data base space will be spent on an unessential field.

One refinement is to create a date-of-update field for whole groups of fields that are updated together, as shown by Figure 49.

In Figure 49, much less data is used for coordination of update between operational- and atomic-level data. The concept of using a single date of update can be extended even further for data that is infrequently updated.

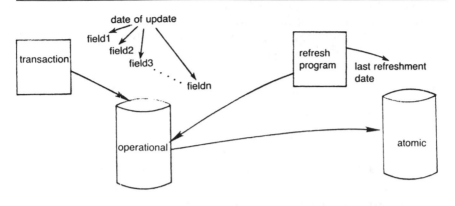

FIGURE 49 Multiple fields are referred to by a single date of update, saving much space.

For example, in the banking environment when basic customer data, such as name, address, phone, changes, the entire record may be flagged for transport to the atomic environment. While update of fields that haven't changed may seem inefficient, since the fields change so infrequently, there is not a terrible waste of resources.

Another option—depending on the type of data being managed—is to reflect only periodic values of data. For example, in the banking environment, the field CURRENT BALANCE changes frequently—on an hour-by-hour basis. It makes sense to track current balance only at preselected intervals—daily, weekly, etc. By not tracking CURRENT BALANCE for each change, the flow of data between the operational and the atomic level is minimized.

In a few cases, the operational to atomic refreshment can be done on an as-needed basis. For example, the exact tracking of CURRENT BALANCE is not needed for nearly all accounts. However, it may be necessary on occasion to actually recreate the movement of CURRENT BALANCE for selected accounts (for legal or auditing reasons, for example). For a few selected accounts, the activity against CURRENT BALANCE is retransacted and stored in the atomic level. Since only a few accounts are selected, the flow of data to the atomic level is kept to a reasonable level.

A further option that may be applicable in a few cases is the transaction of only additions and deletions across the operational/atomic interface.

Updates are not reflected. At a later point in time, a massive refreshment is done to capture the updates that have occurred. This option reduces the volume of data and processing to a minimum, but requires massive resources during the refreshment process.

Redundancy of Data and the Architected Environment

At first glance, it appears that the atomic level of data adds storage (or DASD) requirements to an environment. Indeed, in the transition period, from the time the shop embarks on the transformation from the unarchitected environment to the architected environment, more DASD is required. Figure 50 shows a typical transition from the traditional production, application-oriented environment to the architected environment.

On day 1, dss processing is done directly from production data bases. On day 2, the atomic data base is created from existing production data bases. On day 3, production data bases are converted to subject-oriented data bases. This conversion occurs over a period of time. On day 4, the atomic-level data is fed from subject-oriented operational data bases. In addition, at the dss level, the need for multiple extracts diminishes. Only on day 2, as the atomic-level data is created from current production, application-oriented data, is there a net increase in DASD. At day 3, as application-oriented data bases are converted to subject-oriented data bases, there is a net loss of needs for DASD because of the reduction of redundant data, which is inherent to application-oriented systems, and because of the removal of archival data to the atomic level, which will be addressed later. On day 4, as the atomic and departmental levels mature, there is a further reduction in the need for DASD as the individual level of analysis begins to access atomic and departmental data.

In short, there is *less* total DASD required to support the same amount of processing on day 4 than there was on day 1. Of course, on day 4, the organization is fully enjoying benefits of the architected environment other than the reduction of the total amount of DASD needed. This transformation, taken from the perspective of total amount of DASD, at first seems anti-intuitive. A deeper explanation is needed.

Same Data, Different Structures

From a different perspective, there is no difference in the *types* of data found in the architected and unarchitected environment. There is, how-

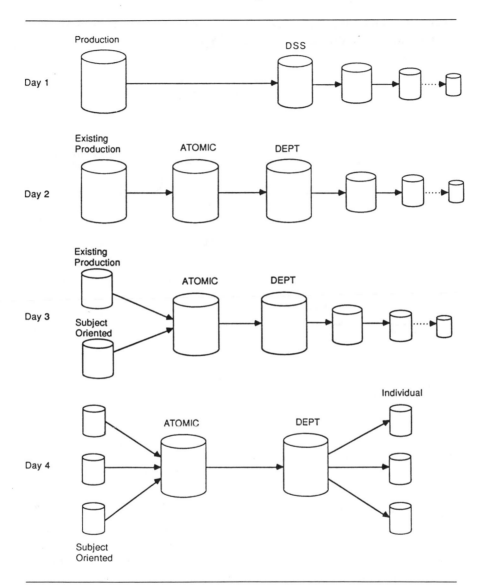

FIGURE 50 A typical transition from the traditional production, application-oriented environment to the architected environment.

ever, a profound difference in the structure of the data (and consequently in the total amount of data). Consider Figure 51.

TRADITIONAL SYSTEMS

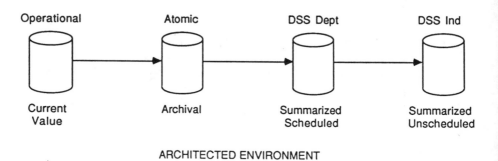

ARCHITECTED ENVIRONMENT

FIGURE 51   Architected environment.

Figure 51 shows the traditional, application-oriented environment and the architected environment. In the traditional application environment, both current-value data (that is, data that reflects the current value of a data element) and archival data are stored at the production level. In the architected environment, the current-value data is stored at the operational level and the archival data is stored at the atomic level.

From the standpoint of the functional use of data, there is *no gain or loss* in comparing the amount of data in the traditional production environment and the architected operational and atomic environments. In other words, that the architected environment adds a new level of data does *not* imply that the architected environment requires any more DASD.

Instead, the architected environment merely recognizes the need to separate current-value and archival data (which have been traditionally freely mixed). To assume that separating traditional application-oriented data into architected data requires more DASD demonstrates a lack of understanding of what is contained in either/both environments.

The Production-Dss Extract

But the issue of redundancy runs deep in the traditional environment, as production data is extracted into data that can be used for dss processing, as shown in Figure 52.

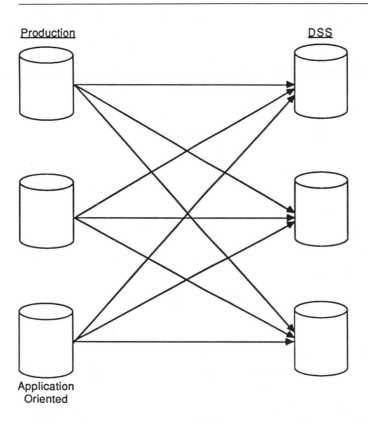

FIGURE 52   Production data is extracted into data that can be used for dss processing.

The simplicity of Figure 52 belies the redundancy that is contained in that environment. The types of redundancy found in Figure 52 are outlined by Figure 53.

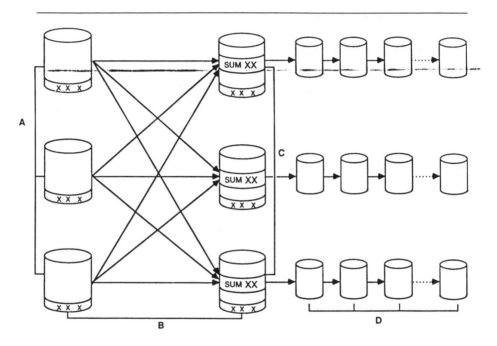

A - Application oriented data - classical redundancy

B - Redundancy of data from OPERATIONAL to DSS

C - Redundancy of Summarized data across summarized files

D - Multiple extracts and analysis of DSS data

FIGURE 53 Types of redundancy found in Figure 52.

There are four types of redundancy found in Figure 53, which represents the traditional production environment. One form is the redundancy found among application-oriented data bases. An inventory application will store part descriptions, quantity on hand, unit of measure, and so forth. Bill of material application data will contain description, subassembly, unit of measure, substitute part, and so forth. Store control data will contain part location, quantity on hand, description, substitute, unit of measure, and so forth. Finally, material requirements planning will contain description, unit of measure, assembly/subassembly, and so forth. Every application contains its own master file, and there is much data that is redundant among the applications.

The second type of redundancy in the traditional environment is the redundancy of detailed information as data is extracted from the production to the dss environment. Because the production data is voluminous and difficult to get to, once the dss analyst gets hold of the production data, he or she grabs as much detailed, current-value data as possible and brings that detailed production data to the dss world. Once in the dss world, the analyst has control of the data and can analyze it to the heart's content. Because of the difficulty in accessing production data, the dss analyst purposely grabs as much data as possible, creating a large amount of data redundancy between the production and the dss environment.

A third type of redundancy encountered in the traditional unarchitected environment is that of "corporate" summarized data stored at the departmental dss level. Each department may calculate and store summarized data, which is likewise summarized and calculated by other departments. In addition to wasted CPU cycles needed for the calculation and the possibility of algorithmic incompatible treatment from one department to the next, there is wasted DASD where there is no central place to store commonly calculated dss data.

The fourth type of redundancy is the redundancy of dss data as generations of extracts are created. The less data there is to feed dss analysis, the greater the need for generations of extracts of data. The types of redundancy found in Figure 53—which are common throughout the traditional DP community—illustrate just how much wasted DASD there is.

Redundancy and the Architected Environment

Now consider the architected environment, as depicted by Figure 54.

In Figure 54, the operational environment is subject-oriented. The change to the subject orientation from the application orientation, in and of itself, reduces redundancy of data and the amount of DASD required. In addition, creating the atomic-level data allows all detailed archival data to be stored in one place, not in many places. There is no need for massive amounts of redundancy between production and dss data bases. The detailed archival information is readily available in the atomic data

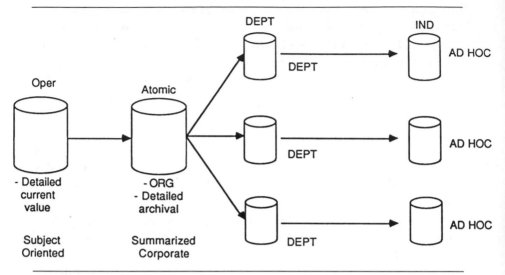

FIGURE 54 The architected environment.

base; thus, the dss analyst has no predisposition to grab as much data as possible (as was the case in the traditional systems development environment).

In addition, the atomic data base provides a convenient place to store commonly used summarized dss data. There is no need to store (or calculate!) the same summary data in multiple places throughout the dss environment.

Finally, because the atomic and departmental data bases provide such a robust (and believable!) source of information, there is a minimal need for generations of extracts. The savings show up as a minimal need for DASD.

The full effect of the lessened need for DASD is illustrated by Figure 55.

There are four cases shown in Figure 55. There is the unarchitected simple case, the architected simple case, the unarchitected complex case, and the architected complex case. The full differences in terms of total amount of DASD are not obvious in the simple case. The real differences in DASD show up in the more complex cases. The more complex the case, the more DASD is needed. There are several reasons for this phenomenon.

The more production (i.e., unarchitected, application-oriented) data bases there are, the more redundancy there is among those data bases.

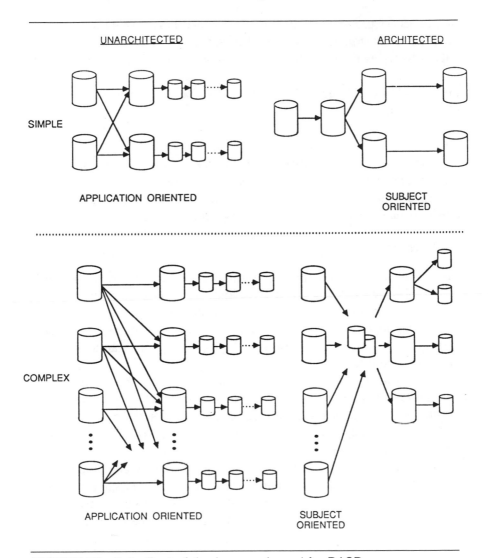

FIGURE 55 Full effect of the lessened need for DASD.

And the more production data bases there are, the more competition there is to access the data. The more competition there is for access, the greater the motivation of the dss analyst to grab and duplicate as much data as possible (thus minimizing the need to return to the production data base for further access of data). In a simple environment, the dss analyst feels free to access production data on an as-needed basis. There is no strong motivation for storage of detailed data at the dss level when production data is freely available. The net result of the above discussion is clear:

Less DASD—much less DASD—is needed for the architected environment.

Of course, this observation is made from the perspective of the entire environment. When the political turf is broken up so that no one entity has global responsibility, then it is easy to dwell on much narrower, much more parochial perspectives that, in a vacuum, do not lead to the conclusions made here by viewing the larger perspective.

SUMMARY

The technical foundation of the information paradigm is seated in hardware, software, and data communications. The foundation may be centralized or decentralized at any level, except that atomic-level data and processing are almost always centralized. The thrust of operational processing for hardware and software is high-performance transactions and high-availability data.

The thrust of atomic processing is management of bulk amounts of data in a sequential or batch mode. In addition, the atomic level needs to interface with a wide diversity of hardware and software.

The thrust of departmental processing is a mixture of processors doing a wide variety of tasks.

Individual processing centers around high flexibility and autonomy.

The data communications component of the technical architecture centers around capacity and capability. Capacity is the issue in flowing data from the operational to atomic levels. Capability is the issue in flowing data from the atomic to the departmental and operational levels.

CHAPTER 4 CONCEPTUAL FOUNDATIONS OF THE INFORMATION PARADIGM

L ike the glacier that is shaped by snow, ice and sun, the information paradigm is shaped by several disparate forces working in concert. It may seem farfetched to equate the union of precipitation with a freezing temperature to the mighty force of a glacier, but farfetched as it seems, there exists an authentic relationship. In the same vein, several seemingly unrelated, innocent concepts form the basis of the information paradigm. The different concepts, and their influences on the information paradigm, will be discussed.

PRIMITIVE/DERIVED SEPARATION

Perhaps the most basic concept underlying the information paradigm is the notion that primitive data and derived data are actually different from each other and should be separated—logically and physically. The fundamental differences between primitive and derived data have been discussed in Chapter 1. The deliberate separation of the two types of data appears to run contrary to one of the most widely accepted maxims of data base—"No Redundancy of Data Should Exist in a Data Base Environment."

The existence of primitive and derived data appears to violate the redundancy maxim. Derived data is inherently redundant, both with other derived data and with primitive data, since primitive data is the source of derived data. But, primitive data *is* essentially different from derived data, and the redundancy maxim must be considered in the historical context in which it was conceived.

Consider the world of explosive growth of master files, as depicted in Figure 34. As the data processing world began to drown in redundant data and a plethora of master files, it was obvious that something had to be done to reduce data redundancy and the problems it brought about. So the maxim of no data redundancy was born and was called the "data base concept." But the redundancy of data that was being addressed at the time, for the most part, was that for operational processing. When the maxim evolved, the vast majority of master files that were creating problems were, far and away, for operational systems. The difference between operational and decision support processing was not clearly recognized at that time. Indeed, derived data was not a real issue in the early days of information technology, since there was little or no basis for derivation of data. In retrospect, the redundancy maxim more properly should have been "No Redundancy of Data Should Exist in an Operational Data Base Environment." But it didn't read that way, and since that time much data base theory has existed that attempts to do away with *all* redundancy of data.

The evolution to the information paradigm is seen no better than in the evolution of data base management systems. The article—DATA BASES COME OF AGE—provides a broad perspective of the ongoing evolution of DBMS productions.

*DATA BASES COME OF AGE**

It is interesting to compare the computer industry with other industries. The computer industry is, after all, new compared with most other major industries. That it is immature is not a disparaging remark—the immaturity of the industry is merely a statement of its age, which is a mere quarter of a century or so.

Contrast the age of the computer industry with those of other industries, such as construction (remember roads that could get you to Rome from wherever?) or accounting (remember the hieroglyphics on the walls of the tombs of the Egyptian pharaohs?). The worlds of software and data base management systems in particular are still in their formative stages.

Compare the data base industry with the automotive industry. In 1910, the automobile marketplace was dominated by a very few models—Model T Fords, for example. The Model T, in 1910, was a general-purpose vehicle. It served to carry chickens to market, the

*By W.H. Inmon, *Computerworld*, September 1987. Reprinted with permission

family to church on Sundays, the salesman from one town to the next and so forth.

Look at the automotive industry today. There is a wide variety of forms of personal transportation—motorcycles, trucks, sedans and Ferraris are but a few. The industry has branched out and created a product for the many niches in the marketplace. A general-purpose Model T in today's marketplace would simply be an anachronism.

Contrast the automotive marketplace with the data base marketplace. In the early dawn of the data base market—around 1960 or so—what did you have? The pioneers that attracted attention in the marketplace were Cincom's Total, IBM's IMS and SAS Institute's System 2000. If you were doing anything on data bases at all, you were using one of these products because that was all there was. At the same time, these were general-purpose products that served whatever data base needs arose. These data base products may be considered the Model Ts of the industry.

AGE OF SPECIALIZATION

But look at the data base marketplace today. What you find is a wide variety of specialized products—Ashton-Tate's Dbase II for microprocessors, Information Builders' Focus for end users, ACP for trans-

action processing and so forth. Predictably, the data base market has reacted just as the automotive marketplace has, by rewarding the specialists. Clearly, the world is staunchly turning toward the specialized data base package.

The result is the storage of data in many forms in many data bases. A by-product of the specialization that has occurred is the prolific redundancy of data. In short order, the specialization of the data base marketplace has mandated that the dual data base approach is the wave of the future.

But there is some curious thinking that can be found in both the marketplace and academia. Many of the mainstream vendors in the market doggedly cling to the notion that a single DBMS will serve all needs. These companies are trying to extend the Model T to serve the needs of hauling hay to market, impressing your date on Saturday night and taking the family on a vacation. The result is a monstrous polyglot that is neither glamorous, efficient nor capable of hauling large loads.

Dual data bases, redundancy of data and specialization rather than generalization are reality, and there doesn't appear to be any turning back. The vendors that firmly entrench their products in concepts rooted in the 1960s are doomed to creating and proliferating museum pieces.

The information paradigm recognizes the difference between primitive and derived data, and it recognizes that primitive data forms the foundation for operational systems and that derived data forms the foundation for decision support systems. The profound differences between operational processing and decision support processing are supported by the paradigm in the physical separation of the two environments.

The information paradigm also recognizes that derived data requires redundancy—redundancy and derived data go hand in hand. Of course, there are classical problems associated with redundant data, but many of them are addressed by the architecture and discipline of processing associated with the information paradigm.

If there is a simple example of the economic justification of the natural separation of primitive and derived data, it may be either the airlines reservation environment or the banking ATM environment. In either of those environments, the importance of online performance is such that the processor on which those primitive processes run is dedicated to them. If derived data and derived processing were attempted on the same machine on which huge amounts of high performance transaction processing is done, the result would be the need for a much larger processor and the larger processor is expensive. The economics of the information paradigm dictate that the processors be separate.

RECOGNITION OF COMMONALITY/PRESERVATION OF UNIQUENESS

A second major concept underlying the information paradigm is the recognition that some data and some processing are common in many places in the environment, and that other data and other processes are unique. Systems built under the information paradigm must account for *both* the commonality and the uniqueness of data and processing. As an example of the commonality of data and processing, consider the processing done for an insurance company that offers several kinds of policies—fire, life, health, and so forth.

There is a tremendous amount of commonality across the different insurance lines—the processing of claims, the management of premiums, and expenses, for example. The systems that recognize the commonality are able to capitalize on the fact that common code and data need be built only once. Of course, in the case of the insurance company, there is much unique data and processing, as well as common data and processing, that must also be accounted for.

The commonality and uniqueness of primitive data is the central focus of the information paradigm. The modeling technique for the recognition of commonality and uniqueness is illustrated by Figure 56.

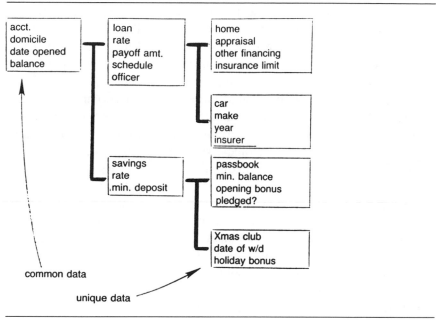

FIGURE 56 Modeling technique for the recognition of commonality and uniqueness.

Figure 56 shows that account information can be for loans or savings. A loan may be a home loan or a car loan, and a savings account can be a passbook or a Christmas Club account. Information that is common to all accounts is shown existing at the account level, such as domicile and date of opening. (In other words, regardless of the type of account, domicile and date of opening must exist and must be processed.) More specific information is at the loan and savings level. All loans have a rate and payment schedule, but rate and payment schedules are specific to loans and not to savings accounts. At the most specific level, car loans identify characteristics of the car and home loans identify characteristics of the home. In Figure 56, the common information exists in the left upper part of the diagram, and the unique information exists in the bottom right part of the diagram.

Carried to its logical conclusion, the recognition of commonality leads the system designer to organize information around the major subjects of the enterprise. Consider how the recognition of commonality and uniqueness has evolved, from a historical context.

In the earliest systems built, the emphasis was on the mimicking of existing manual operations. From that environment rose the development practice of "local" development of systems, in which a limited set of requirements was analyzed and a system was built. The set of requirements used to formulate the system was so small that the commonality of processing with other systems was not recognized. For example, (using the insurance company) one system processes life claims; another system processes Texas auto policy claims; another processes commercial health claims for the government sector; another system processes Colorado auto claims; another system processes health claims from automobile manufacturers, and so forth. Each small system is based on its own, unique "local" perspective, not recognizing that much processing and data are being duplicated among all the different claims systems.

The information paradigm specifically singles out commonality and consolidates it as part of the discipline of the formulation of the paradigm.

The recognition of the commonality of data and processing and the ensuing consolidation that is possible have real economic benefit. For example, a bank creates a single policy system that handles loans, savings, CDs, checking, and so forth. The policy code is written in one and only one place, rather than for each function. Suppose there are 120 different functions that require standard policy management in one form or another. There is a potential economic gain of 10 to 1 by writing policy code in one place.

Subject Orientation/ERD Orientation of the Information Paradigm

The conceptual orientation of recognizing commonality of data and processing leads directly and naturally to the subject orientation/ERD (entity relationship diagram) orientation of the paradigm. The subject orientation/ERD orientation of data and processing refers to organizing data around the major subjects or major entities of the enterprise (rather than the applications of the enterprise). By recognizing the major subjects, the consolidation of requirements—where there is a high degree of commonality—is natural and easy. Figure 57 illustrates the difference between the classical, "local" approach of systems and the subject (or entity) orientation.

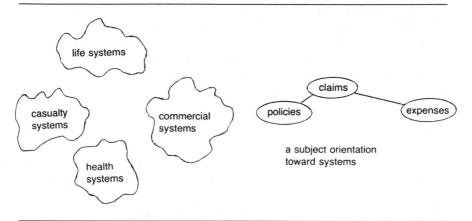

FIGURE 57 Difference between the classical, "local" approach of systems and the subject orientation.

The influence of the business of the enterprise is obvious. Each subject directly represents major areas of business. Indeed, the *complete* set of activities of the enterprise is represented by the subjects of the enterprise.

Data/Process Relationship

The information paradigm takes the philosophy that both data and processes shape the paradigm and are equal partners. Neither data nor processes enjoy a position of hegemony at the expense of the other. The Chinese symbol of Yin and Yang represent the equal, complementary relationship of data and processing.

FIGURE 58 The interrelationship of data and processes is illustrated by the Chinese symbol of Yin and Yang.

Historically, the pendulum of emphasis in the design of systems has swung from process to data and back. In the early days of systems development, there was unquestionably a strong emphasis on process analysis and process design. In those days, it was said that data was a by-product of processing. Indeed, during the explosive proliferation of master files and redundancy of data, data *was* a by-product of processing.

But the emphasis shifted toward a subject orientation of data as the inadequacies of master files became apparent, and the pendulum swung toward data analysis. As master files began to be scrutinized, the technique of data normalization arose. The result of normalization was the organization and consolidation of data according to the relationships of data elements found on master files. Data normalization involves a thorough analysis of data and little or no analysis of processes.

But the pendulum is swinging back from an almost exclusive focus on analysis of data to a more balanced approach with the advent of information engineering. Information engineering (as described in *Information Engineering for the Practitioner*, Yourdon Press, 1988) calls for normalization of processes as well as data, and for the derivation of data and processes from the business of the enterprise (rather than from the master files of the enterprise).

SEPARATION OF ADMINISTRATIVE DATA AND PROCESSING

Another conceptual foundation of the information paradigm is the need for the separation of administrative data and processing from data and processing related to the everyday operations of the enterprise. There is no question as to the existence or validity of administrative information. Certainly, administrative information is valid. But the mixture of administrative and operational information in the information paradigm is discouraged in all but the most stringent cases. Figure 59 illustrates the separation of administrative and operational information.

There has been little mixing of the two environments in the past, and the information paradigm reinforces the separation. [Note: In a few limited cases, administrative and operational information must be mixed. Such a case occurs in the manufacturing environment, where a worker is paid on a piecework basis. The output of day-to-day operations is directly linked to pay, which is an administrative unit of information.]

FIGURE 59 Deliberate separation of administrative and operational information is a regular part of the information paradigm.

Separate Manipulation of Derived Information

One of the foundations of the information paradigm is the separation of primitive and derived data. And much emphasis—data modeling, requirements analysis, and so forth—is placed on firmly establishing the requirements of the primitive data environment. But the derived environment is at least an equal partner to the primitive environment. Some of the major differences between the primitive and derived environments include:

- The primitive environment focuses on efficiency of processing; the dss environment focuses on effectiveness.
- The primitive environment addresses the day-to-day operations of the enterprise; the derived environment addresses the considerations made by the upper level of management.
- The structure of the primitive environment seldom changes (or at least changes at a very conservative pace); the structure of the derived environment changes very rapidly, as quickly as management develops an interest in a new perspective of the enterprise.
- The primitive environment is static and is not adaptive; the derived environment is highly adaptive and relies upon the primitive environment for its basis.

The manipulation of derived data is done in a free-form manner for the most part. Given the tools geared for ease of use and flexibility that are found in the derived environment, and given the need of the dss analyst to constantly change the interpretation, usage, content, etc., of derived data, it makes sense *not* to analyze and architect most of the derived environment. Instead of spending large amounts of analytical resources in the pursuit of defining the details of the architected environment (which change faster than they can be modeled), it is easier and more efficient to simply build the derived systems and heuristically alter them on an as-needed basis. The tools found in the derived environment lend themselves greatly to this orientation.

The derivation of data from its primitive basis is not to be taken as a trivial task, however. The derivation needs to be properly executed. As analysis is done and primitive data is separated from derived data, the basis for derivation from the primitive environment is captured.

For example, the data element Cumulative Monthly Sales is encountered during analysis. Cumulative Monthly Sales is a derived data element, since multiple activities are represented and cumulative sales do not depend on the existence of any given department. The primitive basis is individual sales by date by department. As long as the detailed primitive data is represented in the model, the derived data can be calculated at the departmental level. Thus, derived data elements of major importance do have their primitive algorithmic foundation analyzed and documented. But many derived data elements do not have a carefully delineated foundation outlined in the primitive environment, nor is there a need for such a careful delineation. Consequently, the foundation for derivation of data from the primitive to the derived environment is only partially laid, in the best of cases.

Relational Data Base Organization/Existence Dependency

The information paradigm depends on the discipline in the grouping of data elements. The historical basis for organizing data elements stems from the early days of relational theory. Relational theory calls for the normalization of data. Data normalization mandates that any given data element exists as a function of its key, its whole key, and nothing but its key.

There are several levels of normalization. Most practitioners advocate going to three levels. The first level requires the removal of repeating groups. The second level requires the identification of the immediate dependency of data. And the third level requires the identification of secondary dependencies of groups of data. Figures 60-a through 60-d illustrate the different steps of normalization.

A very similar analytical process for the organization of data elements based on existence dependency criteria is associated with the information

Unnormalized Data Elements

date employee attended school	net pay
school attended	number of dependents
degree sought	married/single?
major	special deductions amount(1)
social security number	special deductions amount(2)
employee number	special deductions amount(3)
cumulative FICA paid	special deductions amount(4)
cumulative annual pay	limits of deductibility(1)
cumulative annual state tax	limits of deductibility(2)
cumulative annual federal tax	limits of deductibility(3)
date of hire	limits of deductibility(4)
location of hire	FICA per pay period
dependent(1) identification	state tax per pay period
dependent(2) identification	federal tax per pay period
dependent(3) identification	insurer number
dependent(4) identification	liability limits
dependent(1) relationship	date of insurance coverage
dependent(2) relationship	accident coverage amount
dependent(3) relationship	illness coverage amount
dependent(4) relationship	death coverage amount
date of pay(1)	
date of pay(2)	
date of pay(3)	
. . . .	
. . . .	
. . . .	
date of pay(n)	

FIGURE 60-a Unnormalized data elements.

paradigm. (Refer to *Information Engineering for the Practitioner*, Yourdon Press, 1988, for an in-depth discussion of existence dependency criteria.) Organization of data elements according to existence dependency criteria mandates that data be organized according to the existence of the data element on the key *and* that the existence dependency criteria of any two data elements grouped together be the same.

For example, using the key Employee Number and the data elements of birth date, sex, date of hire, location of hire, and beginning salary as an example, simple existence dependency allows the data elements to be

Normalized Data Elements—First Normal Form

date employee attended school	net pay
school attended	number of dependents
degree sought	married/single?
major	special deductions amount
social security number	limits of deductibility
employee number	FICA per pay period
cumulative FICA paid	state tax per pay period
cumulative annual pay	federal tax per pay period
cumulative annual state tax	insurer number
cumulative annual federal tax	liability limits
date of hire	date of insurance coverage
location of hire	accident coverage amount
dependent identification	illness coverage amount
dependent relationship	death coverage amount
date of pay	

FIGURE 60-b   Normalized data elements—first normal form.

Normalized Data Elements—Second Normal Form

employee number	(pay history relationship)
date of hire	pay date
location of hire	net pay
	FICA paid
(dependent relationship)	state tax paid
dependent's id	federal tax paid
dependent's relationship	
	(insurance relationship)
(pay relationship)	insurer number
cumulative FICA	liability limits
cumulative pay	date of coverage
cumulative state tax	accident coverage
cumulative federal tax	illness coverage
	death coverage
(education relationship)	
school	(deduction relationship)
degree	number dependents
date attended	married/single?
	special deduction amounts
	limits of deductibility

FIGURE 60-c   Normalized data elements—second normal form.

Employee Base Table	Pay History Table
employee number date of hire location of hire	employee number pay date net pay FICA paid state tax paid
Dependent Table	
employee number dependent id dependent relationship	**Insurance Table**
Annual Pay Table	employee number insurer number liability limits date of coverage accident coverage death coverage
employee number year social security number cumulative FICA cumulative pay cumulative state tax cumulative federal tax	**Deduction Parameter Table**
Education Table	employee number deduction types number dependents married/single? special deduction amounts limits of deductibility
employee number school date attended degree/other	

FIGURE 60-d Data elements that have been normalized and organized into tables.

grouped together. If there is no employee, then there is no birth date, sex, date of hire, and so forth. But existence dependency criteria require that data elements have the same criteria for existence, and sex and birth date have very different existence criteria than do date of hire, location of hire, and beginning salary. Existence criteria mandate that two groupings of data be created, one for each existence criterion.

Another difference between classic normalization and existence dependency criteria is that normalization assumes that data elements are given (usually taken from existing systems), and existence dependency analysis assumes that data elements are to be gathered from an analysis of the enterprise.

The information paradigm supports the notion of normalization in that data at the operational and the atomic level is normalized.

STANDARD WORK UNIT

At the heart of the performance and resource utilization within the architecture is the standard work unit (SWU). The SWU addresses the issue of online performance. It historically appeared as the first large online systems were being built. The first online systems merely mimicked earlier batch predecessors in design, and the result was that, as the online workload grew, performance significantly worsened. The first reaction to poor performance was to tune the system. The first tuning efforts produced (usually!) favorable results, but very soon the effects of tuning produced marginal or negligible results. One of the reasons for the ineffectiveness of tuning is that it attempted to optimize a given workload or configuration of an online system. But the workload and the configuration were constantly changing; consequently, tuning was the equivalent of shooting at a moving target.

The next attempt to achieve performance resulted in the purchasing of more processing power. To some extent, bigger and faster processors did boost performance, but other problems quickly appeared. Purchasing larger processors was an expensive way to boost performance, and the boost usually melted away rapidly. Furthermore, for really large online systems, many shops were already processing on the biggest computer available, so that purchasing more hardware was not an option.

The third approach to achieving good online performance was to address the issues of performance at the moment of design. Thus was born the SWU. The SWU mandates that processing be broken into small units. So the classical large, multifunction batch processes that were put online were broken into a series of small transactions, which separately accomplished a limited function and collectively accomplished the business function. An analogy that explains the dynamics of the SWU is the hourglass, as shown in Figures 61-a and 61-b

Figures 61-a and 61-b show two hourglasses—one with small, regularly shaped grains of sand and another with larger pebbles mixed in with the grains of sand. In the hourglass with normal grains of sand, flow is even and efficient. In the hourglass with pebbles and sand, flow is irregular and inefficient. The hourglass is like an online processor and the grains of sand are like the processes executing inside the processor. When the grains of sand are small and uniform in size, performance is optimal. When transactions of different sizes are mixed together, performance is mixed.

The information paradigm supports the SWU in that primitive and derived processing are separated into different environments. Primitive processing is where online performance is most important and is (fortunately) where processes can be broken into their finest, most granular packaging. Derived processes are typically executed where performance is much less of an issue, and derived processes usually consume large amounts of resources. Derived processes typically are not broken into small units of processing. The result is that the separation of primitive and derived processing is very much aligned with the SWU.

One example of the fine granularity of primitive processes is airline reservation transactions. Even though the clerk can do a whole range of functions, each function is done a small step at a time. From the perspective of the computer, the broad range of functions amounts to a series of related yet separate transactions. And the airline reservation environment is one of the highest-performing environments in existence.

Contrast the primitive processing in the airline environment with the year-end processing of a large retail organization. At the end of the year, *much* derived processing must occur. Annual reports, quarterly reports, and tax accounting are but a few of these derived processes. There are few performance (i.e., online performance) criteria or requirements for year-end derived processing. It hardly matters whether a report finishes running at 2:00 A.M. or 2:02 A.M. The processing that is occurring is packaged in large units that run undisturbed by much else than an occasional checkpoint.

Accuracy of Data and Credibility of Decision Support Processing

Accuracy of data is an issue in the operational environment. If there exists inaccurate operational data, either the enterprise or the customer (or both!) are in for unwarranted surprises. But credibility of data is at the foundation of decision support processing as well, since the decision support environment directly depends on data. If the data in the dss environment suffers from credibility and cannot be believed, then the question must be asked, why even do dss processing in the first place? Credibility of data—both operational and dss data—is a very important force that must be reckoned with.

The information paradigm mandates that the system of record contain nonredundant data. As a consequence, the credibility exposures in this

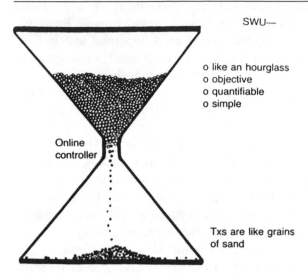

SWU—

o like an hourglass
o objective
o quantifiable
o simple

Online
controller

Txs are like grains
of sand

FIGURE 61-a The standard work unit — transactions (txs) are like grains of sand and the online processor is like an hourglass. As long as only grains of sand flow through the hourglass, the flow is uniform and efficient.

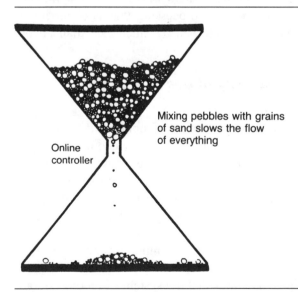

Mixing pebbles with grains
of sand slows the flow
of everything

Online
controller

FIGURE 61-b When pebbles are mixed with the grains of sand, then the flow through the hourglass becomes ragged and inefficient.

environment are minimized. And, since derived data is removed from primitive data in the operational environment, if special measures need to be taken to ensure accuracy in the operational environment, the operational environment is uncluttered by volumes of data. The result is that the operational environment has the minimum amount of data to be managed, thus rendering the most freedom at the design level.

The credibility of decision support processing is supported in the information paradigm by the existence of the atomic level of dss data. If there is ever a dispute as to the accuracy of dss data, the atomic level exists as a basis for reconciliation. In addition, the discipline in the creation and population of the different levels of data ensures that if discrepancies occur, they can be resolved.

One of the paradoxes of processing capability is that while CPU processing has become significantly cheaper and more powerful over time, DASD processing has not followed suit. Instead of more CPU capability, the world of data processing has been stymied by the lack of disk processing capability. What is needed is not faster CPUs but applications that avoid unnecessary I/O (input/output operation).

FROM A BROAD PERSPECTIVE

The information paradigm, then, satisfies several major bodies of thought. It is, after all, the product of several major forces at work. From performance considerations to the subject orientation of data, the information paradigm accommodates—gracefully—the different foundations of information processing. The eclectic collection of forces, like sun, snow, and ice working on a glacier shape the information paradigm into a cohesive, gracefully flowing whole.

SUMMARY

The primary conceptual foundation of the information paradigm is the separation of primitive and derived data. This separation contradicts the notion of a single data base serving all purposes.

The consolidation of commonality of data and the preservation of uniqueness is another concept fundamental to the information paradigm. The result of the consolidation of commonality is the organization of data around the major subjects of the enterprise.

The information paradigm reinforces the separation of administrative and operational systems.

The standard work unit (SWU) greatly reinforces the separation of data into operational and dss processing.

5 IMPLICATIONS OF THE INFORMATION PARADIGM

*T*he information paradigm, that is, data architecture, is the product of a long-term evolution much like the valleys and waterfalls left behind by the glacier. Like the product of most evolutions, the realization of the information paradigm is:

- Slow enough that marginal changes are often missed, and
- Powerful enough that resisting the evolution is not fruitful.

Information systems and technology that are in harmony with the information paradigm prosper; information systems and technology that run counter to the paradigm, in the long run, will be discarded. Thus, the information paradigm is a powerful crucible that can be used to both explain and predict what technology and what systems will succeed and what ones will not. Those vendors and managers that position their systems and technology properly ride the crest of a powerful wave. Those that do not position their systems and technology properly face frustration. This chapter will discuss some successes and failures (and some popular myths) in terms of the information paradigm.

MYTH # 1: "PERSONAL COMPUTERS WILL REPLACE MAINFRAMES"

In the early days of the growth of personal computers, there was speculation that personal computers would replace mainframes (and mini-computers) on a wholesale basis. Indeed, it was noted that the IBM XT and AT processors had the computing power of the early line of the IBM 360 processors (which set the stage for IBM's mainframe growth in the early 1960s). Many analysts viewed the growth of computing power generically, saying that computer power was common across different processors. But the anticipated wholesale displacement of mainframe and minicomputer processors by personal computers simply never materialized. Certainly, there was some marginal displacement, but no wholesale displacement.

The reason for the lack of the predicted wholesale displacement of mainframes by microprocessors can be explained in terms of the information paradigm. The information paradigm clearly separates different kinds of processing. Figure 62 shows the information paradigm and how different processors fit within it.

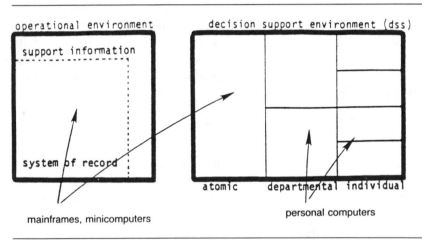

FIGURE 62   The information paradigm and how different processors fit within it.

In Figure 62, mainframes and minicomputers are used in one part of the information paradigm and personal computers are used elsewhere, for the most part. The essential differences between mainframes and personal computers show up in the audience they serve and in the way they are used. They point out that computing power is not generic. In other words, a single mainframe processor with n units of power is not the equivalent of n personal computers with one unit of power.

The early predictions, then, of personal computers replacing mainframes on a wholesale basis did not factor in the differences clearly spelled out by the information paradigm. The growth of personal computers filled a need—that of individual dss processing—but did not displace other processing.

There are, of course, operational systems that reside solely on personal computers. In this case, either the organization using the computer is small enough not to need a larger processor or it coordinates its processing closely over multiple small processors.

In the first case, where there are enterprises whose complete needs are serviced by a personal computer, there usually is not a displacement of mainframe processing because the enterprise is too small ever to have justified a mainframe computer in the first place.

The second type of application, where multiple personal computers make up a network that collectively does operational processing, is not a terribly widespread phenomenon because of:

- The complexity and costs of networking,
- The limitations on the amount of data that can be stored and forwarded on the network,
- The coordination and control needed to establish and administer a system of record,
- The control needed to maintain the "purity" of application code,
- The difficulty in doing classically centralized jobs such as year-end reporting, accounts receivable, accounts payable, etc.

For (at least!) these reasons, there has not been a massive movement to operational systems of the second variety on the personal computer.

MYTH #2: "4GL TECHNOLOGY YIELDS PRODUCTIVITY GAINS OF UP TO 1,000 PERCENT AND IS A TOOL TO REDUCE THE DATA PROCESSING BACKLOG"

4GL technology is designed for ease of use, quick construction of systems, and quick changes of systems. 4GL technology is ideal for the heuristic processing that typifies decision support processing. Unquestionably, 4GL technology is more compact and more powerful than earlier technology, in the sense that one line of 4GL code controls the execution of more machine instructions than one line of third-generation code.

But to say that 4GL technology reaps a 1,000 percent gain in productivity is misleading unless the information paradigm is factored into the equation. When the decision support analyst uses COBOL or PL-1 for heuristic dss processing, 4GL technology probably will yield significant productivity gains. But for the programmer building high-performance online systems, 4GL technology will not yield productivity gains, simply because 4GL technology is not an appropriate tool to be used for those kinds of systems. Figure 63 shows where different software tools fit in the information paradigm.

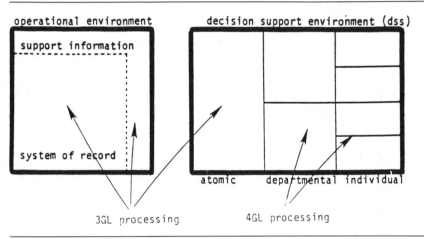

FIGURE 63 Different software tools in the information paradigm.

4GL technology simply is not appropriate to many forms of operational processing, and it is no wonder, then, that it has done very little, if anything, for the data processing development backlog. If the backlog of data processing development is for operational systems, then 4GL technology has no bearing on its reduction. Of course, if the backlog is made up of decision support needs, then 4GL technology will apply. The information paradigm provides a valid framework for understanding what role 4GL technology plays and what productivity gains can realistically be achieved.

The evolution of DBMS products can be characterized as the "march of the dual data bases". For years theoreticians had been proclaiming that a single data base technology would serve all data base needs. While most practitioners paid lip service to that notion, the marketplace strongly reinforced that different types of data base technology would be the wave of the future.

The advent of the information paradigm signals the end of the outdated notion that a single technology best serves the data base needs of the world.

The article—TWO DBMS TYPES SEEN EMERGING—is one of many articles written in the days when the issue of dual data base was in debate.

*TWO DBMS TYPES SEEN EMERGING**

It seems that an evolution is occurring in data bases in the mid-1980s. In the large mainframe environment, the most complete embodiment of the original notion of data base was the "full-function" data base management system (DBMS). This is one that fulfilled the original goals of the data base while interfacing with or containing a teleprocessing monitor and interfacing with a standard operating system. It also handled a wide range of application functions and could handle both small and very large amounts of data. The standard for the full-function DBMS was IBM's IMS.

But there are signs that the DBMS is evolving from a full-function DBMS toward two types of DBMS—a high-performance DBMS and a decision support DBMS (Figure 1). The evolution is shaped by the realization that high-performance DBMS do not make a good foundation for MIS and that decision support systems do not make a good foundation for operational systems.

One trait of a high-performance DBMS is the very high arrival rate of on-line transactions that can be

sustained. In a full-function DBMS, a sustained arrival rate of 20 transactions per second is very good. But in looking at future needs, it is not inconceivable to think in terms of 200 transactions per second.

Another trait of high-performance DBMS is the ability to manage very large amounts of data. The data bases kept by credit bureaus, insurance companies and government agencies fit into this category.

A third criterion for high-performance systems is on-line update data integrity. The on-line update of transactions must remain pure, that is, not interfered with by other on-line transactions acting on the same data at the same time. High-performance systems are optimized to operate on the units of data (segments, records and the like) of a data base rather than on the entire data base. The primary thrust is toward on-line systems, with fast, limited access of data.

Mixing the three criteria is quite challenging. The result is a system that is useful for operational control of a company. Not surprisingly, the high-performance DBMS environment is quite complex. Reading between the lines of IBM's announcements of IMS Fast Path (for IMS 1.3) would indicate that IBM

---

*By W.H. Inmon, *Computerworld*, February 1984. Reprinted with permission.

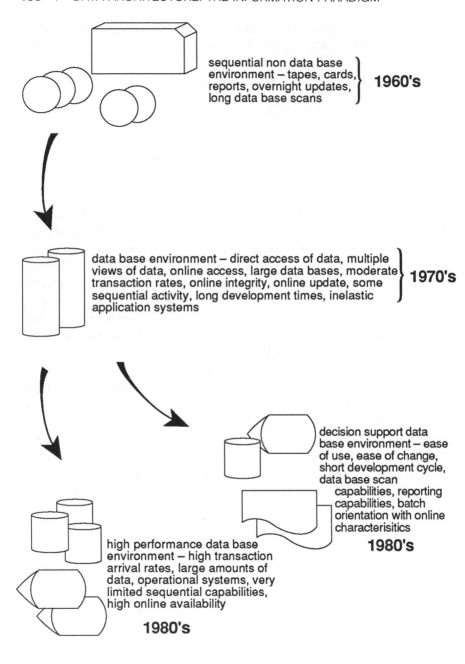

sequential non data base environment – tapes, cards, reports, overnight updates, long data base scans } **1960's**

data base environment – direct access of data, multiple views of data, online access, large data bases, moderate transaction rates, online integrity, online update, some sequential activity, long development times, inelastic application systems } **1970's**

decision support data base environment – ease of use, ease of change, short development cycle, data base scan capabilities, reporting capabilities, batch orientation with online characterisitics

1980's

high performance data base environment – high transaction arrival rates, large amounts of data, operational systems, very limited sequential capabilities, high online availability

1980's

The High Performance Environment

The Decision Support Environment

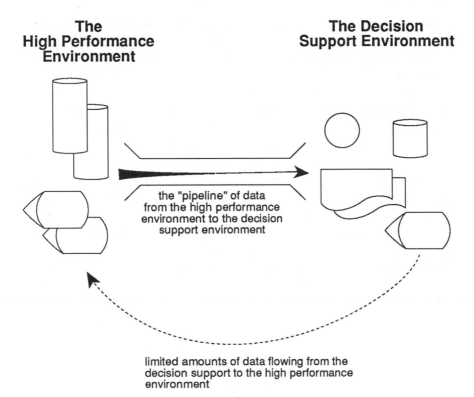

the "pipeline" of data
from the high performance
environment to the decision
support environment

limited amounts of data flowing from the
decision support to the high performance
environment

intends to fill the future needs for high-performance software with Fast Path.

The first-quarter 1984 enhancements of Fast Path extend the capabilities of the previous version significantly. The migration from IMS Full Function to Fast Path is an evolutionary one, not a revolutionary one.

While high-performance DBMS have many operational capabilities, in general they must be used very carefully as they are difficult to change. What is springing up in the void are decision support data base software packages that serve a dif-

ferent audience. Decision support software is easy to change and easy to use in developing new systems.

This software is especially appropriate for unstable environments where the basic form of data is subject to constant and unpredictable change. The difficulties with the long development cycles that are common to high-performance systems are not the same in the decision support environment.

The decision support environment is optimized to manipulate entire data bases in a single request and, to a lesser extent, the units of data within the data base. While there are certain on-line character-istics of decision support software, most of it is designed to operate in a batch or sequential mode.

In environments where there is more than a moderate amount of activity and/or where there are large amounts of data, the activities are restricted to limited queries of data. The full range of decision support activities such as updates, large scans of data and other activities requir-ing many resources are batched and run at night in a sequential mode. Decision support software is typi-fied by IBM's recently announced relational software.

The route from IMS Full Func-tion to relational is made easy by common calls and by extract and load facilities. Like the migration to Fast Path, the path to IBM's re-lational system is evolutionary.

If the very definition of data base is splitting into two directions, what does that portend for existing IMS Full Function applications? By vir-tue of the fact that there are literally billions of dollars of full-function applications in existence today, there is a momemtum that will not easily change.

VENDOR SUPPORT

What will happen is that as full-function applications reach the end of their life cycle, there will be en-couragement by vendors to rebuild the applications in modes other than full function.

High-performance and decision support software will almost cer-tainly not share the same main-frames. If there is a sharing of these resources, it will most likely be on a "duplexed" basis, where the sys-tems run during certain hours of the day in one mode and at other times in another mode. The basic oper-ating characteristics of the systems are such that they are mutually ex-clusive.

High-performance and decision support systems will share data by means of a "pipeline" connecting them. Entire data bases or large masses of activities will flow from the high-performance environment on a periodic basis.

REVERSE DATA FLOW

Limited amounts of data will flow in the reverse direction and under stringent conditions. The reverse flow of data will enter the high-per-formance environment through the sequential capabilities of the high-performance environment as seen in the figure on page 159.

The two types of DBMS operate in essentially different modes, and there will necessarily be wholesale duplication of data between the modes. Within the same mode of operation, there will be an absolute minimum of data duplication.

The direction of other vendors toward the multiple DBMS environment is not as clear as IBM's. The advertisements indicate that the direction is toward both high-performance and decision support at the same time. If that is the case, then Cullinet Software, Inc.'s IDMS appears to be heading for the old idea of a full-function DBMS being all things to all people.

Other DBMS vendors seem suit of their niches in the marketplace. These include Model 204, Mathematica Product Group, Inc.'s Ramis, Focus and others.

Those companies with a clear vision of where their role lies in the mainstream of evolution will prosper, whereas those without a clear understanding of the forces of evolution will wither.

MYTH #3: "BUILD IT QUICK NOW AND WE'LL TUNE IT LATER"

One of the early dogmas of systems development was to build the system quickly and worry about performance later. This attitude stemmed from the need for more and faster systems development that arose chiefly during the proliferation of master files. The medium on which most master files operate is magnetic tape, and batch performance is not at all the issue that online performance is. As the evolution of the information paradigm progressed (especially to the point of development of online systems), it was discovered that performance must be consciously designed into the system prior to building it. Attempting to create a high degree of performance after the system had already been built was folly. The evolution of the information paradigm, then, led to maturity beyond the development/tuning rule.

MYTH #4: "REDUNDANCY OF DATA IS UNDESIRABLE"

As has been previously discussed, the notion that redundancy of data is undesirable stems from the pandemonium that arose with the proliferation of master files. But redundancy of data is absolutely essential in the dss environment in order to achieve the high degree of flexibility and ease of use that is desired.

The information paradigm acknowledges the need for redundant data in the different levels of decision support data.

MYTH #5: "NORMALIZATION OF DATA IS THE FOUNDATION OF DATA ANALYSIS"

Normalization of data is one of the foundations of relational theory. And normalization of data and the similar analytical techniques of existence dependency do apply to the system of record. But normalization does not apply to the information paradigm across the board. Normalization applies almost exclusively to primitive data. Primitive data—reflecting the day-to-day activities of the enterprise—is very stable and structurally very slow to change.

Derived data, on the other hand, is constantly changing—in some cases on an hourly basis. Given the rate of change and the tools that are available, it makes sense to simply create and populate the new structures of data rather than go through a normalization exercise. Because data analysis applies across the spectrum of the information paradigm and normalization applies almost exclusively to primitive data, normalization has limited applicability to data analysis.

Another issue relating to the historical foundation of normalization is that normalization evolved as a technique that applied to the analysis of existing files. Nearly all the early writings on normalization assume that data elements are given. In other words, given data in file layout 1, file layout 2, and file layout 3, normalization was used to show how the data elements in the files could be organized meaningfully. But data analysis—done from a global basis—requires that data be derived from the business of the enterprise itself. In data analysis, in its pure form, data is not given; it is gathered. While normalization techniques can be adapted to treat derived data, a large part of data analysis is in the gathering of data.

Still another shortcoming of normalization is the lack of recognition of the differences between primitive and derived data. The fundamental differences between primitive and derived data are incidental to normalization. In short, normalization is a valid technique of data analysis, but it is only one of the foundations.

Interestingly, the notion of process normalization applies not only to data but to process analysis and design as well. The techniques of normalization can be used to organize massive amounts of program specifications. Process analysis, once normalized, yields a degree of "topdown" flow that is otherwise very difficult to achieve.

MYTH #6: "HARDWARE IS GETTING CHEAPER ALL THE TIME" (ERGO, "I CAN AFFORD TO SOLVE MY PROBLEMS BY BUYING MORE EQUIPMENT")

The unit cost of hardware has been dropping constantly over the years. But this popular myth—used in a self-serving manner by hardware manufacturers—overlooks several important points:

- The decrease in the cost of hardware is more than compensated by the increase in the units of hardware sold.
- The unit cost of hardware that is decreasing (i.e., the manufacturing cost) is almost incidental to the customer cost; in other words, the margin between manufacturing cost and sales cost is so large that the actual manufacturing cost of the hardware is incidental.

Hardware is most rapidly consumed in the attempt to enhance system performance—specifically online performance. When an organization attempts to build systems not in the mold of the information paradigm, there is a never-ending thirst for hardware. As operational and dss processing are mixed together, more and more hardware resources are consumed. But when an organization molds its systems according to the information paradigm, operational and dss processing are separated. The hardware required for operational processing is tuned *only* for operational systems. The result is that the organization is able to squeeze *much* more performance out of its hardware and the hardware budget is used most effectively.

SUMMARY

The information paradigm provides a framework around which many popular myths relating to technology achieve an air of reality:

- "Personal computers will replace mainframes"—in the departmental and individual levels of data, personal computers *will* replace mainframes, but in the operational and atomic levels of data, personal computers *will not* replace mainframes.
- "4GL technology yields productivity gains of up to 1000 percent"— 4GL technology will produce productivity gains in the departmental and the individual levels but not in the operational or atomic levels.
- "Build it quick now; tune it later"—applies to departmental and individual processing, not to operational or atomic processing.

- "Redundancy of data is undesirable"—in the operational and the atomic environments but not in the departmental or individual environments.
- "Normalization of data is the foundation for data analysis"—for atomic and operational data, not for departmental or individual levels of data.
- "Hardware is Getting Cheaper All the Time"—operational performance can be purchased, but only up to a point.

CHAPTER

6 SPECIFICS OF THE INFORMATION PARADIGM

When seen from afar, glaciers appear to have a few simple components: ice, snow, melt. But when examined closely, the components of the glacier appear in wide array. Only when examined closely and finely does the observer appreciate the variety of phenomena that make up the glacier.

The four data levels of the information paradigm—operational, atomic, departmental, and individual—have been described at a gross level in an earlier chapter. This chapter will describe them in much more detail and will present an example of data and processing at the different levels of the paradigm.

OPERATIONAL LEVEL

Data at the operational level is primitive detailed data for the most part. There is a high probability of access of operational data, which is accurate up to the second. Data in the system of record exists nonredundantly, so there is no need for synchronization of processing and no possibility of incorrectly accessing an inaccurate value.

For example, in the manufacturing environment, the date an order is received, who sent the order, the quantity and items ordered, and so forth, are all operational data. For an inventory system in a manufacturing environment, the amount on hand at any moment in time is another example of operational data.

There is a large volume of detailed data at the operational level, oriented toward the major subjects of the enterprise. The physical access of the data is random for the most part. The content is constantly changing; so the data is frequently updated. The structure of the data is very stable, changing only as major alterations are made to the business of the enterprise.

Operational data is designed and implemented so that it can be recovered or reorganized quickly. To achieve quick recovery and reorganization, data is partitioned either at the system or the application level (or at both levels).

Processing that occurs at the operational level can be characterized as primarily update processing, accomplished in small, discrete units. Each process uses a small amount of resources (I/O) and in doing so, creates an environment where high performance can be achieved. All online processing in the operational environment is highly structured; there is no unstructured processing that occurs there. High volumes of online transactions are the norm. The transaction workload is characterized in both total transactions per day and in terms of the maximum transaction arrival rate. While most of the processing in the operational environment is online, there is a batch window for extracts, utilities, sequential processing, and so forth.

Much of the processing at the operational level is for the update of discrete elements of data. Locating and changing data at the detailed level as the business changes is the primary work of the operational environment.

Most of the operational processing is within the system of record. Just as the integrity of data is important, so the integrity of processing is likewise important in the system of record. During the peak period of processing, capacity and the transaction arrival rate are the two main system constraints. During off-peak hours, the length of the batch window and the amount of batch processing to be done within the window are the main constraints. The nature of processing in the operational environment is record-at-a-time, using traditional tools.

A Banking Example

The entire data architecture with its different levels of data centers around the model that serves to unify the disparate levels of data. The data model has three levels of detail: The ERD level, the dis (or mid) level, and the detailed physical level. The ERD—shown at a very high level—for the banking example that will be developed is shown by Figure 64.

FIGURE 64   A very high-level ERD for the banking example.

Note that for the ERD, there is little detail shown beyond the identification of the entities and the relationships between them. The scarcity of detail at this level of modeling is deliberate, as detail at this high level only confuses the model. The emphasis at this point is on the identification of the major entities and the establishment of the major relationship among them.

The mid-level model—the dis—is shown for the accounts of the bank in Figure 65. (For an in-depth discussion of mid-level modeling, refer to *Information Systems Architecture*, Prentice-Hall, 1986.) There will appear a separate dis for each entity found in the ERD.

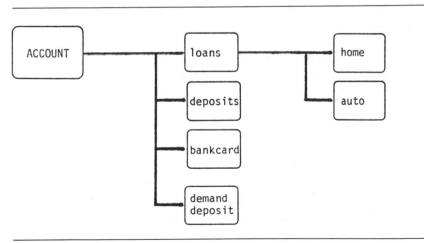

FIGURE 65   A high-level dis for the accounts that are in the banking example.

Figure 65 shows that there are four types of accounts: loans, deposits, bank card, and demand deposit (checking). There are two types of loans: home and car loans. From the dis, several tables of data are created, as shown in Figure 66.

ACCOUNT BALANCE	ACCOUNT-DEPOSITS
ACCOUNT-CURRENT ACTIVITY	ACCOUNT-LOANS
ACCOUNT-QUARTERLY ACTIVITY	ACCOUNT-BANKCARD
CUSTOMER	ACCOUNT-DDA
BANK CALENDAR	ACCOUNT

FIGURE 66 Some of the major files that exist in the operational environment.

Note that the account information is separated into different collections of data. There are balances, current activity, bank card, and so forth. Collections of data are logically related but are physically separate. The groupings of data at the dis level are separated, so that the existence of any nonkey data in a group directly depends on the key of the grouping of data for its existence.

The detailed data that exists in the operational environment is shown by Figure 67.

Figure 67 shows some of the pertinent data elements that can be found in the collections of data. Note that related information shares a common key. Account Number is found in several places but has a subkey to distinguish this grouping of data from other groupings of data, except, of course, for the base information that applies to all accounts.

Separating balance data

Also note that balance data is separated from activity data and other related account data. The separation is because of the performance characteristics of balance, which is one of the most heavily accessed pieces of data in the banking environment. The daily balance is calculated from many pieces of data—all daily activity and the previous balance. But

```
account current activity         account balance
account number                   account number
activity date                    account balance
amount
location
identification                   account
electronic id                    account number
teller id                        statement cycle
                                 customer id
                                 date opened
account loans                    transaction limits.
account number                   account type
officer
type
colateral id
limits
interest rate
terms
line of credit
```

FIGURE 67   Some of the details that exist in the operational environment.

balance is still a primitive data, since it relates to a single customer for a single moment in time.

The data found in the operational environment is, for the most part, current up to the second. Of course, there is a small amount of data found in the operational environment that is archival: the current activity file and the quarterly activity file contain archival data. Current activity is needed for monthly statement processing, and, consequently, its existence in the operational environment is justified. But other less popular archival data is not found in the operational environment.

Quarterly activity is kept in the operational environment because the odds are good that if a customer has an inquiry as to his or her accounts' status or activity, the activity in question will be no older than three months. However, three month's worth of activity in the operational environment is the outer limit, since data older than three months is rarely queried. There is, then, a high probability of usage of the archival data that is stored in the operational environment.

The processing that occurs in the operational environment is depicted by Figure 68.

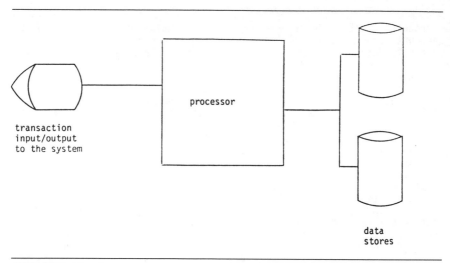

FIGURE 68 Simple processing configuration for the operational environment.

Transactions are entered online and processed—usually updating detailed data. The results of the processing are returned. The processor may be a single processor, as shown, or a series of processors that collectively present a single image. The data is often physically stored in multiple locations. Through the auspices of the model of data, there is close coordination of the content of data, forming a ''logical'' data base that is physically separated.

For example, one record that is processed may be in the southwest region data base; another record will be in the Western data base, and so forth. The physical displacement of data presents no obstacle because the data—and the ensuing processing against it—is controlled by the architecture.

The transaction gathering may be directly from a terminal to the system of record, or, the transaction may be gathered and processed through a front end system.

The emphasis in operational processing is on online transaction processing. The response to the customer is fast and accurate, satisfying his or her needs immediately.

Missing From the Operational Environment

The operational environment that has been described is of interest not so much for what is in it but for what is not in it. Some notable missing components follow.

–Batch processing. There are two kinds of batch processing that exist in the operational environment: batch processes used to support the background utilitarian functions, such as creating backup copies of data, and batch runs used to transform data from the operational to the dss environment. Most classical batch processing used to directly support customer services or usages of the system is gone. A few batch processes remain that indirectly support customer requirements such as monthly statement processing, but the direct, mainline services provided are done so online.

–Archival data. Compared to earlier operational systems built without the utility of an architecture, there is very little archival data found at the operational level in architected systems. The only archival data found at the operational level is the data that has a very high probability of access. The bulk of data that is typically associated with the archival environment is not found in the operational systems.

–Summary data. Like archival data, the only summary data found at the operational level is that used to directly support the customer. Much summary information is pushed off to the atomic or departmental environments.

–Indirect information. Like summary data, much indirect data, such as cost accounting information and general ledger information, is not found at the operational level. The accumulations of information for accounting, financial, and other indirect profiles of the organization are found at the atomic or departmental levels. There is a modicum of indirect information that is found in the operational environment. The very basic classification information—the charging of an expense to an account or the crediting of an asset to an account—is found at the operational level. But only a minimal amount of information of that type is found operationally.

In short, the operational environment carries:

- Information that is directly and immediately useful for customer services,
- Information that has a high probability of access,
- The least amount of summary or indirect information that is possible.

ATOMIC LEVEL

The atomic level is characterized by a high volume of archival data. Data stored at the atomic level is primitive and as detailed as will ever be needed to support dss or archival processing. And it is nonredundant. The source of all atomic data filters through a single extract interface from the operational level.

Data at the atomic level is oriented towards time dependency. Unlike data at the operational level, which is usually current up to the minute, the data found at the atomic level is time dependent. In other words, the contents of data at the atomic level are valid only within the time frame with which they are associated. Generally speaking, there are four ways the time variancy of atomic data is stored. They are:

- Static data, which never changes over time
- Continuous, time-span data
- Periodic discrete data
- Event discrete data

Examples of derived data at the atomic level in the manufacturing environment are order history data, parts usage data (over time), manufacture projections (MRP— material requirements planning—projections for detailed items over time), and inventory stacks per item over time. The primary difference between operational and atomic data is that operational data represents up-to-the-second accuracy whereas atomic data represents up-to-the-second accuracy of data as of some moment in time. For *each* moment of time represented automatically, there will be a measurement of value, whereas in the operational environment, there is only a single value.

(For an in-depth discussion of time variant data and techniques for the storage and manipulation of time variant data, please refer to *Effective Data Base Design*, Prentice-Hall, and *Information Engineering for the Practitioner*, op cit.)

Time Variant Data

Static data is data that never changes over time. For example, in the manufacturing environment, the customer associated with an account number, the date the customer became a customer, and so forth, never changes. Usually there is very little static data.

Continuous timespan data measures the variable (or variables) of data over a lengthy period of time. The variable being measured has one and only one value at any moment in time over a span. Usually only a few variables of atomic data are captured in the continuous format. The continuous format of data is the most complex form to store and maintain.

As an example of continuous time-span data in the manufacturing environment, consider the manufacturing "load" rate for different types of employees. The work done by a manufacturing line can be measured by a rate. The rate is usually the salary of the employees plus overhead divided by the number of units manufactured. Each assembly line has its own load rate. As lines change, contracts change, and as the manufacturing process changes, the load rate changes. The load rate for each assembly line is measured over time—from one change to the next.

The next form in which time variant atomic data is stored is the periodic discrete format. In the periodic discrete format, a periodic snapshot of data is taken. Usually, many values are included in a snapshot. Any change (or changes) of values that a variable might have undergone between one periodic snapshot and another is lost. For example, the bank measures the balance of an account as of the end of the month. Or, the manufacturer measures levels of inventory on a monthly basis; inventory changes of a day or an hour are not reflected, only the month-ending quantities for certain parts. The periodic discrete format is a relatively simple format for update and storage of data. Most atomic elements are stored in such a format.

The last common form for atomic storage of data is the event discrete format. This format stores discrete images of data, as does the periodic discrete format, but in the event discrete format, a snapshot is triggered by an event. In the periodic discrete environment, a snapshot is taken on a periodic basis, regardless or how many or how few events have occurred between snapshots. In the event discrete environment, a snapshot is taken *because* of an event occurring. For example, every time an order is received or a shipment is made, a discrete snapshot is made and stored. Because of the unpredictability of the events that cause snapshots to be made, the number of snapshots is variable, and the data for event discrete snapshots is consequently much more difficult to manage.

Orientation of Atomic Data

The primary orientation of atomic data bases is toward the major subjects of the enterprise, as is the orientation of operational systems. In fact, except for some of the content and the time orientation, there is a strong similarity between operational and atomic data.

Processing of atomic data is fairly straightforward and simple. Data is input from the operational environment and placed in the atomic environment. Atomic data is accessed selectively by the various extract and derivation programs that exist for each department. The process of refreshment of atomic data occurs fairly frequently; in fact, the validity of the atomic data can be no better than that supplied by the latest refreshment. The refreshment of data from the atomic to the departmental level is done at the convenience and schedule of the department requesting the data. Some departments may require daily (or, conceivably, hourly) refreshments. Other departments will have more casual requirements, such as weekly or monthly. Generally speaking, departments extract subsets of atomic data. Figure 69 illustrates processing that occurs at the atomic level.

Along with data input and refreshment, a third type of processing done at the atomic level is the occasional "scrubbing" of the files, in which data is purged from the atomic level. The data is either deleted entirely from the system or is saved on true archival files. When data is removed

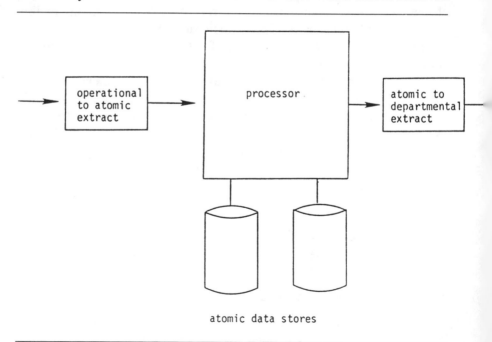

FIGURE 69 Processing in the atomic environment.

from the atomic level, the motivation is a very low probability of access. There is an absolute minimum (if any at all) of online processing in the atomic level. It is surprising to find a legitimate need for online processing in this environment. It is safe to say that 99.99 percent of the processing in the atomic environment is batch.

On occasion, however, there will be a need to access data from the operational environment that exists in the atomic environment. Even though atomic data has a low probability of access, it does not have a zero probability of access. On those infrequent occasions when there is a need to access atomic data, provisions must be made to allow access from the operational environment. The access will not be online in most cases.

The following stores of data would be typical of what might be found in the atomic level for a manufacturing enterprise:

▪ Customer order history—date order received, amount, items ordered, etc.,
▪ Shipment history—date of shipment, amount shipped, lading, shipping line, items shipped, etc.,
▪ Supplier history—quantity supplied, date of supply, rejects, defects, late charges, etc.,
▪ Assembly history—by assembly line, date, completed orders, rejects, etc.

Representing Time Variancy in the Atomic Environment

The time variancy aspects of the atomic level of data are logically represented by various forms of data structures—continuous, event discrete, periodic discrete, and so forth. The basic storage of data may be in a myriad of forms, such as:

Char (6)—YYMMDD (year, month, day)
Char (6)—DDMMYY (day, month, year)
Char (2) Dec Fixed (3.0)—YYDOY (year, day of year)
Dec Fixed (5,0)—Julian Date (Julian Date)

From a simplicity perspective, it makes sense for a shop to adopt a single date storage format that fits all needs. Whatever basic storage format for date-related data is chosen, the internal format is (and should be) independent of the external format—format as seen and perceived by the end user. In other words, a translation from the internal to the external format can be done, if needed, for the purposes of display.

Having a consistent internal data storage format for time variant data makes program logic much easier. Not having to worry about a conversion from one format to another for the usage of data from an atomic data store removes just another layer of complexity facing the user of atomic data.

THE OPERATIONAL TO ATOMIC INTERFACE

The interface between the two levels of data—the operational and the atomic—serves to point out some important dynamics. For example, for discrete data in the atomic environment, there may be many events that are measured or at least noted in the operational environment but that go unnoticed in the atomic environment. For example, suppose that an atomic data base in the manufacturing environment stores—for each part—the maximum amount of inventory, the minimum amount of inventory, and the average amount of inventory for the month. This discrete atomic snapshot will not include much detail, such as withdrawals, receipts or rejects that occurred during the month. Much operational detail will be lost in transforming the data to the atomic level on a monthly basis.

Like the article previously cited in chapter 5, DUAL DATA BASE—THE RIGHT STEP?—is another article that appeared in the days when the issue of a single data base technology or a dual data base technology was in doubt.
The information paradigm—borne of market and technology forces—of course solidly endorses dual data base as the wave of the future.

DUAL DATA BASE: THE RIGHT STEP?*

One of the major issues facing many DP shops today is the dual-data base dilemma. To have dual data bases or not to have them; that is the question.

The dilemma stems from the belief that shops should have one data base management system for operational processing and another for decision support or information center-type processing. Some vendors loudly proclaim that the single data base approach is the best solution, while other vendors voice the merits of the dual-data base strategy. Which side is right?

The controversy can be traced to the very origins of the data base

*By W.H. Inmon, *Computerworld*, June 1986. Reprinted with permission.

itself. Consider the world of master files, where every new application breeds its own set of master files, which usually are redundant. The promise of the data base as a single system of record was made, and soon master files disappeared from the scene.

A single system of record is one in which the content of data resides in its up-to-the-second value at the most detailed level. With a single system of record, the difficulties of master file redundancy and data synchronization are greatly minimized.

With a data base, which was touted as the be-all and end-all for users, there was no need for redundant data strewn all over the DP landscape. Thus, the early and intellectually appealing argument was made for the "truth" data base— the data base that served all data needs. Unquestionably, the truth data base approach was an appealing step in the right direction from the master file concept.

To this day, some data base management system vendors still make the claim that a single data base is the best approach.

But just as the world changed from master files to data bases, so has today's world changed from a single-data base concept to a multiple-use concept of data. The demands on today's data bases are many and varied—from the high-speed uses in bank teller and airline reservations data bases to the analytical needs of a vice-president of planning for decision support processing.

EVOLUTION TO DUAL DATA BASE

The next evolution from the truth data base approach is the dual-data base scenario. The primary division of data base processing is made along the lines of on-line, or operational, data bases, and decision support data bases.

On-line environments typically require a very structured kind of processing, while the uses of decision support data bases are unstructured. To use hardware to its fullest advantage requires the separation of structured and unstructured activities onto different processors.

Systems programmers have long known that IBM's CICS should not be mixed with TSO. Today's data base administrators are making a similar discovery. Cullinet Software, Inc.'s IDMS does not belong on the same machine as Information Builders, Inc.'s Focus.

To even the most die-hard relational advocate, it is apparent that the purpose and uses of decision support data are very different from those of operational data. Thus, the division into a dual-data base environment is a natural progression.

This assumes that there remains a single system of record, which nearly always is in the operational environment. Were there to be multiple systems of record, the advantage of going to data base from master files would be lost. But the dual-data base approach in no way mandates that there be multiple systems of record.

For decision support processing, there simply is no need to have up-to-the-second currentness of data or the level of detail found in the system of record. Thus it is that the dual-data base scenario represents the next step up in evolution.

The world is evolving into not only a physical separation of processors but also a physical separation of types of processors. For example, on-line operational systems are not just being physically separated from decision support systems, but operational systems are dominating the world of mainframes, and decision support systems are rapidly migrating to the micro environment.

An interesting issue is whether IBM has embarked on the dual-data base philosophy by accident or by design. Certainly, with DB2 and IMS Fast Path, IBM is clearly advocating the dual-data base approach. Cynics have suggested that IBM embarked upon that approach merely to protect its many customers that have billions of dollars of applications code tied to IMS.

While it is possible that IBM chose the path of expediency, in this case IBM has chosen the proper next step of evolution. Clearly, the next evolutionary step for the data base is the dual data base.

Another type of detail that is omitted as the transformation is made from the operational to the atomic level of data is the "nonrelevant" details. For example, suppose the withdrawals made against a part are to be stored in an event discrete atomic data base. At the operational level, details such as location of transaction, time of transaction, the using assembly line, ID, electronic identification, and so forth, are stored. For operational processing, these details are necessary, but as the data moves to the atomic level, many of the details of the transaction are unnecessary and are lost in the transformation. Typically, at the atomic level only the most useful details are stored, such as amount of withdrawal and date of withdrawal.

There are occasions in which data is compressed in going from the operational to the atomic environment. For example, suppose a credit bureau stores millions of pieces of information in its operational files.

As it stores its archival data, much data is deleted or summarized. The result is that there is actually less data in the atomic level than there is in the operational level. Of course, a credit bureau is a special kind of information handler, having unique processing requirements not found in other, more typical environments such as a bank, insurance company, or manufacturer.

With a few exceptions, there should be more data in the atomic environment than in the operational environment. Typically, there is a 1 to 2 or a 2 to 3 ratio between the two levels of data.

The processor that is needed for the atomic level of data is one that can handle much data and do sequential processing. The ability to interface with a variety of machines and software is another characteristic of the processing needed for the atomic environment. The processing that is relevant to the atomic level is shown by Figure 69.

The Banking Example in the Atomic Environment

Continuing the banking example in the atomic environment, consider the data bases shown in Figure 70.

Passbook rate	Customer/customer relationship
passbook type	customer id
beginning date	customer id
ending date	year, month
rate	
conditions	**Account balance**
Customer/account	account
	year, month
customer id	ending balance
account	average amount
beg. date	high amount
end date	low amount
Activity	**Customer**
account	customer id
date	address
amount	year, month

FIGURE 70 Some typical atomic data stores.

The passbook rates are the rates the bank pays for passbook accounts. It is a classic example of continuous time-span data. Every time the bank changes its passbook rates, a new time-span record is entered into the atomic environment. Since the rate is infrequently changed, there will be few records in the data base. There will be no logical overlap between any two values in the rates data base, nor will there be any point in time for which there is no rate defined. The key will go down to the day (or whatever unit of time the bank uses for rate changes).

The activity atomic file is an example of event discrete data. Every time an activity is transacted on an account, the information triggers an activity record in the atomic data base. Note that much detail has been lost in the transformation from the operational to the atomic level. Also note that there is a very variable number of occurrences of data from one account to the next and from one month to the next for the same account.

The third data store found at the atomic level is the account balance data. This store of data is a classic example of discrete data. Every month, one snapshot of data is made. The day-to-day fluctuations of the balance field are lost as the data is transformed into atomic data. A certain amount of analysis must be done in the operational environment to provide the basis for this data. The account's high, low, and average balance must be kept from one snapshot to the next. Unlike what happens with event discrete data, the account balance data snapshot occurs with great regularity, regardless of the number of events that have (or have not!) occurred.

Another type of atomic data is shown by the customer/account file. The relationship between customer and account is contained in this store of data. The length of time that a customer has had an account is indicated by the beginning and ending dates. Note that for all active accounts, end date will be high values, infinity, or some value that indicates the account is not yet closed. Also note that if an account is closed and then reopened, there will (logically) be a point in time for which there is no definition. In other words, the data for customer/account will be discontinuous for some period (or periods) of time.

The customer/customer relationship store of data shows a recursive relationship with time variancy added. The year/month time values may form a continuous chain of information, or they may be more relaxed.

The customer atomic data store—the last store shown in Figure 70—shows that customer demographic information is separated from other customer information and is time stamped in a manner that may be maintained either rigorously or casually.

Note that customer data changes much more slowly than account data. Also note that separate time stamps are used for each piece of customer information because the information being tracked can have different time values.

The information in the atomic data base is based on the major subjects of the enterprise, as defined in Figure 70. There is nonredundancy of information within the atomic level. There is a very close relationship between the data in the operational environment and that in the atomic environment, yet it is not the same. The data in the atomic level is time stamped (in different ways). Data at the atomic level is at as detailed a level as will be available for dss/archival processing. Any data lost in the operational to atomic transformation is lost for good.

Data at the atomic level serves as a basis for *all* departmental and individual dss/end user computing. Practically all of the data flow from the atomic level goes into departmental processing. Very little individual processing is done against the atomic level. For small organizations that do very little dss processing, there may be a significant amount of individual processing that occurs. But for most organizations (especially large organizations), the departmental level of processing is a fact of life.

DEPARTMENTAL LEVEL

There is a mixture of primitive and derived data at the departmental level. For departmental data, there may or may not be time variancy that is carried with the data as it is transformed from the atomic to the departmental level. If time variancy is carried with the data, it is no more granular than what exists at the atomic level. (In other words, if data is carried monthly at the atomic level, it cannot be carried weekly or daily at the departmental level.)

The extract and derivation of information will most likely be different for each department. There will be one and only one extract program for each department. The extract program, of course, can be executed as often as needed, usually (but not always) on a scheduled basis.

Typically, the departments doing extract processing include marketing, accounting, finance, and information center (ad hoc, special requests, etc.). Depending on the business of the enterprise, other departmental computing groups might include actuarial, quality assurance, and engineering.

There will undoubtedly be much overlap of data from one department to the next.

The extract from the atomic to the departmental level is a large, general-purpose program. Not only is data selected for departmental processing, but the algorithms needed to derive the data from its primitive basis are actuated here. The level of complexity created by sorting, summing, managing, editing, and filtering data is considerable.

There may be a direct loop back to the operational environment for data that is found to be incorrect or invalid, but, for the most part, the flow of data is one way.

The departmental needs for data are parochial, serving the interests of each department that owns the data. As long as the departmental data can be reconciled to the atomic data, there is no further need for explanation. The data at the departmental level may or may not be subject-oriented. Indeed, if a formal data model is constructed for a department, it may well turn out that the subjects as viewed by the department are different from the subjects as viewed by the corporation. As long as the departmental subjects have an identifiable primitive basis in the corporate data model, then there is no problem. (Of course, the original data modeling effort ensured that any identifiable departmental need has a primitive foundation in the data model of the corporate operational data.)

Most of the processing at the departmental level is batch access and calculation oriented (i.e., analytical processing). The only individual update processing that is done at the departmental level is for departmental needs. (A departmental need is for data that applies *only* to one department and never, under any circumstances, to any other department.)

If there is ever a need to change values or interpretations of primitive data at the departmental level, a public audit trail must be left. The audit trail will be available to *all* parties in the enterprise, including *all* other departments.

There is a combination of structured and unstructured processing at the departmental level. The structured processing that occurs is typically for periodic reporting, management reporting, and specific profiles of data relevant to the department. The unstructured processing that occurs is for special requests, ad hoc trend analysis, and so forth. Generally speaking, *most* of the departmental processing will be structured. For organizations that blend departmental and individual processing, there probably will be more of a mixture of structured and unstructured processing.

To continue the example of the banking environment, suppose the needs of the marketing department are shown in Figure 71.

In Figure 71, there are several types of data being collected. The standard reports, on a monthly basis are:

- The total number of accounts
- The total number of accounts by type of account
- The total number of accounts by branch
- Miscellaneous standard monthly reports, such as

  −number of overdrawn dda accounts
  −number of stop payments issued
  −number of inactive accounts
  −number of "hyperactive" accounts

  Other standard reports for loans include:

- Monthly late payments
- Monthly number of first warnings issued
- Monthly number of second warnings issued
- Monthly number of foreclosures
- Monthly number of extensions
- Monthly old commitments
- Monthly new commitments

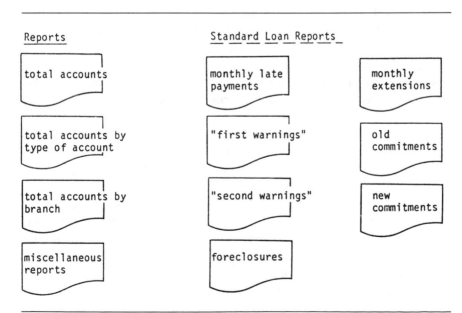

FIGURE 71 Scheduled reports by the marketing department.

Periodically, some other reports are run. One such report is the "promotion" analysis. Whenever the bank has a promotion, such as giving away stuffed dolls for opening an account, a report is run.

Not only are reports run in the departmental environment, but a certain amount of departmental data is collected. For example, the data required to plot the trend of number of accounts on a monthly basis is calculated and stored on a departmental data base.

INDIVIDUAL LEVEL

The individual level of data—in some ways an extension of the departmental level—is oriented toward very fast, very individual processing. The analysis done at the individual level is often done on a spreadsheet on a personal computer. There is a very high degree of autonomy at the individual level. The only real discipline required is that the individual analyst be able to trace the lineage of the data used for analysis. Of course, if there is a question as to the calculations that are made, the analyst needs to be able to trace the algorithms as well.

Far and away, the most common source of data for the individual is departmental. On a few occasions, the individual analyst may access atomic data directly. If the individual analyst accepts data from a source other than the department or the atomic level, the lineage of the data *must* be determined. Otherwise, there is only a small chance at the reconcilability of data.

The type of processing that occurs at the individual level is almost completely unstructured. There is normally little or no scheduled processing at the individual level.

The nature of individual processing is heuristic and iterative analysis. Unlike in operational processing, where the computer is a vehicle for the transformation and usage of data, in individual dss processing the result of processing is a concrete answer.

Relatively speaking, there is only a small amount of data in the individual level. The data that exists is almost 100 percent derived data. The frequency of refreshment is on an as-needed basis. The processing is characteristically done a set-at-a-time in a high-level language. The output of dss processing frequently goes directly to top management.

For example, the individual analyst in a bank may be asked to determine:

- How many loan applications for homes have been received that are over $150,000 and the applicant

  –has more than $75,000 in equity from the sale of a previous home,
  –earns over $55,000 per year,
  –is from a single-earner family.

Another analysis done at the individual level is for accounts whose average balance is greater than $5,000. For those accounts:

- What is the low balance at any time during the month?
- What is the high balance?
- How many accounts of this type are there?
- What other accounts does the customer have?

The analytical activity that is done is actuated by requests from management. Upon the occasion that an analysis is done periodically or on a scheduled basis, the analyst prepares the report to be run departmentally.

There are two departments-worth of data at the departmental level: accounting and marketing. Most of the departmental data is scheduled, periodic data. There is a large collection of departmental trend analysis data. The same data is summarized and stored in many different ways. The flow of data from the atomic to the departmental level is dictated by content of data and the need for data. Some data flows daily; other data flows weekly, monthly, or at other periods.

Individual dss analysis does not occur on a scheduled basis. It is done as a result of the requests of management. Most individual analysis is done from the basis of departmental data. On occasion, atomic or operational data is used. In addition, for certain types of analysis, external information is used. For example, comparing interest rate growth versus GNP growth requires the introduction of GNP growth rates. Information from the Bureau of Statistics is introduced and matched against the trends of interest rates. When external data is introduced, it becomes parochially departmental data. If there is a need to use the external data across departments, then the data will be introduced into the atomic level.

SUMMARY

The details of the operational, atomic, departmental, and individual levels of data have been described in this chapter.

7 MIGRATION TO THE INFORMATION PARADIGM

*I*t is unrealistic to create (or even suggest) an architecture that cannot be fully realized. One of the first (and most pragmatic) considerations of an architecture *must* be the relationship of the architecture to the existing environment and the work required to move the existing environment toward the envisioned architecture. If an architecture—any architecture—cannot accommodate existing systems in a graceful fashion, then it will be, at best, a theoretical success.

One of the most salient and positive aspects of the information paradigm is that it fits conveniently (as conveniently as an architecture can fit) with unstructured, unarchitected existing systems. The migration to the information paradigm architecture from existing systems can be done a step at a time, on a schedule convenient to the enterprise, and with minimum disruption to the existing environment.

The following discussion will outline considerations of migration to the information paradigm and coexistence with existing, unarchitected systems.

MIGRATION TO THE ARCHITECTURE

The steps in the migration to the architected environment are depicted by Figure 73.

The first step in the migration is the construction of the high-level data model. The detailed considerations of the construction of the data model

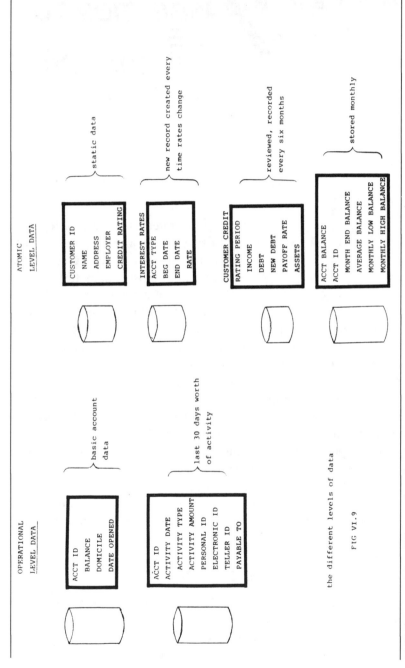

FIGURE 72 The different levels of data.

are amply documented in *Information Systems Architecture*, op cit, and in *Information Engineering for the Practitioner*, op cit. This discussion will only highlight a few of the major aspects of the modeling effort.

The data model that will be used as a foundation for the migration should:

- Have a formally and well defined statement of scope;
- Have different levels of modeling, where detail is separated from abstraction, recognizing the commonality of data while preserving the uniqueness;
- Separate primitive and derived data—the model focuses on primitive data but lays a foundation for derived data;
- Be able to be linked to a process model;
- Identify key structure for all groupings of data.

The first step in the migration process—creating the model—should be done with dispatch. Creating the model should not be a long, tedious affair. Even for the most complex organization, six months is adequate time.

The next step in the migration is the analysis of existing systems with respect to the data model. Existing systems should first be analyzed with the intent of separating primitive data from derived data. In some cases, typically financial and accounting systems, whole systems can be classified as derived and should be moved to the derived environment. In other cases, whole systems can be classified as primitive. But most existing, unarchitected systems have elements of both primitive and derived data and processing. Figure 73 illustrates the separation process.

Existing Primitive Systems/Derived Systems

For those systems that are already aligned with the architecture—those that are already entirely primitive or entirely derived—the least amount of work needs to be done. For existing systems whose primary orientation is primitive, the migration effort focuses on the alignment of the existing system with the major subjects of the enterprise, as described in the model, and how the existing primitive data can feed atomic data bases.

As an example of the migration of an existing system whose orientation is toward primitive, operational data, consider an auto policy premium system for an insurance company. The orientation of the system is toward the management and manipulation of the details of the premiums. As the

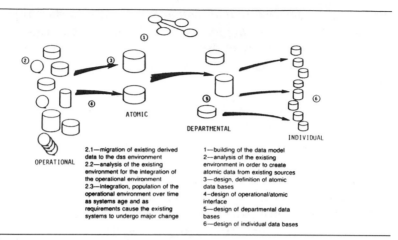

OPERATIONAL

ATOMIC

DEPARTMENTAL

INDIVIDUAL

2.1—migration of existing derived data to the dss environment
2.2—analysis of the existing environment for the integration of the operational environment
2.3—integration, population of the operational environment over time as systems age and as requirements cause the existing systems to undergo major change

1—building of the data model
2—analysis of the existing environment in order to create atomic data from existing sources
3—design, definition of atomic data bases
4—design of operational/atomic interface
5—design of departmental data bases
6—design of individual data bases

FIGURE 73   The steps to achieve the integrated environment.

system is integrated, much data and processing remain the same. Instead of focusing on auto premiums, once the system is integrated, it focuses on insurance premiums, of which certain premiums, such as autos, are a category. Because the existing, unintegrated system contains little or no derived data, it can be fairly easily migrated to an architected system.

For systems whose orientation is primarily derived, the issues of architecture revolve around the source of primitive data and how the primitive data feeds the derived systems. The positioning of existing derived systems into the architected environment is an issue as well; that is, how can the existing unarchitected derived system be placed in the architected derived environment?

As an example of an existing system that centers around derived data, consider a financial system that tracks manufacturing and marketing activity. The existing system receives general ledger information at a detailed level. Each manufacturing expense is classified according to a chart of accounts. Once entered into the financial system, the data is categorized and summarized many ways. When the financial system is moved to the architected environment, the most notable effect on the system is the changing of the source of data input to the financial system. Whole blocks of code that do financial analysis and manipulation do not change as the system moves to the architected environment.

But existing primitive and derived systems that wholly (or very close to wholly) fit the pattern of the architecture are rare. It is much more normal to encounter an existing environment filled with systems that have elements of both primitive and derived data. The architectural considerations for the more normal existing systems begin with how to separate the primitive and derived aspects of the system. The split is mandatory but need not be made at once.

In other words, once the analyst has determined what the primitive and derived components of the existing system are, he or she must then determine how to recreate the derived components of the existing system in the derived portion of the architecture. The derived components can be created in the architecture over a period of time, a step at a time. There is no need to create the derived architecture immediately or on an "all or nothing" basis once the existing systems have been analyzed.

The migration to the architected environment can be considered as two separate (and, interestingly, loosely related) processes. The two processes are:

- migration of operational systems
- migration of derived systems

The operational migration is usually done slowly, a single step at a time, almost in a passive state. The migration to derived systems is done relatively quickly, in an active state. Most existing systems have a strong orientation toward operational processing. The uprooting of operational systems has a direct relationship to the day-to-day business of the enterprise. On the other hand, derived systems do not have as direct a relationship to the day-to-day business of the enterprise. Consequently, there are many more liberties that can be taken with derived systems.

Another factor that affects the rate of change of operational and derived processing is the technology in which systems are written and executed. Existing operational systems are built in languages and technology that are difficult to change, while derived systems are traditionally built in technology that is more amenable to change.

A third factor affecting the rate of migration is that there are often many constraints in the operational environment, such as response time and availability. While there are constraints in the derived environment, they are much more relaxed. The result is that operational systems migrate to the architected environment much more slowly than derived systems.

The classical migration of systems is illustrated by an example depicted in Figure 74.

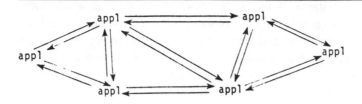

FIGURE 74 The typical flow of data from one application to another in an unarchitected environment.

In Figure 74, there are several tightly interrelated, unarchitected application systems. There is a flow of data between the applications, which has the following characteristics:

- It is caused by the redundant existence of the same data in multiple applications.
- It causes the triggering of events or processes.
- It represents transformations of data as well as passage of raw data values.

As an example of the flow of customer data, suppose that, in a banking environment, a customer changes his or her address. Each application that uses customer address needs to have the address change made. The first application in which the change of customer address is made is responsible for passing the change of address to other systems where it needs to be made (i.e., where the data exists redundantly).

On other occasions, a customer will overdraw his or her checking account. The checking application, of course, first detects the overdraft condition. The checking application then passes news of the overdraft to the loan application, where, in the worst case, the credit line of the customer may need to be reconsidered. In such a fashion, the flow of data between applications is used to trigger events.

In an example of the third type of data flow between applications, a customer makes a loan and pledges the balance of a savings account, as collateral. This event—the pledging of savings—is recorded in several ways: as a function of the making of the loan, as part of the periodic commitment of funds (i.e., accumulated with other loan commitments), and as a part of pledged collateral. The single transaction ripples through the different applications in multiple ways and in multiple forms.

The flow of data between applications represents the single most complicating factor in the migration of operational systems to the architected environment. Any realistic migration plan must account for *all* the flow of data between applications and for all the reasons for it.

Another perspective of the flow of data among applications is from that of a single stimulus activating a chain reaction, as shown by Figure 75.

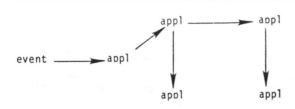

FIGURE 75 An event that has triggered the flow of redundant data.

In Figure 75, an event has occurred that triggers a change in an application. Once the effect of the change is recorded in the application, it ripples into other applications. Figure 75 shows only a single event starting the ripple effect. In actuality, multiple events are often capable of triggering multiple applications, as shown by Figure 76.

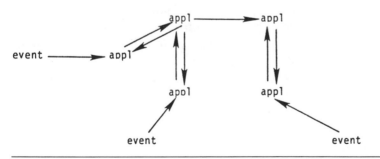

FIGURE 76 Multiple events that trigger data flow in a random fashion.

The level of complexity in Figure 75 is significantly greater than the level of complexity in Figure 74 because of the multiple ripple effects that are being executed at the same time.

The first practical step in the migration of existing operational systems to the information paradigm is the identification of subject areas in the existing application environment—in other words, what existing operational data is there in support of the data model. The identification of existing data as a foundation for the architecture comes as a result of comparing existing systems to the data model, as shown by Figure 77.

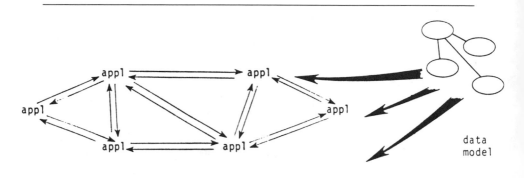

FIGURE 77   Comparison of the data model to the existing environment.

The data model serves as a guide to what data can be used, as is, in the existing operational environment, what data is needed, and what data that already exists needs to be discarded.

For example, an insurance company has existing fire, life, and health applications. The data model specifies premiums as a major subject of the corporation. Based upon the model, premium information from fire, life, and health applications are selected as a foundation for migration.

The comparison of the data model to the existing environment uncovers components of the existing environment that may be used as a basis for the architected environment, as shown by Figure 78.

After the "foundation" in the existing environment has been identified and established, the next step is the population of the atomic environment from the foundation data, as shown in Figure 79.

The foundation data feeds the atomic-level data. It is normal for only a fraction of the atomic data that will ultimately exist to be fed at the outset. As the operational environment matures, the atomic data bases become more fully populated.

As soon as the atomic data bases become meaningfully populated, reports should be run from them. The reporting function is displaced (in

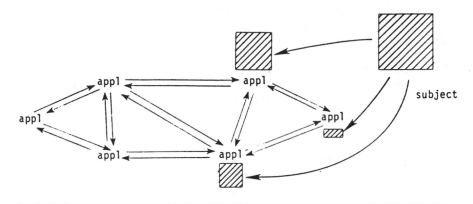

FIGURE 78 The first cut at the subject data within the system of record is found in bits and pieces in different parts of the existing environment.

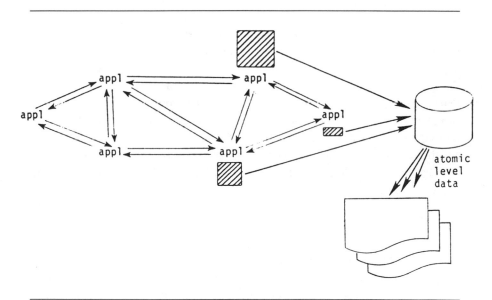

FIGURE 79 As soon as the parts of the existing environment that support the subject data have been identified, the atomic data is populated from the existing environment, and reports (usually those that are regularly scheduled) are run from the atomic-level data.

The information paradigm takes on many forms. One of those forms is 'living sample' data. This specialized form of data is useful for statistical analysis of data and for the formulation of heuristically oriented queries of data. Living sample data is described in the article—USING EXTRACTED SAMPLES IMPROVES INFORMATION CENTER.

USING EXTRACTED SAMPLES IMPROVES INFORMATION CENTER*

FRED L. FORMAN AND WILLIAM H. INMON

Forman is a senior vice president at American Management Systems, Arlington, VA, and director of its Corporate Technology Group. Inmon is a senior principal in Corporate Technology Group at AMS.—Ed.

An increased number of end users is the most obvious factor that has triggered the explosive growth in the demand for computing resources at information centers. Spiraling resource demands may also be due to less evident factors such as the increasing use of fourth generation technology (FOCUS, RAMIS, SAS), which consumes enormous resources while delivering ease-of-use and flexibility.

A dramatic example of the demand that fourth generation tools can place on the information center is illustrated by IBM's recent DB2

performance figures. While a 3090-200 can handle 47 production-type DB2 transactions per second, a 3084Q (roughly comparable in power to the 3090-200) can only handle two to three DB2 *ad hoc* query requests per second.

Another indication of resource consumption is the growing number of files available in the typical information center and the fact that many of those files are growing in size over time. For example, during the year the year-to-date ledger files will grow and other 2files, such as a personnel file, will increase in size with the growth of the organization. The resources required by most 4GL tools are often related to the file size, not just the number of records users are requesting.

The rapid, uncontrolled growth of resources demanded by IC users is endangering the usefulness of the information center as response times and general performance characteristics reach unacceptable levels. This is especially true in organizations that cannot easily increase their IC

*By Fred L. Forman and W.H. Inmon, *Data Management Magazine*, January 1988. Reprinted with permission.

computing resources. Hence, information center managers must look for methods to manage the growth in resource demands.

CONTROLLING IC RESOURCE USE

Until recently, IC managers have concentrated on traditional ways to control the growth in resource demands. Some approaches, such as chargeback to users based on resources actually consumed, have been used. Other traditional control methods, such as limiting the maximum number of users at any one time, are relatively Draconian and not a way to gain new IC adherents.

Another popular idea is to download to data microcomputers. In practice, micromainframe tools are in their infancy and do not support rapid, efficient access to the amounts of data often needed. So far, the use of micromainframe links for IC processing has not significantly offloaded processing from the mainframe. In many cases, it has added new IC users, thereby increasing resource demands.

Another approach to the resource consumption crisis is to wait for performance improvements in the IC software tools. While most vendors are aware of the performance deficiencies in their products, they are far more interested in extending support to new IC environments (such as DB2) than they are in significantly

improving performance. Many of the products have fundamental architectural problems which prevent dramatic performance improvements.

There are other performance "defects" in many of these IC software products which are subtle. For example, some of the products are unable to efficiently handle partial-key access requests and end up scanning the entire file. In such cases, special routines to improve access efficiency have been written.

TYPES OF IC USERS

Hence, squeezing more useful end user results out of an existing IC environment requires learning more about what the end users are actually doing with the IC facilities and finding ways to achieve the same results more efficiently. IC users fall into several categories:

- *Ad hoc* reporting and inquiry is likely the predominant use of the IC's ways to improve efficiency and prepare intelligent summary files based on usage patterns. For example, a detailed ledger file might be summarized to the departmental level by object code to support many types of reports and inquiries. In truth, such an approach is little more than the standard report extract file approach used in many accounting systems. The use of such summary files is especially critical if the primary *ad hoc* reporting and inquiry tool has the partial-key scan defect referenced earlier.

▪ Administrative use, such as electronic mail, electronic calendars and office automation is somewhat more difficult to manage from a resource consumption perspective, with chargeback being the primary weapon in the IC manager's arsenal. Another possibility is to periodically audit the IC environment to ensure that users are conducting important business and not just using the IC for personal business.

▪ Personal computing, such as small custom end user applications or the use of mainframe modeling packages (IFPS from IBM) is another common use of the IC. This area of IC use is difficult to manage with respect to resource consumption. Some IC's try to prevent this type of use by providing read-only access to the IC, although that is a very limiting option. Once the IC is made available for personal computing, there is no turning back, since users will quickly create applications on which they depend for their day-to-day work (i.e., "end-user production" applications).

▪ Statistical analysis, such as salary trend analysis, customer profile analysis and the like is also a common use of the IC. This type of processing often shares the same files as the *ad hoc* reporting and inquiry users.

The focus of this article is primarily on the latter type of IC use, statistical analysis, although some of the concepts are also applicable to *ad hoc* reporting and inquiry. Specifically, the use of a relatively simple and straightforward technique, "extracted samples," can offer immediate and significant payback with little or no loss of effectiveness when applied properly. An extracted sample is data that is a subset of a larger data base, either one that is already available in the IC or a production data base. The subsetting is typically done by selecting only a fraction of the records from the full data base, plus the set of data elements selected may also be reduced. The intent of extracted samples is to reduce resource consumption, while not compromising analytical effectiveness.

EXTRACTED SAMPLE DATA

The resource consumption benefits of extracted sample data are straightforward. Suppose an information center analyst takes 10 hours (i.e., 600 minutes) to process a data base of m units of data. The data base of m units is divided into a smaller subset of n units of data where $n = m/100$. Now the information center can work on the extracted sample data and accomplish the same work in 1/100 of the time (i.e., six minutes). Using extracted sample data, the information center now operates on much smaller collections of data, uses far fewer resources and can effectively achieve the same results.

As an example of the application of the extracted sample technique, suppose a state department of motor vehicles desires to know the average age of a person when they receive their first moving violation and the length of time, on the average, that the person has had their driving license. One approach is to take the driving records of all licensed drivers and calculate the numbers. If there are five million licensed drivers, this process turns into an arduous activity. For the sake of the example, the result of processing five million records turns out to be 18 years, three months as the average age, with license being held for 1.46 years.

Now suppose there was an extracted sample of the motorists so that 50,000 (i.e., 1/100 of the original collection data) records were maintained. The extracted sample is queried, using 1/100 of the resources of the previous study. The end result of the extracted sample query is that the average age is 18 years, four months with the license held for 1.42 years.

ACCURACY OF STUDIES

Undoubtedly, there will be minor discrepancies between the accuracy of the first study and the extracted sample study. But the question must be asked, what is the cost of accuracy and is the cost worth the resources consumed? The first study required 100 times the resources of the extracted sample study to determine that the average age of the ticketed person was 18 years, three months, rather than 18 years, four months (in the extracted sample). Is the precision of the first analysis worth the costs? The trade-off then between precision and resources consumed must be made in the use of extracted samples. In many cases, the precision of processing against huge collections of data is unnecessary and certainly not cost-effective.

Extracted sample processing, then, is very useful for many types of statistical analysis—determining averages, medians, profiles and so forth. And statistical analysis is the very essence of many types of IC processing, such as trend analysis, *ad hoc* reporting, demographic analysis and so forth.

As powerful as the notion of extracted sample processing is, it is not applicable to all forms of IC processing. In particular, extracted sample processing is not useful when:

- Extreme precision is mandatory
- Individual, detailed instances of data must be located
- Subtotals, grand totals, etc., are being calculated
- Audits of detailed records are being processed.

ECONOMICS

The economics of extracted sample processing are fairly simple. In general, the resources consumed by information center processing are directly proportional to the amount of the data on which the process operates. (Strictly speaking, this may not be true. Most processes—IC or otherwise—have a certain amount of overhead required for startup/shutdown that is independent of the amount of data on which the process operates. As long as this overhead is minimal, it is not important.) For example, if n units of resources are required to process m units of data, then m/a units of resources are required to process n/a units of data. The arithmetic reduction in resource consumption then is considerable.

The use of extracted sample processing opens up other resource reduction possibilities. Some IC processing is well suited for execution on a microprocessor. However, microprocessors can handle only relatively small amounts of data. By using extracted sample techniques it is possible that much IC processing can be shifted to the microprocessor that otherwise would have required a larger processor.

Another advantage of extracted sample techniques is that possibilities are opened up when doing "what if" analysis. In the case where much data is subject to "what if" analysis, the large amount of resources consumed by each analysis may become a constraining factor to doing a thorough analysis. Using an extracted sample approach, the analyst can establish one set of criteria, calculate an answer, then adjust the criteria and recalculate. Parametric adjustment and recalculation can continue many times until the analyst has arrived at just the right set of criteria. Had the analyst been constrained by the resource consumption of each iteration, such a heuristic approach that entailed many iterations of processing would not have been possible.

The use of an extracted sample subset of data, then, has many merits in the fact of the appropriate type of processing in the IC environment.

EXTRACTED SAMPLE CONSIDERATIONS

Some of the major considerations of an effective extracted sample environment are:

- The frequency of refreshment of the extracted sample data
- The amount of extracted sample data selected
- The algorithms used to create the extracted sample.

Each of these considerations is examined below.

FREQUENCY OF REFRESHMENT

Extracted sample data is current only from the moment that it is extracted from the main collection of data of which it is a subset. The sample begins to age immediately from the moment of its extraction. Because of the aging that occurs, extracted sample data must be periodically refreshed. The primary factors that determine the frequency of refreshment are the nature of the data and the usage of the data.

For example, daily refreshment of mortgage payment extracted sample data would not make sense because most mortgage payments are normally made on a monthly basis and a day-to-day refreshment would show very little meaningful change from one day to the next. By the same token, a monthly refreshment of stock market fluctuations would miss many important daily swings and changes (although for some purposes a monthly snapshot of stock market data would serve adequately). The analyst must then decide upon the frequency of refreshment based upon the fluctuation of data in the data base and the use of the extracted sample data.

THE AMOUNT OF EXTRACTED SAMPLE DATA

The amount of extracted sample data selected is not a trivial issue. On the one hand, the more data selected, the more resources required to process the data. As a rule of thumb, the extracted sample data should contain only enough data to form a representative and statistically meaningful sample. The amount of data can be determined:

- Mathematically, by using statistical techniques for selection
- Heuristically, by varying the amount selected until the sample size proves to be adequate, or
- Empirically, based on previous experience.

There are several ways to limit the amount of data chosen. Some of these ways include selecting subclasses of data, based on a predetermined need and/or summarizing selected data, where appropriate.

Suppose a large personnel file exists that is to be turned into an extracted sample. The personnel file contains many types of data about the employee, such as name, age, sex, education, height, weight, wages paid (on a week-by-week basis) and so forth. If an extracted sample data base is to be created for the determination of the correlation between education and salary, there is no need to keep other unrelated data such as sex, height, weight, etc., in the extracted sample. The extracted sample would contain only the types of data pertinent to education and salary.

By limiting the types of data stored in the extracted sample, much data is removed from the sample and the extracted sample is then only able to be used for limited purposes. On the other hand, processing the sample requires minimal resources. Such is an example of limiting the type of data in the extracted sample to suit the needs of the analysis being conducted.

Now suppose a study were to be done on the work history of women employees. The sample may include many types of data such as age, salary, education and so forth, but only women would be included in the extracted sample. This preselection of a subset of data (in this case, women employees) greatly limits the amount of data handled and at the same time limits the use of the data.

Suppose a third kind of study were to be done on the personnel data. In this case, the average monthly fluctuations of employee payments to FICA, insurance, the Federal government and the state government must be analyzed. It makes no sense to store weekly data in the extracted sample. Instead, the monthly summarization of the relevant data is stored for each employee. In doing so, the monthly figures can be analyzed in-depth, and much less raw data appears in the extracted sample. Of course, if there ever is a need to analyze weekly data, the extracted sample will be inadequate because it contains only monthly data. The summarization by month of personnel data is an example of the third form of selectivity for extracted sample data.

The preceding three examples illustrate two phenomena:

- For predetermined analyses, the analyst can be very selective in choosing data for the extracted sample, and
- The more selective the analyst is, the fewer uses the extracted sample has.

EFFECTIVE SELECTION ALGORITHMS

The final factor in the effective use of extracted sample data bases is the algorithm used to select data from the primary data collection. Ideally, the algorithm will be efficient in creating an unbiased extracted sample. For example, suppose a primary collection of 1,000,000 units of data were to be reduced to an extracted sample of 10,000 units. The algorithm doing the selection could select every 100th unit from the primary collection of data. In doing so, only a minimal amount of resources would be used in the selection process. But (as is the case with every algorithm) there is the danger that the algorithm will select data in a biased manner and in doing so produce a biased sample.

TREND ANALYSIS

When an extracted sample is refreshed, its data is made current as of the moment the refreshment is done. But there is nothing that dictates that the previous extracted sample must be discarded (other than the cost of online storage). For example, suppose an extracted sample is refreshed each month. By saving each month's sample and archiving those historical samples, the analyst has created a basis for trend analysis. Once several month's samples are stored, the analyst can use the different time variant samples collectively to determine trends. Of course, the more detailed the sample is, the more trends there are that can be analyzed.

MANAGING DIFFERENT ORIGINS

All of the discussion heretofore has centered around the extraction of data from a single large collection of data. But there is no reason why an extracted sample cannot be created from more than one collection of data. Suppose there is a parts file and a supplier file. An extracted sample could be created to reflect part activities and another extracted sample could be created to reflect supplier activities. The two files can be merged together to create an extracted sample reflecting the intersection of part/supplier data. Such a sample might contain information such as the number of times an order was placed to a different supplier, the total amount of parts ordered from a supplier, the average price (and the pricing trends) of a supplier, the number of parts a supplier has fulfilled and so on.

Such merging of two or more files may actually represent great savings, not so much in the amount of data stored, but in the fact that the system is asked to merge the data only once.

GENERATIONS OF EXTRACTS

Every discussion of extract processing, whether for the creation of extracted samples or otherwise, deserves a discussion on generations of extracts. Generations of extracts occur when an extract is made from already extracted data, or an extract is made from an extract which in fact has come from another extract and so forth.

In general, whenever generations of extracts are allowed, in short order the credibility and validity (i.e., the quality of the data) of data is severely weakened. Therefore, extracted samples should not be used for further extractions and all extracted samples should come directly from the original source. (A detailed discussion of the issue of credibility in the face of extract processing will be treated in the forthcoming book by Inmon and Yourdon, *Information Engineering for the Practitioner,* Dow Jones-Irwin, 1987.)

VALIDATION OF THE SAMPLE

In the best of cases, the accuracy of analyzing an extracted sample will be in question (i.e., because the extracted sample is only a subset of a larger collection of data, can the results of the analysis done against the sample be believed?). Such is the nature of sample analysis. One way to verify the validity is to periodically measure the primary collection of data using the same parameters as were used in the analysis of the extracted sample.

For example, suppose the analysis of the extracted sample resulted in an average employee salary of $19,642.31. Management questions the result and the same analysis is run against the primary collection of data. This analysis shows that the average salary is $19,701.46. The numbers are well within range of each other so there is no problem. But if the analysis of the primary collection of data showed that the average salary was $27,846.39, then there would be a significant bias in the results, so much so that the validity of the extracted sample must be questioned.

SUMMARY

The extracted sample technique can be used to save significant resources in an Information Center environment with little or no loss of effectiveness for many forms of analytical processing. The extracted sample is a subset of a larger collection of data that is periodically refreshed. Processing against the extracted sample is much cheaper, in terms of resources, than processing against the larger collection of data, which may also be used for *ad hoc* reporting and inquiry.

The amount of data selected, the frequency of refreshment and the selection algorithm used are all factors in the creation of an effective extracted sample.

---

an orderly manner) from the operational environment to the atomic dss environment at this point. (Of course, some reports that deal *only* with the day-to-day operations of the enterprise will not be displaced. But many reports based on summarizations, merges, selective subsets of data, and so forth, will leave the operational environment.)

After the reporting function has been displaced (or while it is being displaced), the next task is to begin to consolidate existing operational subject data bases and to add on to the subject data bases based on the requirements identified in the building of the data model. The process of consolidation and addition of operational data requires many resources and usually occurs over a long period of time. Figure 80 illustrates the consolidation and addition of subject data.

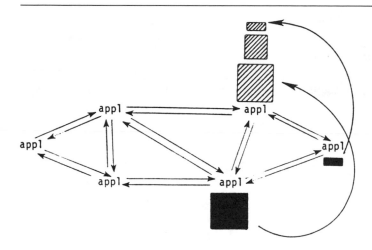

FIGURE 80   Over time, as applications age and are replaced, the subject data is migrated to a single source, forming the subject data base in the operational environment as originally envisioned

One of the major problems encountered in the consolidation process is the operation of existing applications. Consider the displacement of data from an application to a subject data base as shown in Figure 81.

In the figure, the operational subject data is being displaced from an application data base. What happens to the application whose data is being displaced? And what happens to the other applications that are closely intertwined with the data application that is being disrupted? Three options are shown in Figures 82, 83, and 84.

In Figure 82, the stream of input used to create the subject data is fed into two processes—the application and the subject data bases. The code

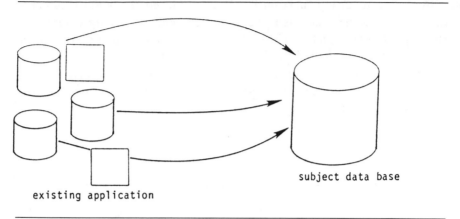

existing application

subject data base

FIGURE 81 The displacement of existing application data over time.

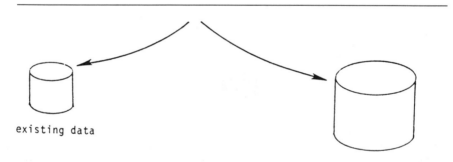

existing data

FIGURE 82 Feed same source of data simultaneously to each data base environment.

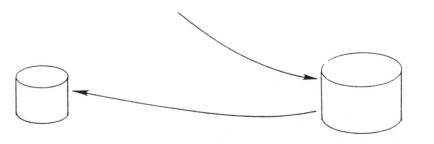

FIGURE 83 Load and update the subject data base and feed the existing environment from the updated subject data.

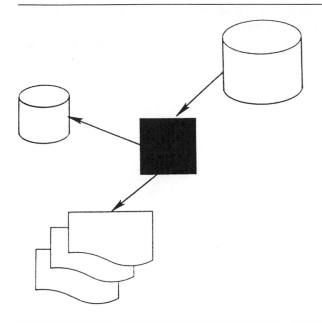

FIGURE 84 Migration of application processing to the subject environment.

needed to update and create the data is now found in two places. But there is minimal disruption to the existing application. At a later time, the business function served by the existing application can be dismantled piece by piece and moved to the architected environment.

In Figure 83, data is updated into the subject data base; then the subject data base serves to directly feed the updated data into the existing application. This approach causes a fair amount of code to be uprooted (e.g., the creation and update function now exists in the processing of the subject data base, whereas it once existed at the application level). This approach tends to "enshrine" the existing application, in that there is little motivation to discard it.

The third approach, shown by Figure 84, shows that the entire application processing is consolidated with the subject data base. Interestingly, in many environments this change is fairly easy to accomplish. In other environments, the change is difficult. Where the change is difficult, one of the other options discussed may be appropriate. In practice, all three options (and many intermediate variations) are used in the migration of existing applications to the architected environment.

Over time, the net result of the migration is as depicted in Figure 85.

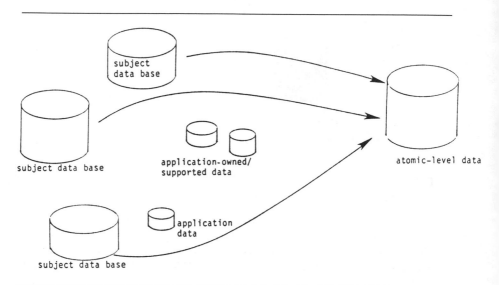

subject
data base

subject data base

application-owned/
supported data

atomic-level data

application
data

subject data base

FIGURE 85 A typical environment during the transition to the architected environment.

In the operational environment, there are subject data bases and a few remnants of the application mode of processing. For example, there might be a customer data base (a subject data base) and a preferred customer list (a holdover from the loans application). The application data would have little or no usage outside the application. Come the moment when a preferred customer list for loans is needed outside of the sphere of loans, there will be a motivation to move the application data into the subject area.

Industry experience has shown that the migration to operational subject data bases is done slowly and a subject at a time. Banks moved from a plethora of applications to customer files. Once the customer files were in place there was a movement to account files, and so on. Insurance companies moved to integrated policy systems. Once integrated policy systems were in place, claims systems were built, and so on. The order of movement to subjects usually begins with the most important subjects or subjects that touch the most applications as the initial impetus for migration.

Design of Atomic Data Bases

After the existing environment has been analyzed and the operational migration is planned, the next step is the design of the atomic environment. Atomic data bases are oriented towards the major subjects of the enterprise. The keys of atomic data bases are used to relate different aspects of the subject. For example, an account atomic subject data base may have related tables for account activity, account ownership, account establishment, and account relationships. The data model that has been created can be lifted, in most cases directly, and used as a basis for the design of atomic data bases.

The general orientation of the keys of atomic data bases is towards time variancy. In general, four types of time variancy are found: static, where the data remains static over time; continuous, where the fluctuations of data are measured over time; event discrete, where a discrete snapshot of data is triggered by an event, and periodic discrete, where a discrete snapshot of data is triggered by the passing of time.

Populating the Atomic Data Bases

After the atomic data bases are designed, they need to be populated. As previously discussed, some atomic data is most likely to be populated directly from existing systems, as shown by Figure 86.

Figure 86 shows that some existing data can be used, as is, for the foundation of atomic data bases. All that needs to be done is writing an extract program moving operational data to the atomic environment. Over time, as existing systems are replaced or rebuilt, atomic data bases will become fully supported, as shown by Figure 87.

The difference between Figure 86 and Figure 87 is that in Figure 87, the operational environment is subject oriented and fully supports the atomic environment, while the environment depicted in Figure 86 is not subject oriented and does not fully support the atomic-level data. In Figure 86, the environment is application-oriented and only in a scattered fashion supports the atomic environment.

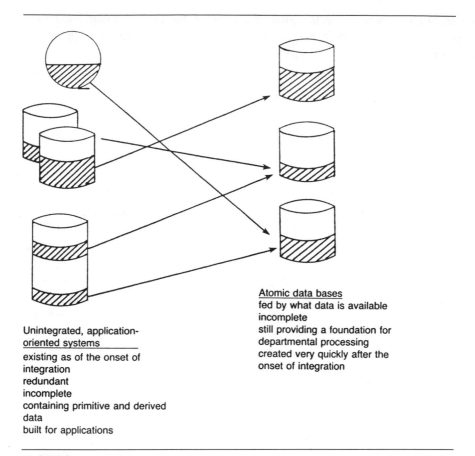

Atomic data bases
fed by what data is available
incomplete
still providing a foundation for
departmental processing
created very quickly after the
onset of integration

Unintegrated, application-
oriented systems
existing as of the onset of
integration
redundant
incomplete
containing primitive and derived
data
built for applications

FIGURE 86 Migration to the atomic environment prior to any integration of the operational environment.

DEPARTMENTAL, INDIVIDUAL MIGRATION

For the most part, the creation of operational and atomic-level data comprises the longest job in the migration from existing systems to the architecture. But there is more to the information paradigm than operational and atomic-level data. Usually, the *formal* migration is for operational and atomic data. The migration to the departmental and individual level is, for the most part, informal.

The departmental migration usually consists of identifying what scheduled reports are required. Next, the reports are categorized by the de-

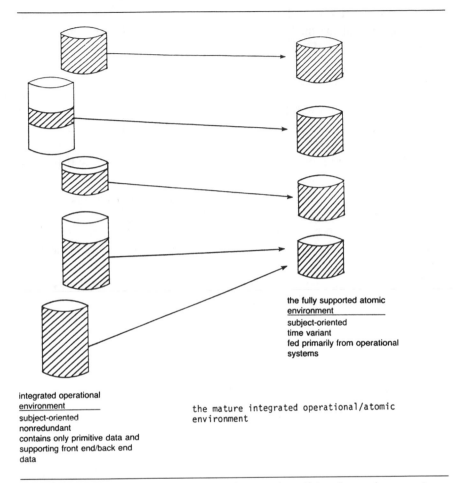

the fully supported atomic
environment

subject-oriented
time variant
fed primarily from operational
systems

integrated operational
environment

subject-oriented
nonredundant
contains only primitive data and
supporting front end/back end
data

the mature integrated operational/atomic
environment

FIGURE 87 The mature integrated operational/atomic environment

partment they belong to. The source for the reports is located in the atomic data base, and the data is extracted to the proper department if the departmental extract does not already contain the data.

Oftentimes, the processing at the departmental level entails creation of summary-level data bases. These data bases are created and updated as the data is transported from the atomic level.

The establishment of the departmental and the individual levels of data comes on an as needed basis, unlike the operational and atomic-level data.

While the migration of operational and atomic-level data occurs as a concerted effort over a relatively short period of time, the migration to (or establishment of) the departmental- and individual-level data occurs as an almost casual effort over a long period of time.

SUMMARY

The first step in the migration to the architecture is building a model of the organization. After the model is created, it is used for a comparison with existing systems. Some of the existing systems can usually be used, as is, for architectured fulfillment. Other existing systems will have to be changed.

Next, the atomic-level data bases are designed. On the basis of the analysis of existing systems, some of the atomic data bases may be able to be immediately populated.

Over time, other existing systems are changed or added, and the atomic-level data is added.

Once the atomic level data is populated, departmental- and individual-level data can be created.

8 ORGANIZATIONAL IMPLICATIONS OF THE INFORMATION PARADIGM

*T*he information paradigm, as a design technique or a general approach to systems, does not exist in a vacuum. To be effective, the information paradigm must become an integral part of corporate culture. There are many organizational implications to the information paradigm, especially as it is implemented.

These organizational implications center around the organizational unit whose responsibility it is to define and direct the implementation of the information paradigm. In some organizations, this task will fall to the data administrator. The classic duties of the data administrator are greatly expanded when the care and tending of the information paradigm become his or her responsibility. The job of the data administrator changes from that of a technician or clerical to that of a high-level managerial business strategist.

In other cases, the task of building and implementing the information paradigm falls to the chief information officer (the CIO). When the CIO is charged with responsibility for the information paradigm, his or her job is expanded considerably by more day-to-day activities than otherwise is normal.

In the case where either the CIO or data administration function does not exist, then an organizational unit needs to be established whose purpose it is to build and tend the information paradigm.

The purpose of the data architecture organization—whether it be part of data administration, part of the office of the CIO, or its own independent organization—is to satisfy the following functions:

- bridging the technical/business gap,
- providing a communication conduit between management and the organization,
- focusing on *both* long-term strategic and short-term objectives,
- steeping the architecture in a realistic technical foundation,
- providing ongoing education/indoctrination.

Each of these major functions will be addressed.

BRIDGING THE TECHNICAL/ BUSINESS GAP

Any architecture that does not take into account *both* the technical and business needs of the organization will ultimately be a failure. The data architect *must* blend both perspectives into the day-to-day job. The data processing industry is littered with technical failures that had little or no relationship to the business of the organization. The data architecture function must combine both sets of needs in a unified, balanced manner.

PROVIDING A COMMUNICATIONS CONDUIT

The data architect has regular conversations with *both* the top management and line workers. It is the job of the data architect to provide two-way communication on a regular basis. Data architecture must be able to translate the global, long-term concerns of management into the detailed, short-term focus of line workers, and vice versa.

FOCUSING ON BOTH LONG-TERM AND SHORT-TERM OBJECTIVES

One of the most important aspects of the data architect's job is understanding long-term goals and translating those goals into short-term objectives. The entire scope of the data architecture effort is in jeopardy if the emphasis is not balanced. If the job of the data architect becomes one of nothing but long-term goals, then it will be a theoretical, "blue sky" job. If the job of the data architect turns into nothing but a series of short-term tasks, then the long-term directions will be lost. The data architect walks a fine line between the major objectives of the job. It is essential that *both* long-term and short-term interests be served.

STEEPING THE ARCHITECTURE IN A REALISTIC TECHNICAL FOUNDATION

The data architect must be constantly aware of technical advances that are being made. There are three aspects of interest: what new technology there is, the cost of new technology, and how and if the technology applies to the information paradigm and the business of the enterprise. Part of the long-term direction of the information paradigm is its ability to be realized within the context of technology. The data architect must be aware of long-term technical directions and opportunities.

PROVIDING ONGOING EDUCATION/INDOCTRINATION

The information paradigm represents a change to the organization, albeit a step toward maturity. The source of information about the information paradigm is the office of the data architect, who plays both a passive and an active role in this regard. In addition, the data architect provides education/indoctrination to very different levels. Some education is aimed at the new employee; other education is aimed at the management infrastructure.

The thrust of education/indoctrination is towards both technology functions and business functions.

THE JOB OF THE DATA ARCHITECT

The first major objective of the data architect is to develop the blueprint of what the data architecture is to look like. The conceptual model (covered in depth in *Information Systems Architecture*, Prentice-Hall, and *Information Engineering For The Practitioner*, op cit. consists of three levels: the ERD level, the dis level, and the physical level. The conceptual model describes primitive data directly and derived data indirectly. And it describes how data is defined over the different levels of data.

The data architect may create the conceptual model either formally or informally. In either case, the model must be created before implementation may occur. (In other words, if the data architect attempts to build the information paradigm *without* a model, there is potential for much confusion and loss of momentum.) After the conceptual model is built, the next step is to apply the model to the organization. It is at this point that there is the greatest challenge and the greatest payoff. The job of "maintaining" the information paradigm over time is an ongoing job. Fortunately, the data architect has a very powerful ally—the forces at work within the organization that naturally push the organization towards the information paradigm. In that regard, the ongoing task of implementing the information paradigm is merely that of a facilitator. The job of the data architect is to recognize the forces of evolution at work and provide graceful continuity between the forces of evolution and the manifestation of the information paradigm.

The information paradigm is the product of a large evolution. The center of that evolution is the end user. In the early 1980's many products were introduced in the name of user friendliness. The mind set was that if the product was user friendly (whatever that meant!) that the product would make the end user happy.
The article—DOES USER FRIENDLY MEAN USER HAPPY?—asks the question—are the two equivalent? In addition the notion of an end user's hierarchy of needs is introduced. Understanding the end user's hierarchy of needs is at the center of understanding the evolutionary forces of the information paradigm.

*DOES USER-FRIENDLY MEAN USER HAPPY?**

User friendliness is easily the most obvious and important trend in data processing in recent years. Its thrust is in two directions—in the development of systems and in the usage of systems. But is user friendliness all there is to user satisfaction? The answer to that question is best addressed in terms of the context of different environments, in particular the on-line, operational environment (as opposed to the decision support environment).

The cost-effective use of workers' time in the on-line, operational environment is unquestioned. What, then, are the parameters of user satisfaction in that environment?

Two parameters are of the utmost importance:

- Consistent, satisfactory on-line response time.
- Consistent, satisfactory on-line availability.

On-line response time is the amount of time required for the system to provide output for an on-line request. On-line availability refers to the amount of time the on-line system is up and available for usage.

When these factors are met, the user then thinks about such things as ease of use, quality of system prompts, value of error messages and so forth. But if response time and availability are not satisfactory, then typical user-friendly factors become secondary.

But if the system is even moderately friendly, performs well and is available at appropriate times, then the system can be successful.

---

*By W.H. Inmon, *Computerworld*, July 1984. Reprinted with permission.

Another way of illustrating this point is to consider the on-line, operational system development life cycle. User-friendly development systems can streamline the first phases of a project. This enhancement of the speed and costs of initial development unquestionably pleases the user, so it is argued that user-friendly systems do in fact enhance user satisfaction. But what happens when the system begins to mature?

As the system matures and goes from design into implementation, the user then wants performance and availability. In running against a small amount of data or with a small amount of activity, user-friendly software usually does not demonstrate any major problems. But when put into execution in a normal, active on-line environment, user-friendly systems often display distressing problems of performance and, in some cases, of availability.

To protect the on-line environment, user-friendly software is either not run at all, or user-friendly features are greatly inhibited. This defeats much of the purpose of the software.

Vendors of some user-friendly software claim it is appropriate to the on-line, operational environment. While there is some truth to that, experience has shown that when user-friendly software is used on-line and operationally, the cost of hardware spirals. This can even call into question the cost effectiveness of using user-friendly software in this fashion.

So a third major criteria—cost —is introduced for user satisfaction. The different criteria for user satisfaction at the different stages in the development life cycle are shown in the figure above.

At different stages, the user wants different things. User-friendly software greatly addresses the first criterion for satisfaction in the on-line operational environment, but usually is inappropriate for addressing the others.

Complicating matters is the fact that performance and availability cannot be addressed after the system is built. Once an on-line, operational system is built, its performance and availability profile are set in concrete. It must be completely rebuilt if the performance and availability profile is to be changed significantly.

A common misconception is that the user assumes that since a system is on a computer, it will perform well. But that misconception quickly dies in the dawn of reality as the user-friendly system competes for precious resources with other on-line activities. The user does not see this competition.

However fast and powerful the computer, the demand for its power soon swallows up any excess capacity. As long as budget, performance and availability remain the criteria for user satisfaction in the on-line, operational environment, then user-friendly software most often will be inappropriate there.

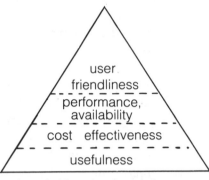

Inmon's hierarchy of needs for users

An interesting analogy can be made to Maslow's hierarchy of needs from the world of psychology. In Maslow's scheme, once a basic set of needs is met, then an individual progresses to a higher set of needs, assuming that the lower level of needs will always be met.

A very simple hierarchy of needs can be drawn up for automation that parallels Maslow's hierarchy. At the bottom of the hierarchy is usefulness. The next factor is cost effectiveness.

For the on-line, operational environment, performance and availability make up the next level of needs. Finally, at the top of the hierarchy, comes user friendliness. Once a system meets these needs, then the issue of user friendliness can become the center of attention.

Implementing the architecture includes, at least, the following rights and responsibilities:

- The review of all new work and/or modification to determine what fit there is between the work to be done, the existing environment, and the information paradigm.
- Close work with the data administrator and the data base administrator to determine what the day-to-day implementation issues are.
- Close work with application developers/application modifiers to determine how application requirements are best determined in terms of the architecture.
- Close work with the end users to ensure that primitive data is providing a firm foundation for derived processing and to determine when private end user data turns into public data.

In addition, the data architect provides focused input into the migration plan—the plan that specifies how today's environment will gracefully be transformed into the architected environment.

There is a conflict here, in that the data architect must have control over some of the classical domains of the application developer. The data architect needs to be able to specify data content and key structure for *all* globally shared data. For data that is not globally shared, there may or may not be any input from the data architect.

The data dictionary is influenced very strongly by the data architect. It is, for all practical purposes, impossible to implement shared data across the organization without some form of data dictionary. The data dictionary should contain, in addition to the classical contents of data dictionary, the formal embodiment of the data model. The different levels of model, the relationship between the levels, the key structure, and other facets of the model should be contained in the data dictionary.

Given that the data architect must have strong influence over part of the application domain, it is easy to predict that there will be resistance from the application development organization. There are three ways that resistance may be minimized:

- By anticipating resistance,
- By clearly defining what the architecture is and how it is to be implemented,
- By clearly defining the rights and responsibilities of both data architecture and applications with regard to data design.

Ambiguity in the face of passive or active resistance tends to strengthen the case of the application developer. So, the data architecture group needs to invest the time required to spell out to applications the exact interface.

The task of data architecture is one of global perspective. Most data processing organizations have similar units with global outreaches, such as capacity planning, systems tuning, training, information center, and so forth. The organization may well structure these organizations together, or it may structure them separately, as shown by Figure 88.

In one case, shown in Figure 84, "global services" are grouped together and are separate from systems or applications. The organizational positioning is appropriate, and the ability to communicate and coordinate across the global services is enhanced. On the other hand, when global

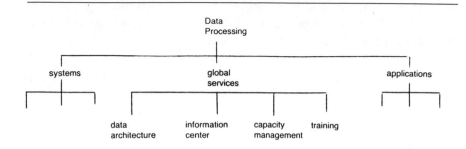

One organization of global services.

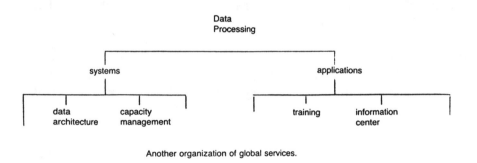

Another organization of global services.

FIGURE 88 Organizations structured separately.

services are removed from systems and applications, they tend to become aloof. In some instances they may be labeled "blue sky." When global services are scattered, as shown in Figure 84, the full impact tends to be lost. Oftentimes, global needs are subjugated to immediate, parochial needs. The conflict between local application needs and global organizational needs is divided on the basis of the organization chart. As a consequence, the most effective organization chart is the one where data architecture, as well as other global services, is separated from application or system organizations.

It is very easy for the data architecture organization to be labeled a blue sky organization. Indeed, the long-term focus of data architecture requires that *some of the time*, a certain amount of blue skying be done. But if *all* the data architecture does is blue sky, then an opportunity has been lost. The data architecture organization must constantly walk a line between short-term and long-term goals. It is a good practice for data architecture to constantly set an agenda of short-term objectives that can be visibly and quantifiably measured. These short-term objectives should be periodically reviewed with management. By creating short-term tasks, the data architecture group can better focus on the short-term side of the equation.

The responsibilities of the data architecture organization and its relationships to other organizational units is shown by Figure 89.

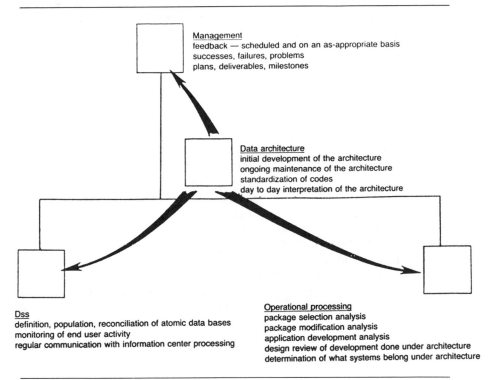

Management
feedback — scheduled and on an as-appropriate basis
successes, failures, problems
plans, deliverables, milestones

Data architecture
initial development of the architecture
ongoing maintenance of the architecture
standardization of codes
day to day interpretation of the architecture

Dss
definition, population, reconciliation of atomic data bases
monitoring of end user activity
regular communication with information center processing

Operational processing
package selection analysis
package modification analysis
application development analysis
design review of development done under architecture
determination of what systems belong under architecture

FIGURE 89   Typical activities of the office of the data architect.

SUMMARY

The information paradigm has many implications for the organization. The data administrator or the chief information officer is primarily responsible for management of the evolution to the information paradigm.

When the data administrator assumes responsibility for the information paradigm, the scope of his or her responsibility is broadened.

The end user is one organizational concern that must be actively managed. Other organizational concerns are data dictionary, education and training, and modeling.

Whatever agency is in charge of managing and monitoring, the evaluation must recognize that there is a balance between the theoretical and the practical that must be struck.

The data architecture imposes new responsibilities on the organization. The formal definition of what task falls into what organizational unit can be very beneficial, especially when there is an organizational realignment of boundaries. The list below sets the stage for conversations about the rights and responsibilities of different organizations.

APPLICATION RESPONSIBILITIES FOR CORPORATE DATA

1. Provide schedules of development for corporate data architecture (i.e., what data structure design is needed when).

2. Provide an estimate of when corporate data bases will be populated and when the corporate data is a responsibility of the application.

3. Provide the code needed to support the business functions for the population and manipulation of corporate data.

4. Provide corporate data architecture with the structural and content changes needed for corporate data.

5. Provide corporate data architecture, with the data element and data structure needs, for the corporate data for which the application is responsible.

6. Ensure that all corporate data is present in the data model that is required by the processes for which the application is responsible.

CORPORATE DATA ARCHITECTURE RESPONSIBILITIES

1. Represent all applications requirements in the data model.

2. Determine what data is to be in the architecture and what data is not to be in the architecture. Once the determination is made, publicly document the decision.

3. Build the model for corporate data (i.e., data that is under the architecture) and maintain the model as the business changes.

4. Ensure that future, as well as current, requirements are reflected by the model.

5. For corporate data:
- Determine what the contents of the model are (i.e., data elements)
- Determine what the key structures are,
- Determine what the interfaces between corporate data will be,
- Determine what the interfaces to corporate data will be from external sources,
- Determine what the "ownership" requirements are, at the element level, for update, creation, and deletion of data,
- Determine what the access requirements are for sensitive data,
- Determine what the cycles of update are.

Manage changes to the content and structure of the corporate data.

6. Determine the source and code for the interface to all corporate decision support data.

9 ECONOMIC CONSIDERATIONS OF THE INFORMATION PARADIGM

*T*he implications of the information paradigm go well beyond the technical and organizational areas. There are major economic implications as well. Like the forces of mass and gravity at work in the glacier, the forces of technology and economics are at work to move the organization to the information paradigm. Indeed, perhaps the biggest motivation at work on today's data processing and end user computing departments is the force of economics.

PEOPLE COSTS

One of the largest expenses of the data processing/end user computing organization is the cost of people. The costs for people are spread over operations, development, maintenance, and technical support, for the most part. Over time, the cost of maintenance alone grows to the point that it is usually the single largest expense, in terms of payroll.

The information paradigm addresses maintenance costs in a strategic and effective manner. As the organization moves to the information paradigm, maintenance costs are (in some cases, significantly) reduced because:

▪ Primitive data is separated from derived data and derived data has a much higher propensity for change.
▪ The information paradigm tends to cause data to be integrated.

Both reasons for the reduction of maintenance will be explored.

The separation of primitive from derived data has the effect of separating stable data from unstable data. Primitive data, on the whole, is much more stable than derived data. Thus, data that is highly likely to change (and hence, highly likely to require maintenance) is insulated from data that is not highly likely to change (but if it does, is highly likely to require only small changes). As an example, suppose a bank has a single application that keeps track, by account, of daily activity and account balances. The application also keeps track of the monthly average balance and monthly high and low balances. The standard account balance information is used for normal day-to-day management of an account, while the high, low, and average account balance is used for decisions on how to manage rate information.

Management decides to take a look at application data from a longer perspective than a month. It will now look at six-month moving averages, annual comparisons, high and low information, and so forth. The application code is affected by this decision. Next quarter, management decides to look at short-term movement of account balances as well, looking at weekly trends—say, Monday, Wednesday and Friday balances. Once again, the application is affected. Each time the application is affected, maintenance of code mounts and people costs rise.

Now, suppose the analyst designing the system had decided to split the operational and decision support processing of the application into separate and distinct components. One application—the operational one—simply does standard account management, keeping track of daily activity and daily balances. An atomic data store is created for the detailed daily activity. New management reports can be written as desired with no effect on the day-to-day processing by accessing and extracting from the atomic data. Maintenance or modification of the original application has ceased because of the separation of primitive and derived data.

Another way the information paradigm enhances maintenance is through the integration of data. Over time, as the organization migrates to the information paradigm, data—at the operational level and the atomic level—becomes nonredundant and integrated. As the degree of redundancy is reduced, the maintenance required drops as well.

There is a factor related to maintenance and the separation of primitive and derived data. Generally speaking, operational systems are written in technology that is not amenable to change and derived systems are written in technology that is amenable to change. For example, in the banking case previously discussed, suppose the original single application were written in IMS, a software product noted for its lack of flexibility. Every time a change needed to be made, IMS code would be disturbed.

However, when the application is broken between primitive and derived data, the operational part of the system can be written in IMS and the derived portion written in some language with a greater flexibility, such as FOCUS. The vast majority of the changes that need to be made will be done in FOCUS.

A third way maintenance is enhanced by the information paradigm is that changes in the operational environment are reflected only once in the atomic data base. If there were no atomic data base, the changes that occur in the operational environment would affect every extract of the production environment and potentially every departmental data base. The infrastructure of atomic data insulates changes in the operational environment from changes in the departmental environment.

While maintenance is a significant cost that is beneficially influenced by the information paradigm, it is hardly the only cost. Development costs are influenced as well.

REQUIREMENTS ANALYSIS

One of the most important aspects of development is the gathering and assimilation of requirements. If requirements are not properly input into the development process, the resulting system has little chance for success. The separation of primitive and derived processing has a very beneficial effect on the requirements analysis process.

Primitive requirements tend to be finite and stable. Once gathered and organized, they tend to remain static. Derived requirements are constantly changing—it is simply the nature of derived data and processing. In fact, it is sometimes said that derived requirements change faster than they can be gathered and organized. A formal requirements definition that attempts to gather derived requirements is a never-ending job. Given the tools used to manipulate derived data, it often makes sense not to formally analyze the data. Instead, it is more efficient to *build* the derived system (assuming, of course, that the atomic foundation is in place to support the derived processing.)

The separation of primitive and derived processing, then, greatly streamlines classical requirements gathering and organization, and thus the development process is greatly accelerated. The result of the acceleration of development is a reduced development cost.

Another indirect enhancement of the development process is the simplification that exists in the face of a subject orientation of data. The application developer in the mature information paradigm environment is free to concentrate on the immediate set of functions that need to be developed. The general structure of the environment is already determined; it does not have to be reinvented by every new development project that comes along.

But the largest enhancement to the development process afforded by the information paradigm is a strategic one. By virtue of the architecture itself, there is the capability of building on previous work that has been done. In other words, the architecture precludes the need to do massive redevelopment. The end result is a very efficient usage of development resources, which is reflected in the budget.

At another strategic level, there is a savings inherent to the information paradigm. Integration of systems is the ultimate result of migration to the architecture. There are some obvious and very large benefits to integration. These benefits—which directly translate to dollars and cents savings—include:

- No need for synchronization of data—the savings are in code development and maintenance.
- Less storage is needed as data redundancy decreases.
- Less processing power is needed—as less synchronization is done, less processing needs to be done.

But there are some benefits of integration that cannot be easily quantified (but nevertheless are very real). These benefits include:

- The quality of data
- The timeliness of data
- The credibility of data

In the long run, the nonquantifiable issues of integration often prove to be more important than the easily quantifiable issues.

As important as the people costs and the issues of integration are, they are hardly the only issues of economics that relate to the information paradigm. The second category of costs (other than people-related costs) that is relevant is the cost of hardware and software. It is in this arena that the information paradigm has great relevance.

The information paradigm greatly enhances the hardware budget in that, by spreading processing power over a wide spectrum, there can be an efficient usage of MIPS. (millions of instructions per second—a standard measurement of processing power). For example, in an unarchitected environment where all processing is done in a single system, it is common to find processing done on a large mainframe. There are two reasons why a mainframe is used: There is a need for a lot of power and the operational aspects of the system require high powered DBMS and TP software that run on a mainframe. The result is that *all* processing is done on a single large mainframe.

One of the principle components of the information paradigm is the extract process. The article—EXTRACT PROCESSING IN DB2—discusses, in the context of DB2, the issues of extract processing.
The article should be read more generically by the reader, as most of the issues discussed apply well beyond the confines of DB2.

*EXTRACT PROCESSING IN DB2**

Extract processing is an integral part of the DB2 environment. Extract processing is necessary to unlock the flexibility that can be achieved in DB2. There is nothing terribly difficult about extract processing from the standpoint of the programmer. The logic required for most extract processing is simple.

But extract processing soon becomes an issue in the face of the volume of data that must pass through the extract programs. In short order the amount of time required for extract processing begins to exceed the amount of time that is available. And the total amount of data that is being extracted soon overflows the DASD that is available. If not carefully thought out and carefully constructed, extract processing soon becomes a large

*By W.H. Inmon, *Data Dialogues* (July 1988). DataBase Programming Design Magazine, Miller-Freeman, San Francisco, CA. Reprinted with permission.

issue in the running of a DB2 environment.

Extract processing in DB2 may be done in a variety of manners, such as—

- using the DXT utility
- using application program logic
- using other utilities such as the DB2 ToolKit, by Innovative Designs.

EXTRACT LOGIC

The logic required for extract processing is simple. The extract program is fed some parameters. The parameters shape the logic that will be used to determine what data will be selected. Usually the selection of data is from a production or operational data base or data bases.

Next the extract program accesses the original production data base(s) that serves as the source of data. The scan through the original data base may be sequential from one row to the next or may be by an index where the program logic is used to select values based on the contents of the index.

After data is selected by the extract program it is transported to the output file. The output file may be in the same order as the original data, or the output file may be summarized, merged, or otherwise altered.

After the extract program has executed and the extracted output file is created, the analyst uses the extracted data as a basis for reports, decision support analysis, for the creation of trend analysis files, or other purposes.

The immediate challenge posed by extract processing is that extract processing can consume a large amount of machine resources, principally in the usage of I/O. In addition much DASD may be used for extracted files.

ARCHITECTING THE EXTRACT PROCESS

The first step in managing the extract process is not do extracts in a random, disorganized manner. The extract of data from one environment to another represents a fundamental transformation of data with many implications in the usage, credibility, and efficiency of processing of the data. For an indepth discussion of these issues refer to chapter 13, INFORMATION ENGINEERING FOR THE PRAC-TITIONER: FROM THEORY INTO PRACTICE, Yourdon Press, 1988. The designer is well advised to carefully consider all the implications of extracts. In short, extract processing should not be an after the fact consideration in the design of the production and decision support DB2 environment.

USING THE EXTRACTED DATA

In some cases the ultimate use and disposition of the extracted data is well known. When the requirements are well established, the designer can design the content and occurrences of the extracted environment with precision. No wasted data should be the goal in this case, as each occurrence of extracted data requires storage and handling.

But in other instances the usage and disposition of the extracted data is not known. In this case the designer can only guess as to what data will be required. Even where there are unknown requirements for extracted data, it is worth the designer's while to try to anticipate requirements.

In the case of unknown requirements if there is a lot of data to be managed, the designer will want to sort data into two categories—data that probably will be needed and data that probably will not be needed. The data that will be needed will be extracted and managed in the normal manner. But the data that probably will not be needed should be stored on a bulk archival medium. If the designer has guessed incorrectly, at a later point in time at least the data that has not been extracted will still be available. The problem is that restoring data from a bulk archival medium is awkward, slow and expensive.

Of course the designer can adopt the stance that ALL data needs to be extracted, regardless of the probability of access. Then the designer must pay the costs of storage and processing of data that is not needed.

The designer should carefully consider the tradeoff between storing too little data and having to restore data from an awkward medium and storing too much data and constantly paying the overhead for data that is never used.

GRANULARITY OF DATA

One of the most important issues the designer faces is the granularity of data as data is extracted. Data in the original (i.e., the unextracted state) is as granular as the data is ever going to be. The designer may want to preserve the same level of granularity as the data in its unextracted state or the designer may want to summarize or otherwise consolidate the data. By consolidating the data upon extract, less

I/O will be used for the loading of the extracted file and less DASD will be needed.

As an example of the considerations of the granularity of extracted data, a designer in a manufacturing environment wants to extract data from the daily usage record for a parts file. Each withdrawal or replenishment of a part is recorded throughout the day in a production data base. One option for extract processing is simply to select each entry of data— each withdrawal and each replenishment—for the extract file. The extracted file can then be used to answer a host of questions—

- what was the largest withdrawal during the day?
- what part had the most activities against it?
- at what time did the most withdrawals occur? and so forth

While these questions may be of interst, they require that data be stored in the extract file at the lowest level of granularity. Each withdrawal and each replenishment must be captured and transported to the extract file. The number of records to be loaded and the amount of DASD required may be significant.

The designer could reduce the level of granularity in the extract file by storing cumulative withdrawal and replenishment activity by part. All daily withdrawals would be added with all daily replenishments for each part. Then the net activity for the day would be stored in the extract file. There would be no savings in the access of the original data, but much less I/O would be saved in the writing out of the extract file. In addition the output file would require much less DASD.

Of course, the analyst could not look at detailed transactions in the extract file. But the analyst still could do much decision support analysis, such as looking at trends of parts usage, for example.

THE RIGHT LEVEL OF DETAIL

There is no right or wrong answer as to what level of detail is appropriate for the extracted file. In general the designer should choose the highest level of detail that suffices for the queries that will be made against the data. The tradeoff is between the type of query that can be made and the cost of extracting and storing detailed data.

The granularity of extracted data and the processing that will be done against the extracted data then are the very first two issues that must be addressed by the designer.

LESS EXTRACTED DETAIL

Not only is the granularity of data an issue in the extraction of data, but the level of detail that is extracted is an issue as well. While there may be cases where entire original records are shipped to an extracted environment, the designer should always assume that not all data elements are candidates for extraction.

For example, suppose a bank has a production data base where account activities are kept. A typical record in the production data base contains the following data elements—

- account identification
- date, time of activity
- amount of activity
- location of activity
- personal identification
- teller window balance at time of activity
- electronic identification
- check number
- "posting" requested?
- payroll activity?

All of these data elements are required for operational processing and rightfully reside in the production data base. But it is unlikely that most of these data elements belong in the extracted file. It is hard to imagine any sort of analytic processing of the extracted file that would require (or even find useful!) data elements such as check number or personal identification. The list of data elements in the original data base may be divided into two categories—those data elements needed for extracted processing and those not needed—

- account identification *[needed]*
- date, time of activity *[needed]*
- amount of activity *[needed]*
- location of activity *[needed]*
- personal identification *[not needed]*
- teller window balance at time of activity *[not needed]*
- electronic identification *[not needed]*
- check number *[not needed]*
- "posting" requested? *[not needed]*
- payroll activity? *[not needed]*

The amount of data shipped to the extract file then is only a subset of the original data insofar as the type of data elements that are shipped is concerned. Of course this weeding out of data does not make the scanning of the original data any more efficient. But the weeding out of data does make the loading of data (and its subsequent access!) more efficient in that less data needs to be loaded. Loading less data implies that the data can be loaded more compactly. The tighter data that can be loaded, the fewer resources required in the loading and access of the data.

The granularity of the occurrences of data and the details that are shipped to the extract file, then, are two issues the designer must come to grips with.

THE HARDWARE ENVIRONMENT

Another consideration the designer has is the hardware environment in which the extract processing will be done. There are two possibilities—

- both the original and the extracted data will reside on the same processor, and
- the original data base will reside on one processor and the extracted data base will reside on another processor.

As long as there is only a modest amount of data and as long as there is only a small amount of processing being done, there is no reason why both the original data base and the extracted data base cannot reside on the same machine. But in the face of much data and/or much processing, it makes sense to split the data across separate machines.

In general the original data will come from the operational, production environment. The extracted data will form the foundation for decision support processing. The generic patterns of processing are very different. Production processing usually entails a fairly static usage of machine resources. Decision support processing entails a dynamic, unpredictable usage of machine resources. Separating the two patterns of machine utilization in the face of volumes of processing makes sense.

When the original data base resides on a separate machine from the extracted data, there can be a beneficial separation of processing. The extract process is broken into two distinct operations—a selection and extract process (from the original file) and a load process (into the extracted file). The actual selection and extract processing takes place on the production machine. The data is then transferred to the machine where the extracted data will reside, and the load process is done there. In such a manner the CPU cycles from two machines share the workload. In addition if there is a need for summarization or other refinement of data the machine on which the extracted data resides can be used.

Separating extracted and original data over multiple machines has another beneficial effect. When the extract process is separated over two machines there is a clarity of processing that otherwise may become blurred if all extract processing is done on a single machine. When extract processing is done on a single machine the extract process itself may become entangled with regular application code. Once the extract process becomes enmeshed

with regular code it is difficult to handle the problems of extract processing independent of the application.

For example, a data base has been designed for an oil company to keep track of shipments of oil. The data base keeps track of oil shipments on a daily basis as the shipments arrive. Billing, refinery, and allocation is done based on the values in the data base. In addition an archiving of shipments is stored in the same data base. After today's shipment is processed, the record of activity is kept in the same data base. The current record is simply written into an archival portion of the data base. The archival of shipment records is used for decision support analysis, looking at historical trends and so forth.

Over time the shipment data base grows, and the volume of processing overwhelms the machine. Attempting to remove the shipment archival processing from the application is a very disruptive thing to do.

Had the application been designed so that current value shipment data not be archived off into the same data base, then managing the problems of volume at a later moment in time would have been much simpler. In the original design of the application, if there had been a separate extract program that periodically examined shipment records for inclusion in a separate archival file, then the problems of volumes of data and consumption of I/O could have been dealt with separately. But trying to separate extract processing at a later point in time is awkward.

THE PIGGYBACK APPROACH

In truth, extract processing usually grows in an undisciplined fashion. But for those organizations that are facing a large amount of extract processing, a disciplined approach is in order.

Consider an undisciplined extract environment. On day one, an extract program is designed to look at a personnel file selecting all male employees. On day two, another extract program is written to look at employees who make more than $50,000 annually. On day three, a third extract is written to look at employees who have advanced college degrees. While none of the extracts consumes too many resources by itself, collectively the extracts consume a fair amount of resources.

The scan portion of the extract could be streamlined in that only one scan of the personnel data base needs to be done, looking for data that fits one or more of the criterion that is being considered. The logic of the scan program determines if the record being examined is a male, makes more than $50,000 an-

nually, or has an advanced college degree. The record is written to as many extract files as there are criteria that are satisfied. There is a wholesale waste of I/O in the scanning of the same personnel data base three times.

The discipline required for the "piggyback" approach mandates that not only current extract requirements be consolidated, but all future requirements be consolidated as well. In other words, whenever a new extract requirement has been identified, the first step the designer takes is to determine what extracts already exist that can be used. The only time the designer specifies a new extract be written is if the extract is against a data base that has no extracts already going against it.

The savings in combining criteria to achieve a single scan of data shows up in the I/O needed for the first part of the extract process. Of course multipurpose scans probably look at data on a record by record basis, rather than accessing data through the index.

INCREMENTAL CHANGES

Some extract processing consists of a blind copy of all data into the extracted format. In this case, the extract appears to be a "snapshot" of data as of some moment in time. There may be a large savings in this type of extract processing if only occurrences of data that have had changes since the last extract are selected for the transportation across the barrier to the extracted file.

As an example, suppose in an Army personnel data base that every six months all officers have their active files extracted into an archived format. This extract (that occurs two times a year) selects all Army officers. The extract takes a long time because there are many officers.

Another approach to the extract is to select only officers who have undergone a change in status in the previous six months. In such a manner many fewer officers could be selected for the extract. For example, if any of the following criteria were met then the officer would be selected for the extract—

- if marital status changed
- if rank changed
- if an advanced degree were obtained
- if there were a change in dependents
- if the officer had received training in a new subject

The selection of only a subset of data based on incremental activity saves processing in both the scan and the load portions of the extract process. Unfortunately such an approach probably will require logic in the loading of the extracted data that otherwise would not have been needed. However the additional logic and complexity is usually worth the savings in processing.

INDEXES AND EXTRACTED DATA

The amount of time required to load extracted data can quickly grow to unreasonable levels if there is a lot of data to be loaded and if the data to be loaded requires that one or more indexes be loaded at the same time. The designer should be VERY CAREFUL of large extracted files with multiple indexes.

The designer should not take for granted that an index is needed for extracted data. Each index should be individually justified.

Certainly clustering the extracted data can reduce the time and DASD required to load one index. But tables can be clustered only once. Clustering an extracted file then, has only limited applicability.

Another approach to managing large extracts of data and their corresponding large indexes is to break the extracted data into multiple separate tables. For example, suppose an insurance company annually extracts the history of claims which have been settled and/or received by the company. Each year the company receives a large number of claims.

One approach to the extract process is simply to load the extracted data into a table and create indexes. But quickly the insurance company discovers that the load and index building process takes an inordinate amount of time.

The designer decides to break the claims table up into twelve categories. There will be a claims table not for the entire year's worth of claims, but for each month in the year. In other words, depending on when the claim was made, there will be a January claims table, a February claims table, a March claims table, and so forth. The resulting tables take roughly 1/12th of the time to load the tables and their associated indexes. Of course the load process still takes as long en toto to execute. But the load process is broken up into units that are much more amenable to normal operations. And there is the possibility of being able to execute the load processes in parallel.

Even though there is no real savings in the division of a table and its associated indexes into small components, there are real gains in the operability and usability of such data.

It is fair to question what the splitting of a table does to program logic that is required to access the table. Consider the request against the single large table of insurance claims—

```
SELECT DATE AMOUNT
   FROMNAME
FROM CLAIMS
WHERE
```

```
CLAIMANT = "Jackson,
Bob'
```

When the table is divided the same request must be run multiple times, as in the following—

```
SELECT DATE AMOUNT
   FROMNAME
FROM CLAIMJAN
WHERE
   CLAIMANT = "Jackson,
   Bob'
```

```
SELECT DATE AMOUNT
   FROMNAME
FROM CLAIMFEB
WHERE
   CLAIMANT = "Jackson,
   Bob'
```

```
SELECT DATE AMOUNT
   FROMNAME
FROM CLAIMMAR
WHERE
   CLAIMANT = "Jackson,
   Bob'
```

```
SELECT DATE AMOUNT
   FROMNAME
FROM CLAIMAPR
WHERE
   CLAIMANT = "JACKSON,
   BOB'
```

```
• • • • • • • • • • • • •
• • • • • • • • • • • • •
• • • • • • • • • • • • •
• • • • • • • • • • • • •
• • • • • • • • • • • • •
```

At first glance the amount of work

required of the programmer appears to have taken an enormous leap. But the requests that are done are repetitive and can easily be generated or otherwise controlled automatically. In addition there may well be some very important performance gains in the accessing of the tables that have been built because each request of the claims data does not have to access the entire table.

When dealing with large tables where three are known requirements to access subsets of the data, it may make sense to create "sparse indexes." A sparse index in DB2 is a construct that is created and supported entirely at the application level. The sparse index most likely is created as the extracted data is loaded.

As an example of the usage of a sparse index in conjunction with extracted data, consider a home mortgage financial institution with a data base that tracks payment activities. Once a month the payment activities are extracted and put in an archival data base.

Most payments are made on time and there is little to say about them. But occasionally a payment is late and a penalty is added. The decision support analyst has a need to track how many loans are late, whether the same loans are chronically late, and what the trend of late payments looks like over a five year period.

One approach is to create an index for all loans that is loaded at the moment the extract data is loaded. Most loans have a penalty payment value of $0.00. But every loan has a late payment record each month. In short there is a lot of index space that is wasted and a lot of time loading the index that has gone for naught.

The designer could have specified a separate table—a late payments table—to be loaded each month at the same time the extract data is loaded. The late payments table contains the identification of the loan that was late and the amount of the penalty. There would be (relatively speaking!) only a few loans in the late payments table, and an index could easily be created for the table. Processing could go against the table for analysis of late payments. And on those occasions where there was a need, the individual late loans could be accessed using information from the late payments table.

The late payments table then serves as a separate adjunct to the regular monthly payments table.

The creation of a "sparse" index does not speed up the extract process. However it does create the opportunity for efficient usage of extract data and possibly precludes the need for the loading of one or more indexes against a large table.

PERIODIC LOADING

Normally extract processing is thought of as an activity that is run overnight or in a batch window. In normal circumstances there is no opportunity to run extract processing during the online day.

But on occasion an extract process can be broken up into fine components and run in the middle of the online day. When those occasions arise it may make sense to do extract processing during the middle of the online day. In a sense the extract processing becomes a "background" type of processing. Note that this option must be considered carefully and does not fit the general case for extract processing.

When an extract can be broken into fine pieces and when there are slack moments of online processing during the production day, then there may be an opportunity to schedule some of the extract processing when there is spare time.

Some of the conditions where this type of processing can be done are where—

- the extract program can "remember" where it last left off,
- no update activity will occur that will destroy the integrity of the extract,

- the extract program can be selectively scheduled,
- the extract program can be stopped and restarted gracefully, and
- there is a production workload with a great deal of variability in the amount of processing power that is used.

The ability to run extract processing during the online day does not shorten or lengthen the total amount of resources spent for extract processing. Instead the capability spreads the demand for resources over a wider timeframe.

COMPACTING DATA

A very useful design technique for the minimization of resources in the load portion of the extract process is the physical compaction of data. When data can be compacted less data is used (saving DASD) and less processor capacity is required to retrieve data.

One of the best techniques for the compacting of data is the creation of arrays of data inside a row. This form of denormalization cannot be used as a general solution. (For an indepth discussion of where this form of denormalization is applicable and where it is not, refer to OPTIMIZING PERFORMANCE IN DB2, Prentice-Hall, 1988.)

As an example of the proper usage

of the creation of an array within a row, consider a payroll history file. In this example employees are paid twice a month. Periodically the past few months of payroll activity are extracted and put onto a payroll history file. The data elements that are extracted include the following—

▪ employee number	char(19)
▪ social security number	char(9)
▪ paydate—yrmoda	char(6)
▪ gross amount	dec fixed(11,2)
▪ net amount	dec fixed(11,2)
▪ FICA	dec fixed(9,2)
▪ state tax	dec fixed(9,2)
▪ federal tax	dec fixed(9,2)
▪ insurance	dec fixed(9,2)
▪ other deductions	dec fixed(9,2)

71 bytes

Each pay period is defined to be another occurrence in the extracted history table for payroll. The data is defined to be in an array so that repeating groups are combined under a single employee, as shown.

▪ employee number	char(19)
▪ social security number	char(9)
▪ paydate—yr	char(2)
▪ gross amount(1)	dec fixed(11,2)
▪ net amount(1)	dec fixed(11,2)
▪ FICA(1)	dec fixed(9,2)
▪ state tax(1)	dec fixed (9,2)
▪ federal tax(1)	dec fixed(9,2)
▪ insurance(1)	dec fixed(9,2)
▪ other deductions(1)	dec fixed(9,2)
▪ gross amount(2)	dec fixed(11,2)
▪ net amount(2)	dec fixed(11,2)
▪ FICA(2)	dec fixed(9,2)
▪ state tax(2)	dec fixed(9,2)
▪ federal tax(2)	dec fixed(9,2)
▪ insurance(2)	dec fixed(9,2)
▪ other deductions(2)	dec fixed(9,2)
▪ gross amount(3)	dec fixed(11,2)

- net amount(3)   dec fixed(11,2)
- FICA(3)   dec fixed(9,2)
- state tax(3)   dec fixed (9,2)
- federal tax(3)   dec fixed(9,2)
- insurance(3)   dec fixed(9,2)
- other deductions(3)   dec fixed(9,2)
- gross amount(4)   dec fixed(11,2)
- net amount(4)   dec fixed(11,2)
- FICA(4)   dec fixed(9,2)
- state tax(4)   dec fixed(9,2)
- federal tax(4)   dec fixed(9,2)
- insurance(4)   dec fixed(9,2)
- other deductions(4)   dec fixed(9,2)

. . . .
. . . .
. . . .
. . . .
. . . .

- gross amount(24)   dec fixed(11,2)
- net amount(24)   dec fixed(11,2)
- FICA(24)   dec fixed(9,2)
- state tax(24)   dec fixed(9,2)
- federal tax(24)   dec fixed(9,2)
- insurance(24)   dec fixed(9,2)
- other deductions(24)   dec fixed(9,2)

---

938 bytes

By storing the payroll history data together in an array where the twice monthly pay information can be stored for an employee, there is both a savings in space and in processing. Space is saved in that there is less total data in the table and that there is 1/24th the amount of space needed for the index. Processing is saved in that one I/O is all that is needed to gather the annual payroll history for an employee. In the case where each payroll entry is its own row, as much as 24 times as much I/O is required.

The practice of blocking data at the application level when applicable saves considerable processing not only for extract loads but for extract scans as well. If a designer is faced with an extract scan that promises to consume huge amounts of resources, the designer is advised to look into the blocking of data in the production data base.

OTHER OPTIONS

A simple (and surprisingly often overlooked) option for minimizing the resources required for extract processing is the possibility of doing extracts on a less frequent basis. This practice does not shorten the length of time required for the extract, but lessens the total amount of resources that must be dedicated to this kind of processing.

Another simpleminded option that often is overlooked is the usage of log tapes as a basis for gathering transactions. The advantages of using logtapes is that the tape can be taken to another processor and processed independently of the online processor.

The disadvantages of using the log tape are—

- only transactions can be captured,
- many computer operations will not allow the log tape to be used for anything other than backup processing,
- the logic of what gets on a log tape may or may not coincide with the needs of the designer, and
- log tapes often contain much extraneous information.

A FINAL NOTE

Even though the following comment does not directly relate to the efficiency of the extract process, it is tangentially relevant. It is good practice to timestamp each extract. The timestamp can often be used to clarify exactly what data has and has not been extracted. By virtue of the fact that a well designed time stamping scenario for each extract of data may save much unnecessary processing, time stamping is a sound design practice.

However, under the information paradigm, processing is necessarily separated; so there is no need to do all processing on a mainframe (unless, of course, that is the most economically efficient place to do the processing). If it is cheaper to do individual processing on a PC, then it can be done there. If it is economically efficient to do departmental processing on a minicomputer, then it can be done there. In other words, because the information paradigm organizes data in a disjointed fashion, there is flexibility to do processing on the most cost-effective processor.

There is another reason why separating primitive from derived processing makes economic sense. Suppose, in an unarchitected directed fashion, all processing is done on a single system. Now, consider the pattern of resource utilization as shown by Figure 91.

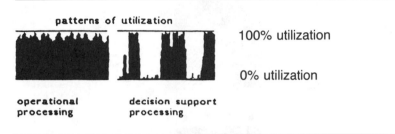

FIGURE 90 The pattern of resource utilization for operational and decision support processing is fundamentally different.

Figure 90 shows that operational processing uses a fairly constant mix of resources and that decision support processing uses a binary mix of resources. In the decision support environment, resources are either being used heavily or lightly. When the two resource utilization patterns are mixed together, as happens in the unarchitected environment, there is an inefficient usage of machine resources, as illustrated by the following example.

Consider the progression of resource utilization as shown by Figure 91.

In the first state, there are plenty of resources available to both operational and decision support processing because there is not much processing occurring. Response time will be good, but there is an inefficient (hence, cost-ineffective) utilization of resources shown in State 1. Now consider State 2. There is an efficient utilization of resources here, but State 2 does not exist very long because the resources required by decision support processing vary so much. State 3 occurs during peak decision support processing. Response time suffers when the decision support processing that is done demands more resources than are available. State 4 shows that a larger processor is required to accommodate the largest amount of decision support processing done, but State 4 is an uneconomic state because much of the processing resources will be idle for a lengthy period of time.

By separating operational from decision support processing, machine

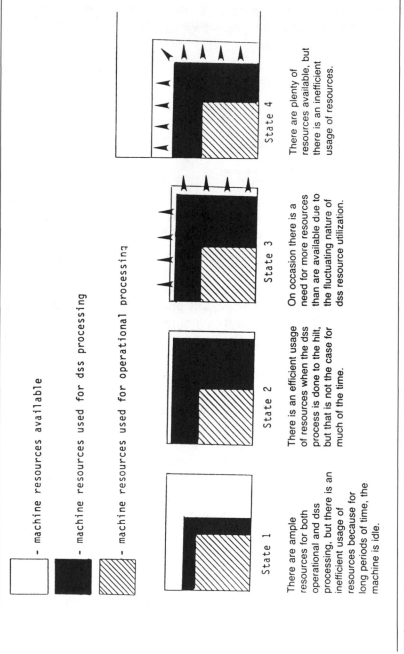

□ - machine resources available

■ - machine resources used for dss processing

▨ - machine resources used for operational processing

State 1

There are ample resources for both operational and dss processing, but there is an inefficient usage of resources because for long periods of time, the machine is idle.

State 2

There is an efficient usage of resources when the dss process is done to the hilt, but that is not the case for much of the time.

State 3

On occasion there is a need for more resources than are available due to the fluctuating nature of dss resource utilization.

State 4

There are plenty of resources available, but there is an inefficient usage of resources.

FIGURE 91 Progression of resource utilization.

resources needed for operational processing remain constant. When decision support processing is separated, it can be moved to a cheaper processor, and the impact of the peaks and valleys of decision support processing is felt only by its users. Furthermore, decision support users are much more tolerant of fluctuations in response time.

The result is that the information paradigm conforms very nicely with the performance needs of the organization and the cost of processors required to achieve the desired levels of performance.

There are some obvious costs related to the information paradigm. One is that of transporting data from one level to the next. If a blanket refreshment strategy is used, these costs will be significant, but if a more normal refreshment strategy is used, then the costs can be kept to a minimum. (refer to Chapter 3 for a discussion of refreshment strategies)

Another obvious cost is the redundancy of data. At first glance, there appear to be massive redundancies of data from one level to the next. In fact, there is a certain amount of redundancy of data, but closer inspection reveals that there is much less redundancy than there is uniqueness. Indeed, it is unusual to find more than a 10 percent overlap of data between levels. With a 10 percent or less redundancy factor, the physical cost of redundancy should not be a significant factor.

SUMMARY

The information paradigm has numerous economic benefits. In general, the more cost-conscious an organization is, the faster it evolves the information paradigm. The costs that are relevant are for hardware, software and people.

Some of the economic considerations of the information paradigm relate to:

- Hardware—separating operational and decision support processing requires an organization to buy the most expensive hardware, mainframes.
- Software—separating operational and decision support processing allows 4GL technology to be used where flexibility is most needed—in the dss environment.
- People costs—the existence of atomic data provides a reusable basis of data, which means people time does not have to be used for redevelopment.

Redundancy of data is minimized in the information paradigm because there is no need to store detailed archival data in multiple departments;

the atomic data base provides an ample basis for storage. The atomic data base also provides a basis for storage for summarized archival data that is used by more than one department. The same summarization does not have to be done by every department. Instead, the summarization is done once, stored at the atomic level, and commonly accessed thereafter. The net result is savings of both storage and processor capacity.

CHAPTER *10* MISCELLANEOUS TOPICS

STRATEGIC SYSTEMS AND THE INFORMATION PARADIGM

Who has not seen the time-honored diagram showing the relationship between strategic, tactical, and operational systems?

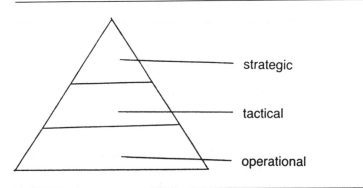

FIGURE 92 Relationship of strategic, tactical, and operational systems.

The triangle shown in Figure 92 implies that strategic systems sit on—or are built on—tactical systems, and that tactical systems sit on—or are built on—operational systems. In addition, it is implied that strategic systems are smaller than tactical systems, which, in turn, are smaller than operational systems.

How does the widely accepted diagram shown in Figure 92 measure up to the information paradigm? Interestingly, in one way, the information paradigm reinforces the popular notion, and in another way, it contradicts it. Both perspectives will be explored.

The information paradigm supports the popular notion of the relationship between strategic, tactical, and operational systems in that operational data feeds atomic data, which provides a foundation for departmental and individual processing. Figure 93 shows this perspective.

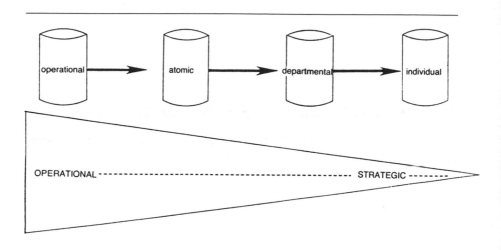

FIGURE 93 The relationship of the information paradigm to the classical organization of operational and strategic systems.

The existence of atomic data and its subsequent usage provides a foundation for reconciliation of dss data. If dss data is taken to be the equivalent of strategic data, then there is a great deal of ambience between the information paradigm and strategic data. But there are many strategic information systems that are anything but decision support. Indeed, some of the most widely discussed strategic information systems are very much operational in nature. Reservation systems, hospital supply systems, and demographic analysis systems are only a few strategically important systems that are operational. In this case, the notion of the relationship between tactical, operational, and strategic systems as depicted by Figure 92 is simply an inaccurate one.

METHODOLOGIES AND THE INFORMATION PARADIGM

Another interesting issue is the relationship of methodologies—primarily development methodologies—to the information paradigm.

Methodologies, such as structured methodologies, information engineering, and business systems planning, relate to the information paradigm as shown by Figure 94.

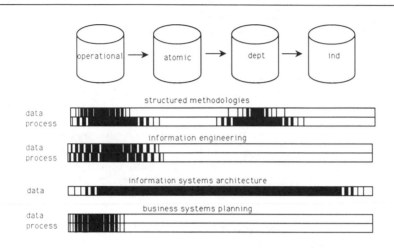

FIGURE 94 The relationship of some popular methodologies to the information paradigm. Where the lines are darkest, the methodology has applicability to the level of the paradigm. Where the lines are lightest, the methodology has little or no applicability to the methodology.

In general, structured techniques apply to operational systems and dss systems. Atomic data is not explicitly recognized by structured methodologies. The strength of structural techniques is in the process/function analysis, rather than in data analysis and design. Information engineering techniques apply almost exclusively to operational data. Even though information engineering techniques can be applied to dss- and atomic-level data, they do not work well because of the constantly changing nature of dss data. As a result, information engineering applies to operational systems almost exclusively.

Information Systems Architecture (ISA) applies across the board to all levels of data. Indeed, ISA is the genesis of the information paradigm. However, ISA has a strong orientation toward data analysis.

Another noteworthy approach is Business Systems Planning (BSP).

BSP applies to only a narrow range of data, primarily because of its crude techniques. (BSP was a pioneer methodology and, as such, is not as refined as other methodologies or as oriented towards results.)

At first glance, it appears that ISA is the ideal methodological approach, based on Figure 90. But ISA has a strong orientation towards data and is most effective when coupled with other methodologies, such as structured techniques that have an orientation towards process modeling and functional analysis.

The evolution to the information paradigm is an organic process. It does not happen in a single step. Instead it happens over time, in a phased approach.
The best example the author has seen of the understanding that the evolution is organic, that the evolution happens in iterations, and that the evolution involves methodologies, existing systems, feedback loops, and the organization itself is illustrated by the diagram provided by Col Wayne Byrd, US ARMY.

ARMY INFORMATION ARCHITECTURE WITH ARCHITECTURAL BUILDING BLOCKS

The dynamics of the architecture interacting with the existing environment is illustrated by the diagram. The future objectives of the business stimulate the analysis of organizational elements, processes and entities. The analysis results in plans for information classes, processes, and organizational elements.

The formalized plans provide a basis for an application architecture and a data architecture which are related by means of a data flow. The data architecture and the application architecture are factored into the geographic needs of the Army and are refined to provide in-

put into individual projects. There is a feedback loop from the projects back into the data and application architectures.

The entire planning process is used as guidance into the migration to the current target configuration, the baseline configuration and the technical objectives. Based on the leadership initiatives and the guidance from the planning process, over time the existing environment evolves into the desired state.

One of the interesting features of the diagram provided by Col Wayne Byrd, US Army is the cognizance of the different components with which a data architecture must interact, as well as the evolution of the architecture over time.

---

*By Col. Wayne Byrd, United States Army.

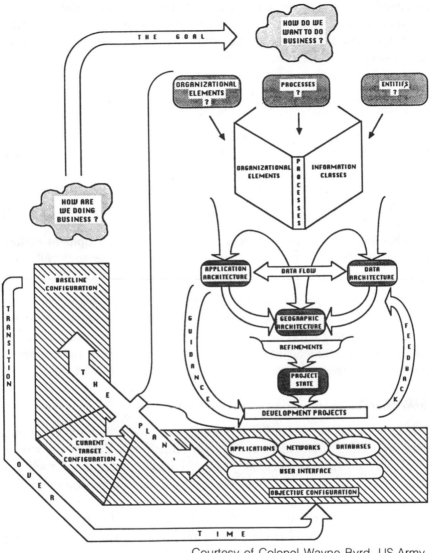

Courtesy of Colonel Wayne Byrd, US Army

RESISTING THE EVOLUTION

The analogy of the information paradigm to a glacier has been used throughout this book. The inevitability of a glacier is likened to the inevitability of the information paradigm. Indeed, organizations that do not acknowledge and gracefully coexist with the information paradigm suffer the same fate as objects that are in the way of a glacier and do not acknowledge its existence.

There are many examples of problems that arise when an evolution is not recognized, particularly when the inevitability of the information paradigm is not recognized. For example:

▪ When an organization dedicates itself to a single data base to serve all needs and attempts to solve its capacity problems with hardware, then the result is large budgets and much frustration.
▪ When an organization attempts to put archival data in operational systems, it is predictable that major availability and capacity problems will arise.
▪ When an organization attempts to use standard development methodologies on dss data that changes faster than it can be analyzed, then disenchantment with the methodologies is predictable.

In short, resisting the evolution of the information paradigm is the equivalent of standing in front of a glacier and hoping for the best. Organizations that understand the evolution towards the information paradigm and gracefully adapt to the evolution are effectively and efficiently positioned to meet the data processing challenges of the future.

SUMMARY

The information paradigm fits very nicely with the notion of operational data supporting strategic data. The consolidation of data at the atomic level allows data to be accurately and efficiently gathered and used in a wide variety of ways. Without the consolidation, organizations either cannot achieve a strategic usage of data or require inordinate amounts of resources in the achievement of the strategic usage of data.

The methodologies that support the information paradigm take many forms. The founder of most of the commonly found methodologies is BSP. From BSP has sprung many variations that address various aspects of data modelling, process modelling, design, and so forth.

Finally, resisting the evolution of the information paradigm is a difficult and risky proposition. The forces that cause the information paradigm to evolve are so strong that in most organizations the information paradigm takes on the character of the irresistible force.

11 DATA INTEGRITY AND PROJECTION DATA

*I*n previous chapters, discussions of credibility have related to historical or "backward looking" systems. Historical systems are those that measure what has already happened; they are the most common type of system. As a simple example of historical data, consider the following data relating to an inventory system.

Part	Month Beginning Balance	Deposits	Withdrawals	Adjustments	Month Ending Balance
0012	250	0	100	0	150
0014	0	10	0	0	10
0016	1,000	15,000	1,300	0	14,700
0019	150	0	125	10	15
.	.	.	.	.	.
.	.	.	.	.	.
.	.	.	.	.	.

The inventory information in the example is descriptive of events that have happened. As previously discussed, atomic-level data working in conjunction with the discipline of an architecture is ideal for creating an environment for reconcilability of historical data.

In general, integrity of historical data is characterized by smaller events or measurements adding up to (or otherwise transforming to) larger events or measurements. This can be represented by—

$$a_1, a_2, a_3, a_4, \ldots, a_n \rightarrow A$$

$$b_1, b_2, b_3, b_4, \ldots, b_n \rightarrow B$$

and so forth.

Whenever the lower-level details support the larger summarizations or transformations, the system is in balance and integrity is intact. But whenever the lower-level events and measurements do not support the higher-level events and measurements, as shown by

$$a_1, a_2, a_3, a_4, \ldots, a_n -//\rightarrow A$$

then the system is out of balance and the integrity of the system has been violated.

The integrity or credibility of historical systems is simplified in that:

- There is a static formula describing the relationship between a_n and A.
- $a_1, a_2, a_3, a_4, \ldots a_n$ represent measurements of finite events and have a single correct value.
- Other than transformations and control of data-related a_n A, there is little confusion as to the correct values of historical data.

PROJECTION DATA

But there is another type of data associated with decision support processing. That data can be characterized as projection data, or future-oriented data. An example of projection (or future-oriented data) is budget and planning data. It is typically found in a spreadsheet environment such as Lotus 1-2-3. Projection data differs from historical data in the following ways:

- Projection data is not based on measurement of past events but on the prediction of future events or measurements.
- Oftentimes $a_1, a_2, a_3, a_4, \ldots a_n -//\rightarrow A$ for projection data.
- The transformation from $a_1, a_2, a_3, \ldots a_n \longrightarrow A$ is not static,

▪ The detail values a_1, a_2, a_3, . . . a_n are projections and, as such, have no specific value.

In other words, oftentimes with projection data, the detail level does not add up to or otherwise transform to the basis for summary data. Integrity of projection data, then, is a very different issue than the integrity of historical data.

The issues of data integrity are much more complex with projection data than they are with historical data. Consider two reasons why projection data integrity is more complicated:

1. When a manager projects that next year's budget for office supplies is $500, exception can be taken due to a whole host of factors. Inflation, organizational growth, organizational patterns of usage, marginal discounts, and so forth, can all be used to argue that the $500 projection should be $450 or $550, or whatever comes to mind. The accuracy of any projected detail is always subject to question because no one really knows. But historical data, once accurately recorded, is not subject to interpretation. For example, when June Foster cashes a check for $125, no one (legally) tries to change the value at a later time to $150.

2. In projections, data is often changed at a summary level, but no corresponding changes are made at the detailed level. For example, suppose a company has asked ten departments—departments A through J—to estimate their staffing needs for the next year. Collectively, the departments will be staffed by 90 people. Management reviews the staffing requirements and decides that there will, in fact, be 75 people for the ten departments. Management is perfectly justified in using the summary number of 75 while the detailed budgets of the departments add up to 90. Of course, at some point there needs to be a reconciliation of the summary to the detail level. But projected summary numbers are regularly changed with no immediate regard for reconciliation at the detail level.

Historical data, on the other hand, is very sensitive to the need for detail data adding up to (or otherwise being transformed to) summarized data. An accountant would no more add up the daily receipts for sales in six chain stores and then summarily alter the number, than the accountant would fly. (Of course, this practice has been tried and is often known as fraud or embezzlement).

There is, then, a fundamental difference in the treatment of the integrity of data depending upon whether it is historical data or projection data.

Integrity of Projection Data

There needs to be a fundamentally different treatment of the integrity of projection data. The following information is required for projection data for each data element where integrity is an issue:

- Reconciled value,
- Moment of reconciliation,
- Current value,
- Owner ID,
- User$_{(1)}$, user$_{(2)}$, user$_{(3)}$, . . . , user$_{(n)}$,
- Algorithmic relationships in which the data element participates.

Each of these types of information, which are necessary for each data element, will be explained in depth.

Reconciled value

The reconciled value is the value of the data element at the point in time when all detail and all summary information is in balance. The reconciled value is valid as of some moment in time, known as the moment of reconciliation.

For example, for Department A, there are four detailed budget items: software, hardware, space, and personnel costs. On December 15, 1987, the manager does a projection of those items for 1988:

Department A:		
	software	$ 450
	hardware	750
	space	125
	personnel	950
	total	$2,275

The reconciled cumulative value for the department budget as of December 15, 1987, is $2,275.

Current value

Current-value data represents the value for the data element at a moment in time. Current-value data may or may not agree with the reconciled value. It can be changed by only one "owner," who is specified by the owner ID.

Suppose Department B has made a reconciled budget, as shown.

	Department B:	software	$ 600
		hardware	1,000
		space	250
		personnel	2,575
		total	$4,425

Now, management adds the total budgeting figures for the two departments—Department A and Department B—$2,275 + $4,425 = $6,700. The system is out of balance at the summarized level.

Management decides that $6,700 is too high and changes $6,700 to $5,800. At that moment in time, the current-value summarization equals $5,800 and the reconciled summarized value equals $6,700.

Department A:

software	$ 450
hardware	750
space	125
personnel	950
	$2,275
total	$6,700

| total | $5,800 |

Department B:

software	$ 600	
hardware	1,000	
space	250	reconciled
personnel	2,575	values
	$4,425	

current
values

Note that the reduction of the reconciled value to $5,800 does not say or imply what line items will have to be changed. The effect on the line items is to be negotiated at a later time (at the next point of reconciliation). Also note that only one agency is allowed to change current-value data. Of course, if management once again wishes to change current-value data from $5,800 to $6,200, that is their prerogative. There cannot be multiple current values.

User$_{(N)}$

The users of the reconciled and the current-value data are listed along with the data. There may be only one list of users, or the users may be divided into two categories—casual users and users to be notified whenever a change to current-value data is made.

A user is merely the identification of someone who uses the data. The purpose of user identification is to allow the user to be notified if a change is made to the data.

For example, suppose the current value data for the 1988 departmental budget has been changed to $5,800. Suppose there are three users of the data: analyst XRK, analyst KRV, and analyst TMR. The owner of the data decides once again to change the value of the current data to $6,500. The current-value data is changed. The system user knows (ID) whom to notify now that current value information has been altered.

Algorithmic relationships

The final field of interest is the algorithmic relationship field. The contents of this field describe (or at least identify) the algorithms in which the data element participates. For example, the data element Departmental Budget participates in the algorithm that describes how to calculate the annual corporate budget.

Public/Private Data

The projection data that has been described—reconciled data and current-value data—can be termed "public" data. Public data is data whose accuracy or integrity is supported by the infrastructure that is being described. The validity or credibility of public data is supported in two ways:

- The transformation of reconciled data is synchronized from the detailed to the summary level.
- Current-value data is synchronized in that there is a sole source responsible for the data, there can be one and only one value of data at any moment in time, and, when changes are made to the data, the users of the data are known and notified.

Even though there may be imbalances between current-value data and reconciled data, there is, nevertheless, the opportunity to believe the data through the workings of the infrastructure.

Private data is any data that is not public. There is no notion of credibility or integrity of private data. Private data reflects the individual opinion or immediate needs of a given analyst and can be created, changed, deleted, and so forth, at will.

For example, suppose a management analyst (who is not authorized to change current-value data) looks at the current-value data for Departments A and B. The analyst foresees a need to buy software that has not been budgeted into the reconciled value of data. He or she privately changes the software forecast to:

Department A			Department B		
software	$ 750		software	$ 950	
hardware	750		hardware	1,000	
space	125		space	250	
personnel	950		personnel	2,575	
	$2,575			$4,775	
total	$7,350				

The data shown is now private data. The analyst is free to do with the private data whatever is desired—do perform "what if" analysis, compare notes to other projections, discuss the results with management, and so forth. But he or she may not represent the private data as being factual—either reconciled or current-value—or as being publicly available. There is no integrity associated with private projection data. The analyst may use the data as a basis for changing (or influencing the change of) current-value data. But the actual changes are made within the infrastructure of public data, where the integrity of the data is supported.

In addition, the individual analyst may interject, create, or otherwise conjure up any other private data that is appropriate. For example, the analyst may compare the privately projected figures to industry profiles.

In short, the work the analyst does privately is not limited in scope. But the analyst may not represent the data as "official" or public.

On occasion, an analyst will calculate or create private data that is of interest or use to another department. At this point, private data becomes subject to the discipline of the infrastructure required for public data. The analyst may create "public" data from "private" data if he or she:

- Assumes responsibility for the accuracy, timeliness, and other aspects of the infrastructure of the data,
- Is not treading on another analyst's turf.

The differences between public and private data are shown below:

Public Data	Private Data
used by more than one department	used in a free-form manner
nonredundant	normally redundant
one and only one owner	is owned by a single analyst
is available for general access	is not available for general access
is aware of different usages	is not "authorized" for general public usage
has integrity	does not have integrity

The moment of reconciliation

From time to time, there will be a point designated as the "moment of reconciliation." A moment of reconciliation is the moment at which:

- All detail adds up to the summary.
- All reconciled values equal the current values.

For example, suppose on December 15, 1987, the reconciled values for the departments have been calculated as previously shown.

But on the 20th of December, Department A decides that hardware expenditures should be $1,050. Unfortunately, Department A cannot change the reconciled value until the next moment of reconciliation. Instead, it changes the current value for hardware expenditures.

On December 21, management decides that the total expenditures of $6,700 are too high and decides to lower the figure to $6,300. The current value is now set to $6,300.

The values of reconciled data and current values are shown below:

Reconciled Values

Department A		Department B	
software	$ 450	software	$ 600
hardware	750	hardware	1,000
space	125	space	250
personnel	950	personnel	2,575
	$2,275		$4,425
total	$6,300		
total	$6,700		

Current Values (as of January 1, 1988)

Department A		Department B	
software	$ 450	software	$ 600
hardware	1,050	hardware	1,000
space	125	space	250
personnel	950	personnel	2,575
	$2,275		$4,425
total	$6,300		
total	$6,300		

On January 2, 1988, the moment of reconciliation is mandated by management. First, Department A's hardware is changed to $1,050. Next, the deallocation of money is made in accordance with management's need to make the total $6,300. The deallocation is made through negotiation. The following figures are arrived at through a balanced cut of money:

Current Value and Reconciled Value—
January 2, 1988

Department A		Department B	
software	$ 450	software	$ 550
hardware	1,000	hardware	4,900
space	125	space	250
personnel	900	personnel	2,175
	$2,475		$3,875
total	$6,300		
total	$6,300		

After the negotiation process is finished, the data is reconciled and the current and the reconciled values are the same. The moment of reconciliation, then, is the moment when all values are in balance.

An example
The dynamics of how the infrastructure that has been described works is shown in an example. Currently, the 1988 budget looks as shown:

Department A		Department B		Department C	
software	$10,000	software	$ 9,000	software	$ 17,500
hardware	18,500	hardware	29,750	hardware	32,100
space	1,550	space	2,750	space	6,900
personnel	22,500	personnel	48,000	personnel	54,000
	$52,500		$48,000		$110,500

The reconciled total 1988 figures are $211,150.

The deadline for the 1989 budget is November 15.

By November 15, Department A and Department C have completed their budgets, as shown.

Department A		Department B		Department C	
software	$12,000	software	—	software	$ 12,750
hardware	21,500	hardware	—	hardware	46,750
space	1,750	space	—	space	7,300
personnel	26,850	personnel	—	personnel	62,500
	$62,100		—		$129,300

For reasons known only to Department B, the 1989 budget is not done. The management analyst is required to submit a final budget by November 18. In lieu of any better information, he or she uses the 1988 budget information for Department B. The total budget to November 15 is then:

$$\$62,100 + \$48,000 + \$129,050 = \$239,150.$$

On November 19, management reviews the projections and adjusts the budgetary figure to $256,000. The current total budget is now $256,000, even though the reconciled budget is $239,150.

Next, the department manager for Department A states that $62,100 is too much. The figure is adjusted to $58,700.

After the figures are in, budget analysts begin to analyze the budget. One analyst looks at the cumulative hardware figures. Another looks at the ratio of hardware to software and the ratio of hardware and software to personnel. Still another looks at the increase in personnel costs from 1986 to 1987, from 1987 to 1988, from 1988 to 1989, and so forth. All of these analysts produce their own private reports, using public data from which to derive private data. After preliminary analysis on November 24, management calls for another moment of reconciliation. To achieve a meaningful moment of reconciliation, the following activities, at the least, have to occur:

- Department B must complete its budget.
- Department A must adjust its budget to meet its manager's goal.
- All departments must adjust figures to coincide with management's figure of $256,000.

The moment of reconciliation is set for December 2. The following reflects the figures as of that date.

Department A		Department B		Department C	
software	$ 11,500	software	$14,000	software	$ 14,500
hardware	20,000	hardware	36,500	hardware	47,750
space	1,750	space	3,500	space	8,450
personnel	26,000	personnel	12,500	personnel	58,550
	$ 59,250		$66,500		$129,250
total	$256,000				

The current and the reconciled values are in agreement as of December 2.

The infrastructure that has been suggested fits very comfortably with the notion of atomic data. The following diagram suggests the appropriate relationship between projection data and the information paradigm:

Atomic	Departmental	Individual
reconciled data	copy of reconciled data	private data
current-value data	copy of current-value data	

Note that there is no projection operational data. The "system of record" for projection data lies at the atomic level. Many departments can access the atomic data and retrieve derived data.

One of the interesting aspects of the atomic-level data becoming a foundation for projection data is that different levels of budgets, plans, and projections can be made.

Management may choose to create its own budget estimate based on Department A's reconciled values, on Department B's most current values, and on the most recent values that can be found for Department C, assuming that Department C has not already made a budget.

Different versions of projections can be made, with many possibilities as to accuracy, timeliness, and credibility of the projection.

A variation on the structuring of data suggested in this chapter is to do away with the notion of current-value and reconciled data, and to simply time stamp every data element used in projections.

For example, Department A creates a budget as of December 13:

```
software    $  975 (Dec. 13)
hardware       650 (Dec. 13)
overhead       250 (Dec. 13)
personnel    2,500 (Dec. 13)

            $4,375 (Dec. 13)
```

Then, on December 14, a change is made to overhead and personnel figures:

```
software    $  975 (Dec. 13)
hardware       650 (Dec. 13)
overhead       250 (Dec. 13)   $  350 (Dec. 14)
personnel    2,500 (Dec. 13)    2,650 (Dec. 14)

            $4,375 (Dec. 13)   $4,625 (Dec. 14)
```

On December 16, another change is made to personnel projections and hardware:

```
software    $  975 (Dec. 13)
hardware       650 (Dec. 13)                            $  675 (Dec. 16)
overhead       250 (Dec. 13)   $  350 (Dec. 14)
personnel    2,500 (Dec. 13)    2,650 (Dec. 14)          2,750 (Dec. 16)

            $4,375 (Dec. 13)   $4,625 (Dec. 14)         $4,750 (Dec. 16)
```

At this point, there are several combinations of budgetary analyses that can be made. At one level, the analyst can ask for the most current budget, which is the one that has the most current value of time associated with it. The most current budget would be:

```
software    $  975 (Dec. 13)
hardware       675 (Dec. 16)
overhead       350 (Dec. 14)
personnel    2,750 (Dec. 16)

            $4,750 (most current)
```

Or, the budget analyst could look at the most current budget, as of December 14:

```
software    $  975 (Dec. 13)
hardware       650 (Dec. 13)
overhead       350 (Dec. 14)
personnel    2,650 (Dec. 14)

            $4,625 (as of Dec. 14)
```

Or, the budget analyst could simply look at the budget for December 13:

```
software    $  975 (Dec. 13)
hardware       650 (Dec. 13)
overhead       250 (Dec. 13)
personnel    2,500 (Dec. 13)

            $4,375 (as of Dec. 13)
```

In short, if each budget entry is time stamped, there are *many* possibilities for analysis. The types of budget, the versions of a budget, and the reconciliation of budgets are all very flexible and auditable when each budget entry is time stamped.

SUMMARY

This chapter has discussed projection data. Projection data is more susceptible to lack of credibility because of the speculative nature of the detailed values, because, oftentimes, the transformation from detailed to higher-level values is out of balance, and because even the algorithm for transformation is open to debate.

Each data element for which credibility is desired needs to have a reconciled value, a current value, and an "owner," and it needs its users identified and the moment of reconciliation recorded. The infrastructure must be maintained with discipline in order to allow projection data to be reconciled.

12 *A TAXOMONY OF DATA*

All data is not created equal. Nowhere is it written that there is a Constitution and a Bill of Rights for data. One of the major complexities and causes of confusion is that, in many early modelling and data administration exercises, the different classes of data have not been recognized. The rules, uses, context, et al., of data vary enormously depending upon the class of data. Trying to apply rules that are appropriate from one class of data to another class of data simply does not work and is one of the underlying reasons why the job of the data administrator has been so hectic and unfulfilling.

THE CLASSES OF DATA

There are three major criteria under which data is divided into classes. The three criteria are:

- private/public;
- historical/projection (or future); and
- primitive/derived

The three criteria can (analogically) be viewed as separate axes of a three-dimensional view of the world, as shown by Figure 95.

The criteria may be identified as:

- public data—data of interest or use to multiple individuals in the enterprise;
- private data—data of interest or use to only a single individual in the enterprise;

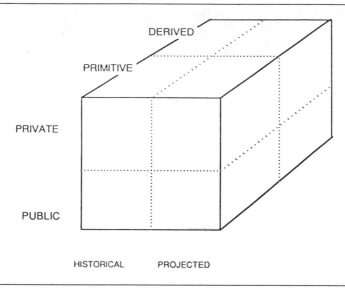

FIGURE 95 Three criteria for data class division.

- historical data—a measure of what has happened;
- projection (or future) data—an estimation of what might happen;
- primitive data—data whose existence depends directly on a single occurrence of an entity of the enterprise; and
- derived data—data whose existence depends directly on multiple occurrences of an entity of the enterprise.

As an example of one of the nuances implied by the above criteria, consider:

- the output of x assemblies of a production line—a historical measure is depicted by last week's output. Once we determine the correct value for last week, it is inarguable. Now consider the projection for next week. The foreman projects that 10,000 units will be produced. The production control manager projects 15,000 units will be produced. There is no such thing as a correct value for projection data, as there is for historical data. The nature of projection data is that it *must* take on ownership, unlike historical data. [Note: historical data has the connotation of ownership in that one organization is responsible for creating the correct value for the historical data. But, historical data has a correct value regardless of what organizational unit is responsible for its update. Projection data, on the other hand, does not have a correct value, so the quantity associated with any occurrence of projection data is relative *only* to the source creating the projection or owner of the projection data.]

Another nuance implied by the definitions is that:

- All derived data is calculated from primitive and/or other derived data, but
- all calculated data may not be derived.

As an example fo calculated data which is not derived, consider the bank account balance of a bank's customer. There is no question that a person's current bank account balance is calculated. It is calculated by starting with the month beginning balance, adding all deposits, subtracting all withdrawals, adding interest and subtracting any penalties. But a bank account balance is still a primitive piece of information because it belongs to a single individual or customer of the bank. If the customer goes away, then the current bank balance goes away.

The deeper one goes into the differences in the types of data based on the criteria set forth, the more nuances there are. In fact, each axis of data has its own characteristics. Each axis serves to emphasize the distinctions between the types of data based on the distinctions. Some of the distinctions are highlighted by Figure 96.

For example, private data tends to contain a relatively low amount of data which has low integrity. If private data is lost or destroyed, it is simply recreated from the mind or records of the owner, rather than being recreated from system sources. Public data, on the other hand, contains a fair volume of data that is managed and maintained with a high degree of integrity.

Historical/Projection Differences

The differences between historical and projection data tend to be very profound. Historical data is based on detailed values which have a correct value. There is no "correct" value for projection data. Another major difference between historical and projection data is that the algorithms used in the management of the data either may or may not vary. For example, with historical data, there may be an algorithm:

daily sales = sale(1) + sale(2) + sale(3) + . . . + sale (n)

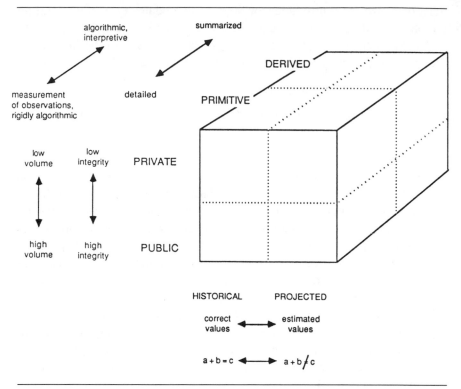

FIGURE 96 Distinctions between the types of data.

But with projection data, a projected sales may be estimated by adding up all the detailed projections.

projected sales = projected sales, dept(1) + projected sales, dept (2) + . . . (n)

After having calculated projected sales by adding up all the detailed projections, management then makes its own cumulative sales projection, which is very different than the one calculated. In other words:

projected sales = projected sales(1) + projected sales(2) + . . . Projected sales(n)

mgmt projected sales ≠ projected sales

The very algorithms used in projection data do not follow the same rules of algorithmic rigidity which govern the order of our arithmetic.

Primitive, Derived Differences

The differences between primitive and derived data are well known and widely documented. (Refer to INFORMATION ENGINEERING FOR THE PRACTITIONER, Yourdon Press, 1988, chapter 13). Some of the more obvious differences between primitive and derived data stem from the detailed nature of primitive data and the summarized nature of derived data. Another major difference between primitive and derived data stems from the fundamental nature of the data. Primitive data is essentially detailed. As such, it represents the measurement of details. Typically primitive data might be the date and time of a transaction, the amount of a transaction, the location the transaction occurred at, the teller managing the transaction. Each piece of primitive data is a measurement or observation and is not subject to discussion as to the validity or accuracy of the data.

Even in the case of calculations used to determine primitive values, the algorithms are well established and not open to speculation. Such is not the case at all with derived data. All derived data is calculated and the algorithm used for calculation may well be open for speculation. For example, an accountant adds up the monthly revenues. A simple formula is used:

$$\text{monthly revenues} = \text{revenues received}$$
$$= (\text{revenue}(1) + \text{revenue}(2) +$$
$$\text{revenue}(3), \ldots + \text{revenue} (n)$$

However, the accountant notes that $900,000 of revenues are from the sales of an office in Atlanta, not from regular receipts based on sales of regular goods and services. So the accountant lowers monthly sales to $4,100,000. The accountant has used an "interpretive" approach to arrive at a derived value of data, not a strictly algorithmic approach. And the practice of rearranging data at the derived level is not questioned. Some of the "cubes" (or sections) created by the sectioning shown in Figure 95 are of interest because there is very different data in each sector. Figure 97 shows some of the more interesting sectors.

For example, the sector for primitive, public, historical data contains the operational data that forms the backbone of classical data processing systems. Bank teller systems, reservation systems, manufacturing control systems are all found in this sector.

Another interesting sector is the public, derived, projection sector. In

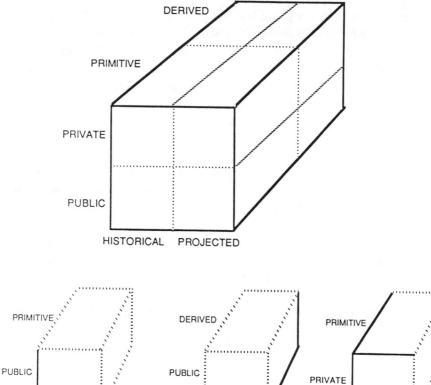

DERIVED

PRIMITIVE

PRIVATE

PUBLIC

HISTORICAL   PROJECTED

PRIMITIVE

PUBLIC

HISTORICAL

Where classical
operational data
is found

DERIVED

PUBLIC

PROJECTED

Where organizational
dss analysis data is
found

PRIMITIVE

PRIVATE

HISTORICAL

Where personal
detailed information
is found

FIGURE 97   "Cubes" created by sectioning.

this sector is found the dss analytical data of the corporation. Such systems as budgetary systems, sales and revenue projections, forecasts and the like are found in this sector.

Each sector has its own personality. Consider the primitive, private, historical sector. This sector is where one would expect to find personal computers keeping track of individual items, such as the mileage travelled in the past year in a person's frequent flyer club, the expenditures on office expenses that are reimbursable, the record of miles driven for business, and so forth.

Each sector then has its own unique flavor.

It is noteworthy that the divisions of data that have been described are equally applicable to processes as well. There is nothing unique about the sectors insofar as data is concerned. The categories apply to processes every bit as much as they apply to data. Another interesting aspect of the criteria is that they can be subdivided further, or other criteria can be used to create other sectors. For example, data could be sectored according to whether it is administrative or operational. Or derived data could be further sectored into data that is interpretively calculated and data that is rigidly calculated. While the criteria that have been suggested appear to separate data most profoundly, the criteria are hardly the only criteria there are.

A final question must be asked—so what? Why is it important to perceive data as being divided into sectors? There is a very important point to be made and it is that the rules for managing (even understanding) data change profoundly depending on what sector one is in.

Consider the following:

Requirements definition makes sense as long as the requirements are stable. But for projection data and some derived data, requirements analysis and definition simply does not make sense because of the heuristic nature of processing.

High performance tools make sense for public, private data, but do not make sense elsewhere.

High integrity tools make sense for public data but not for private data. Spreadsheet technology makes sense for projection data but not historical data.

Data modelling makes sense for primitive data but not derived data. Redundancy of data makes sense for derived data, but not for primitive data, and so forth.

The tools, techniques, approaches, et al., all make sense only in the context of a sector.

IN SUMMARY

Data (and processes) can be fundamentally divided along three axes— private vs. public, historical vs. projection, and primitive vs. derived. The three criteria can be used to "sector" data. Each sector of data has its own unique characteristics and flavor. The techniques and approaches that apply to one sector do not apply to other sectors.

BIBLIOGRAPHY

Amdahl, Gene. "The Early Chapters of the PCM Story," *Datamation*, February 1979.

Bachman, C. W. "The Programmer as Navigator," *CACM*, Vol. 16, November 1973.

Benbirat, I., Dexter, A., Drury, D., Goldstein, R. "A Critique of the Stage Hypothesis: Theory and Empirical Evidence," *CACM*, Vol. 27, May 1984.

Chen, P. P. S. "The Entity Relationship Model—Toward a Unified View of Data," *ACM Transaction Database Systems*, No. 1, March 1976.

Codd, E. F. "A Database Sub Language Founded on the Relational Calculus," *ACM SIGFIDET Workshop on Data Description*, 1971.

———. "A Relational Model of Data for Large Shared Data Banks," *CACM* Vol. 13, June 1970.

———. "Further Normalization of the Data Base Relational Model," *Database Systems*, Courant Computer Science Symposia Series, Vol. 6, Prentice-Hall 1972.

———. "Normalized Data Base Structure: A Brief Tutorial," *ACM SIGFIDET Workshop on Data Description*, 1971.

———. "Recent Investigations into Relational Data Base Systems," Proceedings IFIP Congress, ACM Pacific Conference, 1974.

———. "Relational Completeness of Data Base Sublanguages," *Database Systems*, Courant Computer Science Symposia Series, Vol. 6, Prentice-Hall 1972.

Dahl, O. J., Dijkstra, E. W., Hoare, C. A. R. *Structured Programming*, Academic Press, 1972.

Date, C. J. *An Introduction to Database Systems*, Addison-Wesley, 1982.

DeMarco, Tom, *Structured Analysis and System Specification*, Prentice-Hall, 1979.

Drury, D. H., "An Empirical Assessment of the Stages of DP Growth," *MIS Quarterly* June 1983.

Finklestein, Clive. "Information Engineering" (Parts 1–6), *ComputerWorld*, May–June 1981.

————. "The User Wave in Information Engineering," *ComputerWorld*, September 1982.

Gibson, E. F., Nolan, R. L. "Managing the Four Stages of EDP Growth," *Harvard Business Review*, January/February 1974.

IBM Corp. "Business Systems Planning," *Information Systems Planning Guide*, 1978.

Inmon, W. H., Bird, T. J. *Dynamics of Database*, Prentice-Hall, 1986.

————. *Information Engineering for the Practitioner*, Yourdon Press, 1988.

————. *Information Systems Architecture*, Prentice-Hall, 1986.

————. *Integrating Data Processing Systems: In Theory and In Practice*, Prentice-Hall, 1986.

————. *Management Control of Data Processing*, Prentice-Hall, 1982.

————. *Technomics: The Economics of Technology and the Computer Industry*, Dow Jones-Irwin, 1986.

Jobs, Steve. "When We Invented the Personal Computer," *Computers & People*, July/August 1981.

King, J. L., Kraemor, K. "Evolution and Organizational Information Systems: An Assessment of Nolan's Stage Model," *CACM*, Vol. 27, May 1984.

Kroenke, D. *Database Processing: Fundamentals, Modeling, Applications*, SRA, 1977.

Loper, M.L., Inmon, W.H. "A Unified Data Architecture for Systems Integration," *ISEC Conference*, Washington, D.C., February 1988.

Lucas, H. C., Sutton, J. A. "The Stage Hypothesis S Curve: Some Contradictory Evidence," *CACM*, Vol. 20, April 1977.

Martin, James. *Strategic Data Planning Methodologies*, Prentice-Hall, 1982.

Myers, Glenford J. *Reliable Software Through Composite Design*, Petrocelli/Charter, 1975.

Nolan, R. L. "Managing the Computer Resource: A Stage Hypothesis," *CACM*, Vol. 16, July 1973.

————. "Managing the Crisis in Data Processing," *Harvard Business Review* March/April 1979.

————. "Thoughts About The Fifth Stage," *Database*, 7, 2, 1975.

Orr, Kenneth. *Structured Systems Development*, Yourdon Press, 1977.

Rockart, J. F., Bullen, C. V., Levantor, J. L. "Centralization vs. Decentralization of Information Systems: A Preliminary Model for Decision Making," Center for Information Systems Research, Alfred P. Sloan School of Management, MIT, Cambridge, MA, 1976.

Satler, J.F., Wozniak, S. "Understanding the Apple IIe," *Quality Software*, March 1985.

Swanson, E. B. *Evolutionary Information Systems*, North Holland, New York.

Tsichritzis, D. C., Lochovsky, F. H. *Data Base Management Systems*, Academic Press, 1977.

———. "Hierarchical Data Base Management: A Survey," *ACM Comp. Surv.* *8*, No. 1, March 1976.

Warnier, J. D. *Logical Construction of Programs*, Van Nostrand Reinhold, 1974.

Williams, B. D. "An Experiment in Business Information Systems," paper presented at the GUIDE and SHARE Applications Development Symposium, Monterey, CA, 1979.

Yourdon, E. *Design of Online Computer Systems*, Prentice-Hall, 1972.

———. *Managing the System Life Cycle*, Prentice-Hall, 1972.

———. *Nations at Risk*, Yourdon Press, 1986.

———. Constantine, L. *Structured Design*, Yourdon Press, 1978.

———. *Structured Walkthroughs*, Yourdon Press, 1977.

———. *Techniques of Program Structure and Design*, Prentice-Hall, 1975.

———. "Whatever Happened to Structured Analysis?" *Datamation* Vol. 32, June 1986.

———. *Writings of the Revolution*, Yourdon Press, 1982.

Zloof, M., "Query by Example," *Proceedings NCC*, May, 1975.

INDEX

4GL technology, 82, 85, 87, 117, 155–156
Access, 119
Accuracy, 74, 149
  of data, 44
Ad hoc, 3, 90, 116
Administrative, 142
ADP, 79
Airline reservation, 149
  environment, 138
Algorithmic
  calculation, 21
  extract differences, 34
  stability, 20
Amount of data used in normal processing, 20
Application, 44, 48, 81, 192, 208
  -oriented, 132
  -oriented data bases, 130
  -oriented data, 129
  -oriented environment, 128
  -oriented systems, 126
  by-application development, 49
  code, 51
  design and code, 93
  developers, 218
Architected environment, 35, 126, 128, 131–132, 134, 144, 187, 190, 193
Architecture, 2, 39, 50, 76–77, 121, 123, 171, 189, 190–191, 194, 214, 228
Archival data, 13–14, 113, 126
Archival, 30–31, 169, 171, 175, 179, 252
Arrival rate, 166

Assembler, 81, 117
AT, 154
ATM, 11, 109, 138
Atomic data base, 15, 50, 209
Atomic data, 36, 181–182, 184, 209–210
Atomic environment, 209
Atomic level, 14–16, 49, 111, 113, 126, 210, 253
Atomic, 3, 13–15, 17, 21, 22, 24, 26–31, 35–39, 82, 111, 114, 117, 119, 120, 122–125, 128, 131, 132, 147, 151, 165, 172–181, 185, 194, 204, 209, 211, 226, 227, 248–249, 263
Audit trail, 182
Auditable, 265
Autocoder, 85
Automation, 86
Autonomous, 75, 116
Autonomy of processing, 16, 20, 75
Autonomy, 44, 86, 89, 115, 184
Availability, 19, 20, 40, 43, 47, 48, 82, 85, 89, 90, 110, 116, 191

Back end processor, 110–111
Back end system, 110
Background processors, 11
Backlog of system, 86
Backup, 116, 171
Batch window, 116
Batch, 44, 118, 148, 161, 166, 171, 175, 182
BSP, 249, 250
Budget, 87, 254, 256, 262–265
Business systems planning, 249

Capacity planning, 219
Capacity, 166, 252
Card sorters, 81
Centralized configuration, 90, 91, 94, 95, 111
CIO, 213–214
Classical normalization, 147
COBOL, 81, 116, 156
Common source, 28, 39
Commonality uniqueness of data, 138–139
Commonality, 138, 140
Community of users, 20
Complexity due to generations of extracts, 34
Conceptual model, 215
Concurrency, 19
Consistency, 29
Consolidates, 140
Consolidation process, 205
Continuous time-span data, 172–173, 180
Continuous, 175, 209
Corporate data, 131
Corporation, 182
Cost of hardware, 163
Costs of processing, 87
CPU, 131, 151
Credibility, 32–39, 44, 74, 82, 149, 151, 253–254
Current value, 264
Current-value data, 128, 256
Customer file, 12

DASD, 81, 82, 86, 126, 129, 131–134, 151
Data administrator, 24, 213, 218, 222
Data analysis, 142, 162
Data architecture, 1, 48, 78, 166, 214–215
Data base, 82, 85, 86, 117
    administrator, 218
    concept, 32, 136
    machine, 110
    management systems, 116
Data communication, 121–122
Data dictionary, 219

Data element, 13, 19, 123, 144, 145, 147
Data flows, 114
Data management, 20, 117
Data model, 25, 166, 182, 187, 189, 194, 205, 219
Data modeling, 143, 182
Data normalization, 82, 142, 144
Data ownership, 13
Data redundancy, 136
Data split, 92
Data transmission, 94
Data update, 20
Data, 20
Day-to-day activities, 162
    operations, 143
DBMS, 81, 82, 86, 93, 229
Decentralized configuration, 90
    analyses, 45
    arena, 89
    needs, 156
    support processing, 44, 85
    systems, 3, 138
Decision support, 14–15, 29, 44, 47, 136, 149, 161, 243, 245, 248, 254
Definition of data, 20
Demographic analysis, 27, 180
Department, 115, 174, 182
Departmental level, 16, 111, 181, 185, 211
Departmental, 3, 13–18, 21, 22, 24, 26, 30, 31, 35, 38, 39, 82, 114, 116–119, 120, 122, 132, 165, 174, 181–182, 184, 210, 212, 248
    data, 16
    dss, 116
    extract, 211
Derivation of data, 17
Derivation, 15, 142, 144, 174, 181
Derived, 16–26, 49, 51, 135–136, 143–144, 149, 162, 172, 181, 189–191, 226–227, 242
    data, 17, 21, 143, 151, 215, 225
Designer, 47
Development backlog, 156
Direct access of data, 118

dis, 166–168, 215
Discrete, 180
Distributed
  atomic environment, 113
  centralized, 91, 94
  system, 12
Distribution of, 92
  data, 113
  processing, 93
dss
  analysis, 15, 132
  analyst, 133, 143
  data, 45
  environment, 44–45, 143, 149
  history, 51
  processing, 39
  systems, 249
Dss, 13–15, 27–28, 32–38, 45–50, 75,
    82, 86, 89–90, 111, 116, 118, 129,
    131, 134, 151, 155, 161, 163, 171,
    184, 204, 248–249, 252
Dual personality, 20, 24

Economic, 138
  benefit, 140
  justification, 138
Education, 215
  indoctrination, 214–215
Effectiveness of processing, 86
Element of data, 36, 147
End user, 2, 48, 50, 76, 176, 218, 222,
    225
  computing, 3, 16, 85
Enterprise, 3, 19, 24, 25, 44, 47, 87,
    140–143, 162, 173, 181, 204, 209
Entities, 16, 167
ERD, 140, 166–167, 215
Event discrete, 175, 180, 209
  data, 172, 180
  format, 173
Evolution, 1, 2, 30, 47, 78, 82, 85–89,
    161, 216, 252
Existence criteria, 147
Existence dependency criteria, 145, 147
Existence dependency, 147
Existence, 145

Existing
  data, 209
  environment, 76, 194
  operational systems, 191, 194
  system, 77, 187, 189, 191
External, 28, 38, 185
  data, 27
  format, 176
Extract and load philosophy, 32
Extract program, 181, 209
Extract, 32, 35, 38, 116, 131, 166, 174,
    181, 227

Finite events, 254
Flexibility, 227
Flow of data, 14, 81, 121, 192–193
FOCUS, 227
Fortran, 81, 85, 116
Foundation data, 75, 194
Fourth generation languages, 85
Freedom to do processing
    individually, 76
Frequency of execution, 119
Front end processors, 11
Front end, 109
Functional analysis, 250
Functional, 15

Generations of extracts, 35, 38
Global model, 77
Granular, 14, 149, 181
Groupings of data, 168

Hardware, 90
Heuristic, 16, 20, 75, 116–117, 144,
    155–156, 184
  dss, 26
  spread, 3
High probability, 13, 21
  data, 13
  of access, 165, 171
Historical, 13
  data, 255
  file, 52
  systems, 253, 254

Horizontal compatibility of technology, 121
Horizontal integration, 119
Host processor, 111

I/O, 166, 241
IBM 360, 154
IBM, 85
IBM XT, 153
Immediate dependency, 144
IMS, 227
Independence, 110
Index, 241
Individual, 3, 21, 24, 26, 30, 35, 38, 119, 126, 165, 182, 248
 data, 13, 16, 22
 dss, 17–18, 185
 dss/end, 181
 level, 82, 116, 184, 210–212
Information center, 219
Information cycle, 22–24
Information engineering, 142, 249
Information paradigm, 1–3, 13, 16–17, 20, 24–29, 30, 36, 38–40, 43–52, 75–78, 85–89, 119–122, 135, 138–144, 149, 151, 153–155, 161–165, 187, 194, 213, 215–216, 218, 222, 225–229, 242, 245, 247–249, 252
Information processing, 40, 151
Infrastructure, 20
Integration of systems, 228
Integrity, 82, 256
Intelligent disk controller, 110
Internal, 176
ISA, 249, 250

Key, 144–145, 168, 189, 209

Larger cycle, 22
Level, 2, 19, 32, 121, 128
Line workers, 214
Lineage of the data, 184
Local development of systems, 140
Logging, 116
Lotus 1-2-3, 254

Machine cycles, 40
Magnetic tape, 81, 161
Mainframe, 91, 111, 113–116, 122, 153–155, 229, 242
Maintenance, 44, 51–52, 81, 85, 225–227
Major subjects, 173, 181
Management, 143, 185, 214, 226
Master file, 32, 81–82, 85–86, 136, 142, 161
Maturity, 215
Maximum transaction, 166
Mechanical devices, 79
Methodologies, 248–249, 250, 252
Microfiche, 31
Migration, 44, 76–77, 93, 187, 189, 191, 193, 208, 210–212, 219, 228
Minicomputer, 114–115, 122, 153–154, 242
MIPS, 229
MIS, 81–82, 85, 87
Modeled, 144
Moment of reconciliation, 256, 260, 263

Network, 155
Nonprocedural languages, 117
Nonsystem of record, 3
Normalization, 144, 162

Online performance, 148–149
Online response time, 82
Online, 13, 21, 40, 44–45, 48, 82, 85, 111, 119, 138, 148, 156, 161, 163, 166, 170, 175
Operational, 3, 10–11, 13, 14, 17, 21, 24, 28–29, 35–36, 39, 40, 44–50, 75, 109, 117–119, 122–125, 131, 136, 138, 147, 151, 155, 156, 163, 165, 166, 168, 169, 171–178, 189, 191, 193, 204–205, 208, 210, 226, 227, 243, 247–249, 252, 263
 base, 34
 costs, 95, 252
 migration, 209
 processing, 109
 system, 93

Organization, 2, 27, 82, 85–87, 91, 92,
    181, 182, 213–216, 221–222, 225,
    252
Organizational, 19, 24, 26, 30, 213

Paper tape, 79
Paradigm, 26, 30, 44
Path lengths, 119
PC, 242
Peak period, 166
Performance, 19, 20, 40, 43–46, 82, 85,
    89–91, 94, 116–118, 138, 148,
    161, 163, 166, 245
Periodic discrete data, 172, 175, 185,
    209
Personal computer, 35, 82, 85–87, 116,
    153–155, 184
Philosophy, 20
PL-1, 81, 116, 156
Planning data, 254
Plans, 263
Political turf, 134
Primitive, 16–22, 24–26, 49, 135–136,
    138, 143, 144, 149, 151, 162, 165,
    172, 181, 182, 189, 190, 191, 225–
    227, 242
  conceptual, 26
  data, 215, 218
Private, 24, 258, 259
Probability of access, 30, 31, 40, 175
Procedure-oriented software, 116
Process model, 25, 189, 250
Process normalization, 162
Processes, 149, 166
Production, 47, 126, 130–134, 227
Productivity, 155–156
Program specifications, 162
Program, 119
Projection data, 254–256, 258
Projection, 3, 262–264
Public, 24, 27, 38, 115, 218, 258, 259
Punched cards, 79

Quick system development, 50

Rate, 82
Reconcilability, 253
Reconciled, 35, 36, 258
Reconciliation, 10, 36, 38, 75, 151, 248,
    256, 265
Record-at-a-time, 117, 166
Recovery, 40, 116, 160
Recursive relationship, 180
Redundancy, 14, 15, 19, 32, 49, 81,
    126, 129, 130, 131, 135, 136, 138,
    161, 226, 245
Refreshment, 122–126, 184, 245
Regularly scheduled, 16
Relational data, 82
Relational, 144, 162
Reliability, 94
Reorganization, 40, 116, 166
Repeating groups, 144
Report writers, 82
Requirements, 81, 143
Resistance, 219
Resolution, 36
Resources, 149
Response, 191, 243
Reusability, 50, 51

Scheduled processing, 16
Scope, 189
Scope of Integration, 17
Second order derivation, 17
Secondary dependencies, 144
Semiconductor, 81
Separation, 227
Sequential access of data, 118
Sequential processing, 111, 166, 179
Sequentially-oriented, 118
Set-at-a-time processing, 117, 184
Sheet analysis, 3
Singular existence, 10
Snapshot of data, 36, 173, 180, 209
Sources of data, 34
Speed of application development, 44, 48
Split data, 93, 94
Spreadsheet, 82, 117, 184, 254
Stable, 226
Stage, 78, 87

Static data, 19, 172, 209
Storage medium, 81
Strategic economy of consolidation, 49
Strategic, 247–248
Structured
  methodologies, 249
  programming, 81
  techniques, 250
  usage of, 48
  unstructured processing, 182
Subjects, 140–141, 166, 182, 209
  areas, 194
  data bases, 205, 207–208
  data, 113, 205
  orientation of days, 151
  orientation, 77, 82, 131, 140, 142,
    209, 228
  oriented, 29, 91, 126, 131
  of enterprise, 16, 48
Summarized dss data, 132
Summary, 171
Supporting system 110
SWU, 148, 149
Synchronization of redundant
  elements, 51
System of record, 3, 10–15, 17, 24, 31,
  48–49, 76, 82, 85, 86, 90–91, 93–
  94, 109–111, 116–120, 151, 165–
  166, 170
Systems development practices, 51, 142
Systems tuning, 219

Tactical, 247–248
Technician, 2
Telecommunications, 91
Teleprocessing, 82, 116–117
Terminal access, 91
The dis, 167
Throughput, 44, 110
Tightly coupled processors, 91–93
Time
  dependency, 172
  sharing, 116
  stamped, 180
  stamping of data, 75

variancy, 14, 175, 180–181, 209
  atomic data, 173
  variant, 14, 36, 176
Timing, 34, 36, 123
Tools, 143
Topdown flow, 162
TP, 229
Training, 219
Transaction, 21, 45, 109, 119, 123, 125,
  138, 149, 166, 170
  integrity, 20
  is, 44
  oriented systems, 3, 44, 116
  per second, 116
  processing rate, 117
  processing systems, 44
  processing, 10, 11, 44, 117, 118
  response time, 44
Transistor, 81
Transition, 20, 21, 24
Trend analysis, 3
Tuning, 148

Unarchitected environment, 76
Uncontrolled sources of input, 34
Unidirectional, 22
Uniformity, 29
Unscheduled processing, 116
Unstable, 226
Unstructured, 184, 187
Update, 116, 119
Usage structure, 19
User-friendly languages, 117

Vacuum tube, 81
Vendor, 121, 153
Version control, 95
Vertical compatibility of technology, 120
Vertical integration, 119
Volume discounts, 121

What if analysis, 259
Workload distribution, 93
Workload, 92, 93, 148